WITHDRAWN
UTSA LIBRARIES

DENHAM IN BORNU

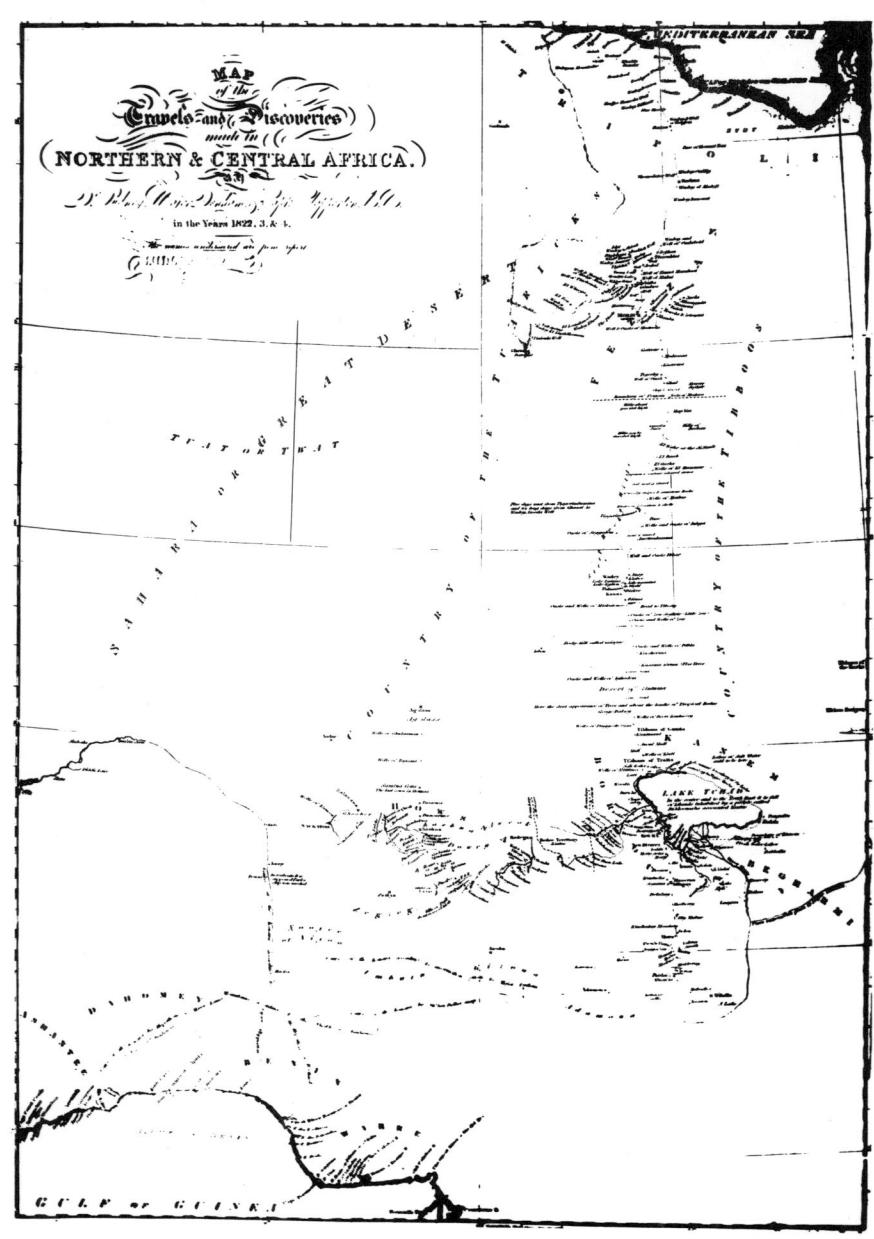

Denham's original map of his journey across the desert and of Bornu.
(First printed 1828)

DUQUESNE STUDIES

African Series

4

DENHAM IN BORNU

*An account of the exploration of
Bornu between 1823 and 1825 by
Major Dixon Denham, Dr. Oudney
and Commander Hugh Clapperton
and of their dealings with
Sheik Muhammad El Amin El Kanemi*

by

H.A.S. Johnston and D.J.M. Muffett

Distributed by Humanities Press, New York
for
DUQUESNE UNIVERSITY PRESS, PITTSBURGH

Copyright 1973, Duquesne University Press
ALL RIGHTS RESERVED

Library of Congress Cataloging in Publication Data

Johnston, Hugh Anthony Stephens.
  Denham in Bornu; and account of the exploration of Bornu between 1823 and 1825.

  (Duquesne studies. African series, 4)
  Bibliography: p.
  1. Bornu—Description and travel. 2. Sahara—Description and travel. 3. Denham, Dixon, 1786-1828. 4. Oudney, Walter, 1790-1824. 5. Clapperton, Hugh, 1788-1827. I. Muffett, D. J. M., joint author. II. Title. III. Series.
DT515.9.B6J63   916.69'4   72-97469
ISBN 0-391-00314-3

First Printing

Manufactured in the United States of America

Foreword

The year 1973 marks the hundred and fiftieth anniversary of the first entirely successful exploration of West Africa—that of Oudney, Denham and Clapperton—to be undertaken during the modern era, excluding, of course, that of Mungo Park in 1795. Such an anniversary should not go unmarked.

It was with this happy coincidence of dates in mind therefore, that after the untimely death of "Tim" Johnston in 1967 deprived both his many friends and African scholarship of one of those most remarkable and invaluable of all historians, the gifted, dedicated and informed amateur, I accepted an invitation from Mrs. Johnston to assume the responsibility of editing, expanding and bringing certain notes which he had assembled to final publication.

As was to be expected of their compiler, the notes which Johnston left behind were voluminous and meticulous. Thus it was also with a consciousness that I was embarking on a work of some magnitude as well as with a sense of great personal excitement and anticipation that I undertook my task.

As it proceeded it became an enduring pleasure, whilst it also afforded me an excellent opportunity of observing at close quarters the scope and reach of the scholarship of the man who had conceived the work in the first place and whose sense of history and simple humanity had made him such a distinguished public servant.

After entering the Colonial Service in 1936, Johnston was granted a release in order to join the Royal Air Force on the outbreak of World War

II. In this Service his career was quite outstanding and led him *via* the Siege of Malta and the D Day landings (and two awards for gallantry) to a Staff post in the Air Ministry, from whence, hostilities being ended, he returned to the Nigerian Administrative Service once again.

Here too his rise was almost meteoric and he very shortly found himself first Senior Resident in Charge, Kano, then Secretary to the Premier and Head of the Civil Service and finally Deputy Governor.

Yet it would be true to say that none of these positions of eminence gave to him the same sense of personal satisfaction which he had enjoyed as a "bush" District Officer and it was in this latter capacity especially that Johnston acquired the almost uncanny perception and comprehension of the attitudes and mores of the Hausa and Kanuri peoples, rich and poor, high and lowly, prince or peasant which characterized him. This knowledge illuminated all his work, both administrative and scholarly and can be distinguished, in the present one, by the skill with which he etches, in brief but vivid portraits, the character of Shehu Muhammad El Amin El Kanemi and of his courtiers and in his *vignettes* of the life and living of the people of the day.

In the field of history in Africa in particular, the contribution to scholarship and learning made by amateurs has always been significant. As it was with Burton, Palmer, Burdon and Harry Johnston, so it was with Tim.

> Several colonial administrators who made an avocation of investigating the history and culture of the people whom they administered won the respect and gratitude of academic scholars. After nearly a decade since the British and French colonial systems in Africa were dismantled, this new example of the old *genre* comes as something of a surprise.*

Much before it became popular to think of African History as a valid area for original research and certainly long before anyone else had given thought to the need for an authoritative and comprehensive study of nineteenth century Hausaland or for the urgency to assemble "oral data," Johnston was gathering material and preparing the manuscript of what was to become his major work, *The Fulani Empire of Sokoto* (Oxford, 1967), in respect to which the tribute given above was first applied.

* *American Historical Review* Vol. 74, Oct. 1968, p. 243-44. Review of Johnston's *The Fulani Empire of Sokoto* (West African History Series) Oxford University Press, New York 1967.

It was an endeavor which was to be subjected to many vicissitudes, some of which were by no means unconnected either with problems of ignorance and apathy on the part of publishers or with picayune jealousies on that of professional academicians and, as a result, it took more than fifteen years for the finished manuscript finally to reach the press.

During that time Johnston also busied himself first with the production of a children's book, *Zomo the Rabbit* (published under the *nom-de-plume* of "Hugh Sturton" by the Atheneum Publishers, New York and by Hamish Hamilton, London) and, secondly, with that of *A Selection of Hausa Stories* (*Clarendon, Oxford* 1966). In this latter sphere, his consumate knowledge of Hausa and his encyclopedic understanding of the folk-tales, legends and oral traditions of that area of Hausaland which he knew the best—Sokoto and Kano—placed him far above and quite immune to any of the somewhat waspish criticism which was often flung at him.

Much of this criticism has centered upon assertions that Johnston was unduly influenced by his adherence to the "Hamitic myth," namely the view advanced by that group of historians who believe that migrations of either Berber, Nilotic or Hamitic origin, occuring sometime around the fourth century or even earlier and continuing for several hundred years, had a profound and decisive effect on the political and sociological development of that area of modern Africa broadly described as the Western Sudan and contained generally in a rough rectangle west from Lake Chad and approximately from 5-15° of latitude north of the Equator.

Opponents of this train of thought, who deny the validity of any such hypothesis, have been vehement in their condemnation both of it and of those who incline towards it, or even of those who give it passing credence. Though never articulated in these terms, they seem to have formed themselves into an exclusively "Negritic School," whose philosophy has at least a distinct element of racism and ethnocentricism in its make up and which they appear to advance on occasion in a manner that borders almost on the frenetic.

To this author, who firmly rejects identification with either stream, but to whom it would be inconceivable that the interaction first of time and environment and then of military, sociological and population pressures would not to be reflected in the development of African political and social institutions in a manner analagous to that which can be seen in any other geographical division of *homo sapiens,* the polemical and assertive perjoration which has often accompanied the exposition of the view of the "Negritic School" has done much to undermine any appreciation of the purely intellectual validity to which it may otherwise purport.

It seems hardly to be comprehended that a similarly diverse admixture to that which, for example, created a Briton or a Spaniard should be denied as being capable of operation in respect, say, of a Hausa. No Briton can logically deny the influences, social, political and physical, of the Dane, the Angle, the Saxon, the Celt, the Norman or the Roman, *inter alia*, in his national admixture. How then can a Hausaman, or for that matter a Yoruba, a Manding or a Fula, especially when—whether the "Negritic" historian likes it or not—the legends and the traditions of each of those different peoples is so positively affirmative on the issue? As far as the present volume is concerned however, the situation which it represents can be divorced from almost any considerations of this nature, except as mere asides and I have not conceived it my duty to alter the text, whenever it was definitive, on this account.

When he died, Tim Johnston had been working on what is actually commentary—a reduction to contemporary relevance as it were—of the journals of Major Dixon Denham and Commander Hugh Clapperton. These two travellers published what is really the first account of Hausaland and Bornu as seen through the eyes of a European—though they were certainly not the first Europeans to have had the opportunity to make these observations.

Johnston had in mind two volumes. The first was to deal with the sojourn in Bornu and the second was to embrace Clapperton's journey on to Sokoto in 1824 and his subsequent return and death at Jungevi during his second visit. Unfortunately, although this latter volume would have constituted an especial labor of love, it does not exist in anything other than the most rudimentary form and its reconstruction would be quite impossible. Happily the first case was entirely a different matter.

As so often happens, Johnston's notes throw a great deal of new light on the personality of the principal subjects of the study—Denham and El Kanemi. In addition, they alerted me to one other point, not new perhaps but rather hitherto merely unremarked, a point which could be of immense importance.

Tucked away in the concluding chapters of Denham's narrative, to a large extent swamped by the overburden of his detail and certainly not fully appreciated before, lies a reference which Denham makes, almost casually and *en passant,* to the common and apparently quite usual presence of Americans far inland from the West African coast and engaged day to day in trade in slaves and gum arabic.

Employing a local knowledge of the area to which Denham refers, it is now possible to suggest, on the basis of this evidence, that American traders were habitually penetrating as far inland as the Oyo, Ilorin, and Nupe areas *and that they had been doing so over a considerable period of time.*

If this is so, since Denham was writing of the years 1823-25 then it argues that it was the Americans and not the British agents Mungo Park and Hornemann who first penetrated to the periphery of the Sokoto Caliphate and its dependencies and to the valley of the Middle Niger. Who then were these people? Where are the records of their journeys?

It is not the purpose of this work to endeavor to answer those questions. It should properly be left to American scholars to re-discover the involvement in the area of their fellow countrymen which Denham so categorically reports. But if, on the 150th anniversary of the journey of exploration which this work now chronicles, the question is raised anew and a fresh spark of enquiry thus becomes ignited, then Johnston's efforts in initiating the study which led to these enquiries will be well rewarded, as will also the part which the present writer has played in supporting his endeavors.

D. J. M. Muffett

Duquesne University
Institute of African Affairs
Pittsburgh, Pa.
29 November, 1972.

Table Of Contents

FOREWORD 5
INTRODUCTION 13
Chapter I. PREPARATIONS IN TRIPOLI 27
II. THE SAHARA 38
III. LAKE CHAD 51
IV. BORNU 61
V. KUKA AND NEW BIRNI 80
VI. EXCURSIONS IN BORNU 91
VII. QUARRELS AMONG THE ARABS 106
VIII. SOUTH TO MANDARA 113
IX. MANDARA 121
X. A DISASTROUS RAID 133
XI. THE MANGA REBELLION 148
XII. THE ONSET OF THE DRY SEASON 165
XIII. LIFE IN KUKA 176
XIV. HARD TIMES 193
XV. EXCURSION TO LOGONE AND THE DEATH OF
     TOOLE 207

XVI.	EXPEDITION TO KANEM	222
XVII.	THE SHUWA ARABS	235
XVIII.	THE JOURNEY HOME	243
	EPILOGUE	262

Introduction

The rock drawings of the Sahara show that at one time the country had a rich and varied fauna which included elephant, rhinoceros, hippopotamus, antelopes of many kinds, horses, goats, sheep and cattle. There is also plenty of evidence that what is now desert supported a sedentary population and enjoyed enough rainfall to have had a river system. This belonged to a prehistoric period however, for by classical times the region, though perhaps rather less arid than it is today, already had insufficient rainfall. 'Libya is full of wild beasts' wrote Herodotus in the fifth century B.C. 'while beyond the wild beast region there is a tract which is wholly sand, very scant of water, and utterly and entirely a desert'. To Pliny, five centuries later, it was 'a desert abandoned to the sand and swarming with serpents'.[1]

At this period there were still enough wild animals in North Africa to furnish the circuses of the Roman world but two important commodities—gold and slaves—were for the most part imported from the interior. The introduction of the camel at about this time made the desert passage a little easier it is true, but the Sahara remained such a formidable obstacle that the Romans knew little or nothing of the people who lived beyond it.

With the decline in the power of Rome, the coherence of the classical world had already been lost before the Arab conquests of the seventh century divided the Mediterranean between Christendom and Islam. In

1. E.W. Bovill, *The Golden Trade of the Moors*, London, 1958, pp. 1-15.

North Africa the Islamic tide flowed westward to Morocco and thence turned south to Mauretania and Senegambia. Similarly in the east it made some progress in the Nile Valley. But then, for a time, it lost its momentum so that it did not reach the people of the Sudan, the long corridor that runs from east to west between the Sahara and the equatorial rain forests of the Congo basin and the Guinea coast, until a much later date.

Although the existence of gold in the countries of the Sudan had been known from time immemorial, it was not until Mansa Musa the ruler of Mali set out in A.D. 1324 to make the pilgrimage to Mecca that the world at large realised how great this wealth was. Mounted on horseback, he was preceeded by 500 slaves each carrying a staff of gold weighing 500 *mithqal* or nearly four pounds. In addition there was a train of between eighty and a hundred camels each laden with nearly three hundredweight of gold. This prodigal display naturally made Mansa Musa and his country celebrated throughout the Islamic world and caused his fame to spread even to the courts of Europe.[2]

At the beginning of the fifteenth century the financing of Europe's growing trade with India, China, and the Spice Islands raised the demand for gold and caused the thoughts of European bankers to turn to the Sudan. By 1470 the representative of one of the great Florentine banking houses, Benedetto Dei, had not only crossed the Sahara but had established himself as a merchant in Timbuktu.[3] So far as is known, he was the first European ever to reach the Sudan. In locating the source of the gold, however, he was no more successful than the innumerable Arabs who had been there before him.

At the same time the Portuguese were trying to outflank the Sahara by opening a new sea-route to Guinea.[4] As a boy, Prince Henry the Navigator had read of the gold caravans and as a young man, campaigning in Morocco, he had heard more about them at first hand. Now he resolved to find a way to reach the gold by sea and began to organize the voyages which made his name famous. Hitherto European sailors had been deterred from going beyond Cape Bojador by the superstition that certain destruction awaited any man who ventured past it. Prince Henry's cap-

2. Ibid, pp. 87-8. An approximate valuation would be over $48 million.
3. Ibid, p. 116.
4. The word 'guinea' probably derives from the Berber word for negro, *aguinaou*. The English golden guinea, which first appeared in 1662, was minted from gold imported from West Africa and owed its premium over the sovereign to the excellence of the metal. Ibid, p. 119.

tains, having exploded this myth, pushed their discoveries steadily south. By the end of the century the Portuguese had established a number of trading posts round the coast from Cape Blanco to the Bight of Benin but everywhere they found the way inland barred to them by malarial swamps, almost impenetrable forests and implacably hostile tribes. In short, the interior proved to be just as inaccessible from the west and south as it had always been from the north.[5]

In 1550 the publication in Italy of Leo Africanus's famous *History and Description of Africa* caused a new surge of interest in the mysterious countries beyond the desert. But the discovery of America and the opening of the sea routes to India and the East Indies had created such glittering opportunities in other parts of the world that the attention of Europe was soon distracted away from Africa. In the middle of the sixteenth century, it is true, a party of Portuguese did succeed in reaching the gold mines but none of them returned to give an account of what they had found.[7] The mystery therefore remained. Moreover, with Peru now satisfying Europe's need for gold, the urge to solve it diminished. Instead, the adventurers of Europe either contented themselves with the not inconsiderable profits to be made out of the slave trade or else sought their fortunes further afield.

Meanwhile, in the Mediterranean Tripoli, Tunis and Algiers had been absorbed into the Ottoman Empire and with the great seige of Malta in 1565 and the battle of Lepanto in 1571 the fighting between Moslem and Christian had reached a new crescendo of fury. Of the Moslem countries only Morocco, with its seaboard on the Atlantic, had succeeded in preserving its independence from the Turks; this had the additional effect of making it the chief *entrepot* for Europe's trans-Saharan trade with the countries of the Sudan and Guinea.

In 1578, Portugal became engaged in a war with Morocco and one of the decisive battles of history took place at El Kasar El Kebir (Alcazar) in 1580, when the ill equipped army of Portugal was annihilated, less than 100 out of a total of 26,000 escaping death or capture.

Abid el Malek, the Shereef of Morocco was killed on the field, but before he succumbed he nominated his younger brother Mulai Ahmed to succeed him.

5. Ibid, pp. 117-120.
6. Leo's book was translated into English by John Pory and published in London in 1600.
7. Bovill, pp. 200-01.

Taking the title of El Mansur (The Victorious) Mulai Ahmed now became Shereef of Fez. He was quick to set about consolidating his position, which at first was somewhat precarious. He received recognition from Elizabeth of England and from William of Orange, as well as from Portugal (who could do little else) and from Spain. The Spanish gift to mark his accession was said to be a ruby as big as a man's hand and an emerald as large as an apple, as well as a casket of huge pearls. Slowly but surely El Mansur consolidated his position until it was unassailable. In this he was much assisted by Elizabeth who, cheerfully ignoring the Papal ban on trade in munitions with Islam, was most willing to supply Morocco with guns (in exchange for saltpetre, for which this was her only source of supply) and with ship's timber, cannon balls, oars and even ship-wrights.

Meanwhile Portugal, as a result of its defeat, was inexorably drawn into the Spanish orbit almost as a client-state and the accretion of Portuguese sea power to Spanish control certainly assisted in the preparations for the dispatch of the Spanish Armada.

As soon as the destruction of the Armada had removed any threat to his rear, Shereef El-Mansur decided to embark upon the annexation of the western Sudan and thus to bring the sources of the gold and slaves under his own direct control. He therefore assembled an army of 4,000 men, sustained by 8,000 camels and 1,000 packhorses, and launched them across the desert.[8]

In the Western Sudan during the previous millenium three great Empires had followed one another: first Ghana with its capital at Kumbi, about 250 miles west-south-west of Timbuktu; then Mali, with its capital at Niani also on the upper Niger; and finally Songhai with its capital at Gao on the middle Niger about 250 miles east-south-east of Timbuktu. Each in turn had controlled the trans-Saharan trade of the whole region between the Atlantic and Hausaland, with Songhai's control extending close to the border of Egypt. Now in 1591 Askia Ishak, the ruler of Songhai, assembled a large army with which to bar the way of the Moorish invaders. The Songhai lacked firearms however and were decisively defeated in two battles.[9]

For a short time the Moors were masters of the western Sudan but they were unable to hold what they had won. Their numbers, small at the start, were further depleted by the casualties of battle and the ravages of

8. Ibid, pp. 148-9.
9. Ibid, pp. 156-162.

17 | INTRODUCTION

disease. Their only chance of success lay in preserving and ruling through the administrative machinery of the Songhai Empire but the destruction of the army and the death of the Askia caused this Empire to disintegrate. The subject peoples took every opportunity to throw off their allegiance; inter-tribal fighting broke out on all sides, brigandage became rife and a region which had enjoyed peace and good government for the past three generations dissolved into anarchy.[10] The Moors, isolated and demoralised, retired to Timbuktu. There a series of Pashas continued to rule in the name of the Shereef of Morocco until 1660, when this last link, which for long had been little more than a formality, was at length severed.[11] After a brilliant initial success the Moorish invasion became a costly fiasco. In Morocco it served only to disturb channels of trade which had previously been functioning satisfactorily. In the Sudan it substituted chaos for order. And in Guinea it left the secret of the gold mines inviolate.

The gold was in fact located in the southwest corner of the continent's great western bulge, between Senegal and Ashanti. The Arabs and Europeans tended to believe that it all came from a few very rich mines but in fact the alluvial workings were small and widely scattered, the majority being situated in the upper basins of the Niger, Volta, Gambia and Senegal Rivers.[12] The tribes who mined the gold were glad to exchange it for salt but they were so suspicious that they not only refused to allow foreign merchants to come anywhere near their diggings but even declined to have normal commercial intercourse with them. Instead they insisted on a system of silent barter whereby the visiting merchants laid out the salt and any other merchandise that they had brought to the appointed place and then retired half a day's journey, returning on the following day to collect the nuggets and gold dust that had been offered in exchange.[13] This arrangement, which was first described by Herodotus and afterwards by many other authorities, enabled the primitive peoples of this region to guard their secret from the world for over two thousand years.

In the seventeenth and eighteenth centuries the overseas interest of the European nations was concentrated on the Americas, Canada, India and the East and West Indies. In Africa they were still very active in the

10. Ibid, p. 165.
11. Ibid, p. 175.
12. R. Mauny, *Tableau Geographique de l'ouest Africain au Moyen Age*, Dakar, 1961.
13. Ibid, p. 195.

maritime slave trade, particularly the British, but this involved only the most superficial contacts with a group of middle-men potentates at the chain of trading posts that was established along the coast. As for the interior, Europe had temporarily lost interest. Towards the end of the eighteenth century, however, a number of circumstances combined to attract European attention once again. Some of the motives, such as the advancement of geographical knowledge and the substitution of legitimate commerce for the slave trade, were altruistic; others, which hinged upon national rivalry and the quest for markets, were less high-minded.

In England, more than anywhere else, these influences were powerful and served to turn public awareness once more towards Africa and particularly towards West Africa. Rivalry with France was at its height. In India and Canada the French had been decisively defeated, but in the United States they had helped the Americans to win their independence. In Africa the issue was still undecided. In 1758 the British had captured the two main French posts of Goree and St Louis and had established the colony of Senegambia, but in 1770 the French had recaptured St. Louis and reasserted their authority over Senegambia.[14] Neither side realised that the gold was already almost exhausted and so both were eager to obtain control over it or, failing that, at least to deny that control to the other.

At about the same time a similar impulse originated from a completely different quarter. In 1783, eleven years after the famous Somerset judgement delivered by Lord Chief Justice Mansfield which had made the state of slavery illegal in England, a group of Quakers formed themselves into a committee to work for the liberation of slaves in the West Indies and towards the discouragement of the traffic from Africa. In 1787, after accepting Wilberforce and others as new members, the committee decided to campaign for the complete abolition of the slave trade.[15] Their propaganda aroused wide interest and their doctrine that everything possible must be done to encourage legitimate commerce as a substitute for the slave trade was later adopted by the British Government and became the corner-stone of its African policy.

A third impulse came from the world of scholarship and science. The eighteenth century was the age of rational curiosity and one of its main manifestations, particularly in Great Britain which was then in the proc-

---

14. Robin Hallett (Editor), *Records of the African Association 1788-1831*, London, 1964, p. 9.
15. Ibid, p. 11.

ess of acquiring its Empire, was a new and more searching interest in geography. The remote and little known parts of the globe attracted special attention and here the continent of Africa loomed ever larger in men's imagination. Indeed, after the discovery of Australia, Africa presented easily the greatest unsolved mystery. Its outline had been established and its extremities explored, but of its interior—apart from the lower Nile valley—the world knew virtually nothing.

By 1788 there was enough concern for the subject in the United Kingdom for the *African Association* to be founded. Its moving spirit was Sir Joseph Banks, who had sailed with Captain Cook to Australia and was a man of wide scientific interest. The other founding members, though their only common links related to the scientific and commercial concepts which had originally brought them together in a dining club, had much to contribute. Two were peers, two more had sat on the Board of Trade and all but two of the rest had some political experience. They included in their number, besides Banks who was a botanist, a successful doctor, an economist and statistician, as well as a Bishop who had held the chairs of both chemistry and divinity at Cambridge. No fewer than six of them were members of the Royal Society. As a body, they were liberal and humanitarian in outlook; some of them had ties with the Evangelicals and most of them supported the Abolitionists. Among their friends were both Wilberforce and the Prince Regent.[16]

Two years after the founding of the Association, James Bruce, the Scottish explorer who had discovered the source of the Blue Nile and who had spent two years in Ethiopia, published a monumental account of his travels. No other European of that age had penetrated so deeply into the interior of Africa. His exploits therefore aroused immense interest, not only in the United Kingdom but all over Europe and his account of them whetted the curiosity of the public about the mysterious continent.[17]

The African Association's full title, which defined its primary aim, was 'An Association for Promoting the Discovery of the Interior Parts of Africa'. To achieve their objective, the members first had to draw up a programme of exploration and then to find men capable of carrying it out. As Bruce was believed to have discovered the source of the Nile and as in any case the lower Nile valley was familiar ground, the thoughts of the members turned naturally to the other great river of northern Africa,

16. Ibid, pp. 12-15.
17. Ibid, p. 10.

the Niger. Except that it lay beyond the Sahara and was associated with the gold-bearing regions of Guinea and with the shadowy Sudanese states mentioned by the Arab geographers, nothing whatever was known about it.[18] Leo Africanus had asserted that it flowed from east to west, but even this question was in doubt, for no-one knew where it rose nor where it reached the sea, or indeed whether it ever did reach the sea.

* * *

The African Association's initial enterprise was extremely ambitious and shows that the members did not at first appreciate how formidable a task it was that they had undertaken. They proposed to quarter the whole northern part of the continent by launching one explorer southward from Tripoli and another westward from the Nile. For the first mission they recruited Simon Lucas, a man with an unrivalled knowledge of North Africa who, having been captured as a boy by Barbary corsairs, had served after his release from slavery as the British Vice-Consul in Morocco. For the second mission an American called John Ledyard was engaged, who had sailed with Cook on his third expedition and afterwards had tried to reach Alaska through Siberia. But the dual venture proved to be a complete fiasco[19] because Ledyard died in Cairo while making preparations for his journey and Lucas, on the pretext that the Bedouins in the desert had revolted and cut the caravan route to Fezzan, refused to stir from Tripoli.[20]

All that the Association salvaged from the wreck of this enterprise was some useful information about the Sudan which Lucas had picked up in Tripoli. This, supplemented by reports from two Moors and from the British Consuls in Morocco and Tunis, suggested that "Hausa" (it was not yet understood that this was a generic term embracing all the states of Hausaland) and Bornu were populous and thriving kingdoms, that Timbuktu was still a great commercial centre and that the trans-Saharan trade was valuable enough to be worth competing for. To the members of the Association it now seemed that, in order to circumvent the Moors and reach the gold of Guinea and the busy markets of the Sudan, all that was necessary was to open a new road from the west.[21]

The less grandiose but more precise and realistic aims of the Associa-

18. Ibid, p. 25.
19. Ibid, pp. 25-6.
20. Ibid. From what Hornemann, a later explorer, said ten years afterwards, it is clear that he did not believe Lucas's excuses. Ibid, pp. 188-9.
21. Ibid, pp. 27-28.

tion's second venture were to explore these regions of the western and central Sudan. As their explorer, the members chose Daniel Houghton, a middle-aged Irish army officer whose qualifications were that he had been to Morocco and that as a young man, he had spent three years at Goree, the garrison post between the mouths of the Senegal and Gambia rivers which had been captured from the French in 1758 but which was subsequently restored to them. Houghton set off from the Gambia in 1790 and was well received by the ruler of the little state of Bambuk. He pushed on past Ka'arta but within a year, exhausted by the ill treatment that he received at the hands of the local Moorish war-lords, he was dead. His mission had not been a complete failure however, for he had succeeded in sending some information back to the Gambia, notably news of Bambuk's desire to trade with England and of the direction of the Niger's flow. This, he said was eastward and not westward as Leo Africanus had asserted.[22]

At the General Meeting of 1792, the Association passed a resolution that Houghton's discoveries should be exploited in the commercial interests of the Empire. Members believed that the first step was to establish a British Consulate in Bambuk and they used their influence to persuade the Government to contribute £3,000 a year for two years towards this scheme. Just when it was about to be launched however, war again broke out with France and the Government's intervention was postponed indefinitely, in fact never to be executed. Instead, the Association, having found a successor to Houghton, despatched him in Houghton's footsteps.

The Association's new recruit, a young Scottish doctor named Mungo Park, was soon to make his name famous throughout the western world. Setting out from the Gambia at the end of 1795 and travelling alone he not only reached the Niger but traversed it for some distance along its course. But he too, as an avowed Christian, suffered the greatest hardships at the hands of the fanatically Moslem Moors. Their hostility prevented him from reaching Timbuktu and on his way home he very nearly died of fever and privation, though after an absence of two and a half years he at last struggled back to the Gambia. His journey constitutes one of the most remarkable feats of courage and endurance in the whole history of exploration. Hardly less admirable was the book which he afterwards wrote to describe his adventures. Informative, restrained and yet intensely vivid, it scored an immediate success and did much to stimulate further the growing public interest in Africa.[23]

22. Ibid, p. 28.
23. Ibid, p. 29.

Mungo Park was so long in the Sudan without any news of him reaching England that the members of the Association, fearing that he too had perished, cast about for another explorer. Their choice fell on Frederick Hornemann, a young German recommended to them by Professor Blumenbach of Gottingen, the father of the science of ethnology. Their objective was still the central and western Sudan, but, believing that Park as well as Houghton had been lost on the western route, they decided to try the desert road again. They also agreed to Hornemann's being given six months special tuition at Gottingen in subjects which would be useful to him and then to his staying in Egypt for a further period in order to learn Arabic. These proposals were carried out but in 1798, while Hornemann was in Cairo, Napoleon invaded Egypt. So great was the animosity against Christians that this action aroused in the Islamic world that Hornemann decided to assume the character of a Moslem merchant when he set out on his travels.[24] Soon afterwards, in this disguise, he joined a caravan for the Fezzan, on the northern edge of the Sahara south of Tripoli. Arriving there, he made a special journey to the coast in order to send a progress report to the Association and then returned to Murzuk, the Capital of the Fezzan, where in April 1800 he joined a caravan bound for Bornu. Nothing more was heard of him for nearly twenty years and not until 1819 did the world learn that he had reached Bornu safely, had travelled on to Katsina and beyond, but had died of dysentery in Nupe while on his way to Ashanti. His journals perished with him and so the fruits of his heroic expedition, which would have entitled him to a place in the front rank of African explorers, were lost.[25]

The Association waited nearly five years for news of Hornemann before abandoning hope and planning a new venture. Then, having had one failure from the west and two from the north, they decided to try an approach from the south. For this enterprise they recruited a man named Henry Nicholls and in 1805 despatched him to Calabar with instructions to strike north to Hausaland and Bornu. On the coast he was well received by the local chiefs but the climate proved too much for him and within three months, before he had even left Calabar, he too was dead.[26]

In the meantime however, the Association had not forgotten Mungo Park's comparative success in the west. At the annual General Meeting in 1799 Banks, in a lengthy address, spoke of the Association having opened

24. Ibid, pp. 30 and 185.
25. Ibid, p. 30.
26. Ibid, p. 31.

a gate into the interior of Africa through which it would be possible for every nation to enter. Five hundred British troops, he suggested, could force a passage from the Gambia to the Niger and once embarked on the Niger would be able to withstand any force that might be sent against them. British merchants thus established in riverain forts, would then be able to take over the gold trade, reckoned to be worth a million pounds a year and by introducing more efficient methods would doubtless raise production. The increase in prosperity which would be brought about would then in turn create a new demand for British manufactures. "Is not this prospect" he asked "of at once attaching to this country the whole of the interior trade now possessed by the Moors, with the chance of an incalculable future increase, worth some exertion and some expense to a trading nation?"

This was an historic speech because Banks was the first man to suggest that it might be in Great Britain's interest to acquire possessions in the African interior. The Association passed an appropriate resolution and the proposal was urged upon the Board of Trade. For three years there was no response and then, believing that they might be forestalled by the French, the Government suddenly acted. An ambitious plan was drawn up whereby Mungo Park was to lead an expeditionary force to Bambuk in order to establish British Military power in the western Sudan and open a trade route to the Niger. When Addison's administration fell however, the new Government cancelled the original enterprise although it agreed to provide and finance a military escort for a civil expedition.[27]

In 1805 Mungo Park accordingly set off on his second journey. This time, instead of being alone, he was accompanied by a large party consisting of four carpenters, two seamen and thirty-six British soldiers under the command of a Lieutenant Martyn. His plan was to march overland to the Niger during the dry-season, to build two boats and then, when the annual rise of the river occurred in the rains, to sail downstream until he reached the sea. Had he been able to keep to his timetable he might perhaps have succeeded. As it was, however, a series of delays threw his plan completely out of phase with the result that most of the overland journey had to be accomplished during the rainy season itself. In the whole history of exploration there is surely no more terrible march than this. Compared with Park's estimate of six weeks it occupied one hundred and eleven days and of the forty-four Europeans who left the Gambia only eleven even reached the Niger. By the time they were ready to sail

27. Ibid, pp. 31-2 and 230.

three months later, their numbers had been reduced to five, one of whom was out of his mind. Nevertheless, despite a falling flood and repeated attempts by the inhabitants to waylay it, Park navigated his ramshackle craft right round the great bend of the Niger and brought it safely to Yauri, on the southern borders of Hausaland. But on the next stage he and his remaining three companions perished in the rapids near Bussa.

The Association soon heard of the early disasters to Mungo Park's expedition, though news of the final catastrophe did not reach them until 1811. After three years of silence, however, any hope of success had faded and so in 1808 the Association accepted the offer of a young Swiss, J.L. Burckhardt, to follow Hornemann's route to the central Sudan. He left England in the following year and, with the Association's approval, spent nearly three years in Syria learning Arabic and acquiring enough knowledge of Islamic custom to be able to pass himself off as a Moslem. But he was unable, for various reasons, to carry out his original plan. Instead he made an adventurous journey which took him up the Nile, thence to Suakin on the Red Sea, and finally, disguised as a pilgrim, to Mecca. Back in Cairo in 1817, he was preparing to set out with a caravan bound for the Sudan when he too succumbed to dysentery. He left behind him five scholarly volumes on his travels in the Middle East but he was deprived by an untimely death of the opportunity of solving any of the riddles of Africa.[28]

Before Burckhardt died, the Napoleonic Wars, which had been hampering the work of exploration for over twenty years, at last came to an end. Freed of its military burden and anxious to find an outlet for the country's growing manufactures, the British Government now devoted some of its surplus resources to the exploration of the Niger and of the countries of the central and western Sudan. As a result of its efforts, Laing was to reach Timbuktu in 1826 and first Dr. Oudney, Major Denham and Commander Clapperton and later the Lander brothers at last to clear up the mysteries of Lake Chad, Bornu, Hausaland and of the course of the lower Niger. Finding itself superseded in this field, the African Association thereupon transferred its attention to the White Nile. To this end it engaged three more explorers but unhappily all its ventures ended in failure. In 1831 the members decided to merge themselves in the newly created Royal Geographical Society which, fittingly enough, was destined to play a similar role in the second phase of African exploration to that which the Association had played in the first.

28. Ibid, p. 33.

Unknown Africa exerted an extraordinary fascination over the minds of some of these early European explorers. Mungo Park, happily married and the father of a young family, found no peace in his quiet Border practice but, as if drawn by some Siren's song, abandoned everything in order to undertake his second disastrous enterprise. Rene Caillié, who reached Timbuktu in 1828, confessed later that the exploration of Africa had become a ruling passion to which he sacrificed all else.[29] Clapperton, after enduring months of sickness on his first journey, emerged from the shadow of death only to hurry back to Africa on his second and fatal one. There was an obsessional, almost mystical quality in the devotion that they brought to their self-imposed tasks. For example when Mungo Park, on his second journey, saw again the distant hills which enclosed the Niger, he became oblivious of sickness and privation; he forgot the trail of exhausted and dying men that he had left behind him; he ignored the unmistakable portents of further calamities ahead; and he thought only of his goal:

> The certainty that the Niger washes the southern base of these mountains made me forget my fever and I thought of nothing all the way but how to climb over their blue summits.

There is no doubt that unless these early explorers had been imbued by this almost fanatical devotion, the task of opening up Africa and bringing its people into the main stream of human progress would have been delayed for several generations. The risks that they accepted were higher than those which, in our own age, have hitherto attended the exploration of space: out of the nine men engaged by the African Association, no fewer than seven were lost, not to mention the forty-three companions of Mungo Park who shared his fate. Dangers apart, the African explorers had to endure every kind of hardship—hunger and thirst, sleepless nights, the torments of flies and mosquitoes, debilitating illnesses—and submit to every form of indignity and persecution that suspicion, greed and religious bigotry could devise. In all the annals of history there is nothing to surpass the courage with which they faced the dangers, the fortitude with which they suffered privation and the resolution with which they drove themselves forward into the unknown.

No expedition displayed more of these qualities than that which assembled under the leadership of Dr. Oudney, Major Denham and Commander Clapperton the story of which is now to be examined in detail.

29. Felix Dubois, *Timbuctoo the Mysterious*, London, 1897, pp. 330-1.

I
Preparations In Tripoli

By 1815 Great Britain had two compelling reasons for giving direct encouragement to the exploration of Africa. First, the reestablishment of peace after twenty-five years of almost continuous war meant that the Government was under a strong compulsion to find new outlets for the industries which had been developed to sustain the military effort of the allies. Second, having made the slave-trade an illegal pursuit for its own nationals and being moreover determined to use its naval supremacy to suppress the maritime traffic altogether, the Government felt bound to do everything in its power to fill the resultant vacuum by fostering the growth of legitimate commerce.

These two aims were complementary but it was obvious that, so far as Africa was concerned, they could only be encompassed when preliminary surveys had been made of the opportunities that existed and of the obstacles that stood in the way. Even during the war the Government had been willing to furnish money and military resources on a small scale in order to mount Mungo Park's second expedition. Now, with the advent of peace, they were ready to be more lavish. Moreover two men in high and especially influential positions had a genuine enthusiasm for exploration—Lord Bathurst, the Colonial Secretary, and John Barrow, the Second Secretary at the Admiralty.[1]

The Niger was regarded as the key to the Sudan but the course which it took below Bussa, where Mungo Park had perished, was still a mystery

1. Hallett, p. 230.

about which there were several conflicting theories. As the mouth of the Congo had already been discovered, though the existence of the river itself was as yet unknown, one school of thought maintained that so great a discharge of water could flow only from the Niger. Mungo Park had come to believe in this theory and Banks also inclined towards it. On the other hand Rennell, the most eminent English geographer of his day, believed that the Niger never reached the sea at all but terminated in the inland sea (Lake Chad) which was known to exist in the Kanem-Bornu area. Barrow shared this belief up to a point but differed from Rennell in thinking that the Niger flowed on eastward past Lake Chad and merged its waters with those of the Nile. Finally there was the theory which a German geographer, Reichardt, had put forward in 1803 that the Niger flowed into the sea in the Bight of Benin. This happened to be the correct explanation but as the creeks of the delta dispersed and concealed the flow of the current, it found few supporters when it was first propounded and Rennell was able to produce a number of plausible reasons for rejecting it.[2]

To solve this mystery the Government planned two ambitious expeditions. The first, organised by the Admiralty and placed under the command of a naval officer, Captain Tuckey, was to attempt to sail up the river which Banks believed to be the Niger but which we now know to be the Congo. The second, arranged by the Colonial Office and placed under the command of Major Peddie, was to follow Mungo Park's line from Senegambia to the upper Niger and then embark on the river. Somewhere, it was hoped, the two expeditions would meet and join forces. In the event both proved to be costly failures. The Congo party made their way upstream for about 200 miles but then came upon rapids which there were no means of circumventing. They therefore returned to England but not before the climate had taken a heavy toll. The Senegambian expedition, on the other hand, met the same unmitigated hostility on the part of the African population that Mungo Park had encountered. Despite great persistence and heavy losses among the Europeans, they failed to reach the Niger and in the end were forced to abandon the enterprise and return home.[3]

Meanwhile a naval officer, Captain W. H. Smyth, who had been given the task of surveying parts of the North African coastline, was sending back reports which revived interest in the northern route. Tripoli, he said, would make a good base for an expedition to the Sudan. The Fezzan,

2. Ibid, pp. 255 and 285.
3. Ibid, p. 231.

which lay athwart the main caravan road and which had previously been independant, was now under the Pasha's direct control. The Sultan of Fezzan, moreover, had recently led a raid to the Sudan and was said to be preparing another which a European traveller could join. Early in 1817 the Admiral in command at Malta sent these reports to the Admiralty which passed them on to the Colonial Office.

The British Consul in Tripoli, an able and enterprising official named Warrington, was instructed to sound the Pasha on the proposition and reported that he was so eager to ingratiate himself with the Prince Regent that he had offered to promote an expedition to Timbuktu. Lord Bathurst, the Colonial Secretary, thereupon agreed to provide the necessary funds and asked Sir Joseph Banks to recommend a suitable person to undertake the journey. The choice again fell on a young Scots Doctor, Joseph Ritchie, and early in 1818 he was given an official appointment as Consul in the Fezzan, and a naval officer, Lieutenant George Lyon, was seconded to accompany him. From Tripoli they travelled inland to Murzuk, the capital of the Fezzan where Hornemann had stayed twenty years earlier. While they were waiting there for a caravan however, Ritchie fell ill and died, whereupon Lyon returned to Tripoli.[4]

By this time Tuckey's expedition had already ended in failure and Peddie's was clearly making no headway. The British Government therefore decided that the best prospect of success clearly lay in the northern route and that a further attempt was justified. After what seems to have been a rather perfunctory search, Walter Oudney, another Scottish doctor, was selected as the leader of a new expedition.

In many ways Oudney was an admirable choice. A man of humble origin he had started life as a surgeon's mate on a man-o'-war and had served during the recent hostilities on the East India station. Though still professionally unqualified he had been promoted first to Assistant Surgeon and then to Surgeon. With the peace, however, he had found himself back in the United Kingdom on half pay. He had therefore returned to his native Edinburgh to study and in 1817 had qualified as a doctor of medicine. To earn a living he had then entered a private practice but his hopes were actually set on becoming a University lecturer. Moreover, in addition to medicine, he had studied chemistry and natural science and he had a special interest in botany. It was no doubt this combination of qualifications and interests that particularly commended him to the Colonial office and to their advisers.

4. Ibid, pp. 231 and 286-7.

Oudney was now thirty years of age and he is described as being of medium height and slight build with a pale, grave face and pleasing manners. He was unmarried but his mother was still alive and seems to have been dependent on him.[5] In spite of his apparent suitability however, Oudney's personality was not strong enough for leadership nor was his physique tough enough for the rigours of African exploration. It was known that he had certain constitutional weaknesses but his assurance that, as a doctor, he could treat himself was believed and he was not rejected, as he almost certainly ought to have been, on account of these disabilities.

The second member of the expedition was Hugh Clapperton, another naval officer also of Scottish descent. Since 1817 the Navy had found no employment for him and he had therefore been living at home on halfpay. Though he owed his appointment to his friendship with Oudney, he was a man of a completely different stamp. Where Oudney was frail, quiet and studious, Clapperton was robust, gregarious and gay. He came of a good Border family but he had had a chequered boyhood and received little formal education. In the Navy, though he had not been present at any of the great battles, his career had still been full of adventure and incident. In age he was slightly senior to Oudney and like him, was still unmarried. Now in his early thirties, he was physically in his prime and possessed a splendid physique and a face that was strikingly handsome.[6]

In the autumn of 1821 Oudney and Clapperton made their way to Tripoli by way of Malta. On arrival they were met by the Consul, Warrington, who put them up in his own house and showed them every consideration. There they began the preparations for their journey and waited for the other members of their party to join them.

* * *

With the Arab conquest in the middle of the seventh century Tripoli had become part of the Islamic world. In 1510 A.D., it is true, the city was reconquered for Christendom by Ferdinand of Castile and in 1528 was entrusted to the Knights of St John of Malta. The Knights soon found themselves hard-pressed however, and in 1553 they were forced to abandon the place to the Turkish corsairs, Dragut and Sinan. For the next century and a half Tripolitania, like its neighbours to the east and west, was a Province of the Ottoman Empire, governed by Pashas appointed by

5. DNB.
6. Ibid.

the Sacred Porte. But in 1714 the Pasha of the day, Ahmed Karamanli, threw off his allegiance and founded a dynasty which was to rule the country for over a century. He and his descendents still styled themselves Pasha, it is true and continued to send presents to Constantinople. They paid no tribute however and obeyed no orders, so that in all but name they were independent.

Geographically the Tripolitania of the early nineteenth century was generally coterminous with the modern state of Libya. It was bounded on the west by Tunisia and on the east by the desert which separated it from Egypt. Apart from the Fezzan, which had been tributary since its subjugation a decade earlier but which still enjoyed a degree of independence, there were four provinces. The population was made up of Berbers, Arabs, Turks, Jews and Negroes. The Berbers, peasants and craftsmen, were to be found in both town and country. The Arabs lived mainly in the interior. Many of them, indeed, were still nomadic or semi-nomadic pastoralists, descendents of the original Bedouins of the Beni Hilall, who followed their flocks and were governed through their Sheikhs. The Turks, descended from the soldiers of the Ottoman period, continued to provide the Pasha with most of his troops. On the other hand the majority of the petty civil officials, both in the palace and the public service, were not Turks but were negro slaves or freedmen. Also some Jews lived in the towns and followed their traditional pursuits.[7]

The population of the city of Tripoli was estimated at this time to be about 25,000. During the long struggle between Christendom and Islam, its seamen had come to regard the ships of Christian nations as fair game. During the seventeenth and eighteenth centuries they continued to prey on shipping and from time to time this provoked retaliation. In 1675 for example, Sir John Narborough, being sent to teach them a lesson, bombarded the port and sank four ships.[8] There were other similar incidents but most of the Christian nations preferred to pay subsidies to ensure that their ships were not molested. But this expedient did not always ensure immunity and in 1801 the United States had had to declare war to defend its interests and even schemed to overthrow the Pasha of the day and have him supplanted by a rival.[9]

So long as they enjoyed the protection of Turkey, the Pashas could take considerable liberties with the Christian powers and yet be fairly

---

7. E. Blaquiere, *Letters from the Mediterranean,* London 1813, 11, pp. 1-58 and 97.
8. Ibid.
9. Enc. Brit.

certain that nothing worse than reprisals would follow. The war with the United States however, seems to have brought home to them that their independence had dangers as well as advantages. Consequently when Great Britain, which had earlier won popularity amongst the Moslem world by compelling the French to evacuate Egypt, emerged from the Napoleonic Wars as easily the strongest maritime power in the world, it was natural that Tripoli should have sought its friendship. A feeling of dynastic insecurity, rather than his professed admiration for the Prince Regent, explains why the Pasha was now so ready to assist the British Government in its plans for African exploration.

* * *

In November, 1821, Oudney and Clapperton were joined in Tripoli by the other two members of the expedition. The first was Major Dixon Denham, an army officer of thirty-five who had volunteered to make the journey to Timbuktu but who had been assigned instead to Oudney's expedition. With him he brought William Hillman, a shipwright stationed in Malta who had volunteered his services and who had been engaged on a salary of £120 per annum.

Denham was a keen and enterprising addition to the party. He evidently enjoyed keeping a log of the journey and, while they were all together, his companions were content to leave the task to him. Consequently the greater part of the account of the expedition which was later published as a book, is his work.[10] Clapperton's contribution was confined to an account of the journey he made from Bornu to Hausaland and Sokoto and Oudney's to a single early chapter about an excursion in the Fezzan.

Denham, warmly received by Warrington, was greatly impressed by the influence that the Consul had established over the Pasha:

> Of this gentleman it is not too much to say that, by his cheerful and good-humored disposition, his zeal, perseverance, and extraordinary good management, we owe in a great degree that influence which England possesses with this government far beyond that of any other of the Barbary powers. The English name, in fact, is of such importance in Tripoli that there is scarcely a point to carry or a dispute to settle in which the Pasha does not request the interference of the British Consul.[11]

10. Dixon Denham, Hugh Clapperton, and Walter Oudney, *Narrative of Travels and Discoveries in Northern and Central Africa*, London, 1826, 2 vols..
11. Ibid, 1, pp. 2-3. Denham employed the word 'Bashaw' but in this book the more familiar 'Pasha' will be used.

33 | PREPARATIONS IN TRIPOLI

The tribute to Warrington's efficiency was well merited and the explorers were later to have reason to be thankful for having such a man behind them.

Now that the members of the expedition were all assembled, Warrington arranged for them to be received in audience:

> On a day appointed we waited on the Pasha. After passing the court-yard, crowded with guards and several groups of Arabs in the passages and ante-rooms playing at cards or dice, we were introduced to the audience chamber where the Pasha, sitting cross-legged on a carpet, supported by his two sons and attended by armed negroes, received us kindly, ordered us to be served with coffee, and expressed himself in the most favourable manner on the subject of our mission, which he promised to forward in safety into the interior of Africa.[12]

On another day, at the Pasha's invitation, they joined him in a hawking party.

The winter was the best time for crossing the Sahara but the season was already so far advanced that there was no hope of making the passage that year. The explorers therefore took their time over their preparations and it was not until early March 1822 that they at length set out for Murzuk, the capital of the Fezzan, which was their first destination.

After thirteen days, when they had covered about half the distance and were approaching the town of Sokna, they saw their first caravan, of slaves marching northward:

> The uniformity of the journey was somewhat enlivened, by meeting with a *Kafila* of slaves, from Fezzan, in which were about seventy negresses, much better looking, and more healthy, than any we had seen near the sea-coast. They were marching in parties of fifteen or twenty and, on our inquiring of one of those parties from whence they came, the poor things divided themselves with the greatest simplicity and answered, 'Hausaland, Baghirmi, and Kanem', pointing out the different parcels from each country as they spoke. Those from Hausaland had the most regular features, and an expression of countenance particularly pleasing.[13]

---

12. Ibid, p. 6.
13. Ibid, p. 13. Denham often used the word 'Sudan' when he was actually referring to Hausaland. Nowadays, however, when the Sudan has become a general term applied to the whole savannah region between the Sahara and the tropical rain-forests, such usage is misleading. So in this and many other quotations, where the real meaning is plain from the context, 'Hausaland' has been substituted for 'Sudan'.

At this stage the party numbered twelve. Beside the four Europeans, there were three Africans whom the officers had engaged in Tripoli as their personal servants. Having already obtained their freedom, they now wanted to make their way back to their homes. In addition there were four camel drivers and a Gibraltar Jew called Jacob who acted as a store-keeper and factotum. Later Denham recruited a native of the island of St Vincent who brought the party's number up to thirteen. His real name was Adolfus Symkins but, because he had travelled widely, he was known by the nickname of Columbus. Beside three European languages, he spoke excellent Arabic. More important, being staunch and loyal, he was to prove a most valuable member of the expedition.[14]

In previous expeditions, it will be remembered, Houghton and Mungo Park had travelled as avowed Christians and as a result had suffered severe persecution from bigoted Moslems. Hornemann and Burckhardt had therefore passed themselves off as Moslems and had aroused no hostility. Ritchie and Lyon could not pretend to be anything but Christians in Tripoli but it seems to have been their intention, when they reached the interior, to assume the character of Moslems.[15] Oudney's party, however, rejected such deception and decided to make no secret of their race and faith.[16] They always wore European dress, though they sometimes modified it with Turkish trousers or an Arab burnous and Denham and Clapperton had uniforms with them which they donned on special occasions.[17]

The distance from Tripoli to Murzuk is a good 500 miles. The country has few features and the travellers found it dreary and uninteresting. As they penetrated further south, so the water became more muddy, bitter, and brackish. Once they went three days without finding any water at all and soon afterwards they were overtaken by their first sand-storm. These experiences, though not very severe, gave them a foretaste of the hardships that lay ahead. At length, on 7 April 1822, after having been over a month on the road, the party reached Murzuk.[18]

* * *

14. Ibid, p. 51.
15. Ibid, p. 14. Referring to a Turk who had been helpful to Ritchie and himself in Tripoli, Lyon wrote . . . 'He was perfectly qualified to caution us on many points which, had we remained in ignorance of them, would inevitably have betrayed us to be Christians to the people of the interior'. See Hallett, p. 183n.
16. Denham, 1, p. 14, and II, pp. 186-7.
17. Denham, 1, p. 27 and Clapperton, 11, p. 265.
18. Denham, 1, pp. 16-18.

35 | PREPARATIONS IN TRIPOLI

The Fezzan, of which Murzuk was the capital, had once been the country of the Garamantes, whom Herodotus described as a powerful people and later as the province of Phazania it had become part of the Roman Empire. Since the Arab invasions of the seventh century however, it had passed into the Islamic world. In the middle of the sixteenth century, when the Turks were establishing themselves in Tripoli, a Shereef from Morocco had founded a dynasty which had lasted two and a half centuries. The country had sometimes been in conflict with Tripoli and intermittently had had to pay tribute. But generally it had preserved its independence. In 1811 however, there had come a serious clash with Yusuf Pasha in which the Fezzaneers had been defeated, their Sultan killed and the dynasty extinguished. Yusuf had thereupon annexed the country and installed his own general, El-Mukkeni as the new Sultan. Since then, though it had not quite been reduced to the status of a province, it had been virtually completely subservient to the Pasha in Tripoli.[19]

When the travellers reached Murzuk, they were lodged in the same house that Ritchie and Lyon had occupied three years earlier. As soon as might be they went to call on the Sultan, Mustafa. Though he received them affably, his news was far from encouraging. Contrary to what they had been led to believe, he said there was no prospect of an expedition leaving for the Sudan in the near future. For a journey to Bornu an escort of two hundred men was necessary and a force of this size could only travel during the cool weather. In any case he himself had been summoned to Tripoli and his instructions were to arrange for the safety and comfort of the expedition until his return.[20] The explorers had supposed that the Pasha had made arrangements for them in advance and that when they reached Murzuk they would find everything ready for an early start. Consequently they were all the more dispirited by this setback, particularly when they recalled that Ritchie and Lyon had been held up here for six months until Ritchie's death had caused their expedition to be abandoned.[21]

Later in the same week the travellers had their first meeting with Abubakr Bu-Khalum, a Fezzan merchant of considerable wealth and influence. Like the Sultan, with whom he was on very bad terms, he was about to go to Tripoli to see the Pasha. He said that the Sultan could

19. Encyclopaedia Britannica.
20. Denham, I, pp. 20-21.
21. Hallett, p. 287.

easily arrange for them to go to Bornu but, as he did not choose to do so, it would be best if, without revealing where the suggestion had originated, they asked the Pasha if he, Bu-Khalum, could accompany them. If this could be arranged, a hundred other merchants would join them and no escort would be necessary. Impressed by the man and his proposals, Oudney lost no time in dispatching a letter to Warrington in Tripoli.[22]

Next day Bu-Khalum, followed by a train of 500 slaves and 30 laden camels, his present for the Pasha, started for Tripoli. A few days later the Sultan, accompanied by no fewer than 1500 slaves, set out after him. Between them they had stripped Murzuk almost completely bare. After enduring the heat and the flies for a month, the explorers decided that there was nothing for it but for one of their number to return to Tripoli and demand of the Pasha that he should fulfil the undertakings he had given in return for the subsidies made to him by Great Britain. For this task the choice fell on Denham and by 12 June 1822, after covering the ground in twenty days, he was back in Tripoli.[23]

On the following day, accompanied by Warrington, Denham had an audience of the Pasha. He protested in the strongest terms at the delay to which the party was being subjected in Murzuk and demanded that a definite date should be set for their journey to Bornu. Otherwise, he said, he would travel straight to England and inform the British government of the Pasha's breach of faith. In reply the Pasha denied that he had broken his word and ascribed the delay, not very convincingly, to the will of God in visiting the Sultan of Fezzan with sickness.[24]

Dissatisfied with this answer, Denham took ship for Marseilles. The reaction of the Pasha to this move showed how concerned he was to retain the confidence and friendship of Great Britain. Not knowing Denham's destination, he sent despatches after him by three separate vessels saying that he had appointed Bu-Khalum and an escort to convey the explorers to Bornu forthwith. Denham received one of these messages while still in quarantine in Marseilles and feeling that he had achieved his object, he returned at once to Tripoli. From there he took the road south again, this time in Bu-Khalum's company and by the end of October he was back in Murzuk.

During Denham's absence his three companions made a long excursion to the west. This had given them some experience of desert travel and had

22. Denham, I p. 23.
23. Ibid, pp. 22-25.
24. Ibid, p. 26.

helped to pass the time. Moreover, by getting them away from the mosquitoes and flies of Murzuk, it had kept them fit. As soon as they returned to the town however, they succumbed to malaria and dysentery, the twin scourges of African travellers. When Denham returned therefore, none of them was well enough to ride out and welcome him. What was particularly ominous was that Oudney, having caught a cold on the excursion, was also having serious trouble with his weak chest.[25]

The Pasha had promised Bu-Khalum and his charges an escort of two hundred men. The most loyal and obedient of the Bedouin tribes in Tripolitania had been given orders to furnish men in proportion to their strength and these now began to muster in Murzuk. There were eleven different contingents and, apart from one of seventy men, the numbers in each varied between ten and thirty.[26]

In the European party the officers had furnished themselves with horses but Hillman was content with a mule. Of the servants, Columbus and Jacob also seem to have been mounted but the others were not. As for the Arabs, some had horses but the greater number went on foot. None, surprisingly, had camels of their own. For the desert passage, however, two camels were required for every mounted man and one for every man on foot.[27] Before the expedition could set off therefore, Bu-Khalum had to mobilize a very large baggage train. Mindful of the peremptory orders that he had received from the Pasha, he threw himself into the task with the greatest energy and in the short space of four weeks he had completed all his preparations. During this period the expedition was reinforced by the accession to it of merchants from Tripoli, Sokna and Mesurata, as well as from Murzuk itself, all wishing to take advantage of the presence of an escort in order to travel to the interior with their merchandise.[28] Towards the end of the month everything was ready for the start.

25. Ibid, p. 49.
26. Ibid, pp. 51-56.
27. Ibid, p. 21.
28. Ibid, p. 51.

II

The Sahara

On 29 November 1822 the caravan, commanded by Bu-Khalum and accompanied for a short distance by every inhabitant of Murzuk who could muster a horse, left the town by the south gate and set off along the Bornu road. Among the Arabs, Fezzaneers and Africans, the little group of Europeans must have been thinking of all their predecessors who had been swallowed by this enormous continent and wondering how many of them were destined to return.

It was not long after passing through Traghan, a walled town near Murzuk, that the travellers had their first taste of real desert travel. They found that the experience was not without its compensations:

> Starting at sunrise we had another fatiguing day over the same kind of desert without, I think, seeing one living thing that did not belong to our caravan—not a bird or even an insect. It is difficult to give the most distant idea of the stillness and beauty of a night scene... The burning heat of the day is succeeded by cool and refreshing breezes and the sky ever illumined by large and brilliant stars or an unclouded moon. By removing the loose and pearl-like sand to the depth of a few inches, the effects of the sunbeams of the day are not perceptible and a most soft and refreshing couch is easily formed. The ripple of the driving sand resembles that of a murmuring stream... The luxury of an evening of this description is an indescribable relief.[1]

1. Ibid. pp. 114-5. Denham habitually used the word *Kafila* (= coffle) but it never gained currency in English and so here and elsewhere 'caravan' has been substituted for it.

THE SAHARA

To escape from Murzuk, where they had all been ill, Oudney, Clapperton and Hillman had gone ahead to Gatrone. When the caravan caught up with them Denham found that their health was not much improved. Clapperton's fever had not left him, Hillman had had two such violent attacks that Oudney had given him up as lost and Oudney himself was suffering from a bad cough and still complaining of his chest. Even Denham felt himself to be debilitated after a severe attack in Murzuk but he found that compared to the others, he was strong. They were in poor shape for the rigorous journey that lay ahead of them but their determination to press on was unimpaired.[2]

Three days later, at Tegerhy, the caravan entered Tubu country. The Tubus were a people of mixed Arab and Negro blood who spoke a language akin to Kanuri.[3] They now inhabited a large area of the eastern and central Sahara round Tibesti. They lived rather precariously off their flocks and herds and on the profits of the salt and natron trade which they conducted with the Sudan and the tolls that they levied on trans-Saharan caravans. These pursuits brought them into frequent collision with the Tuaregs, a Berber people of much purer descent, who controlled the rest of the desert. As the Tuaregs were the fiercer and more predatory they generally emerged as the victors from these encounters and currently were gaining ground at the Tubus' expense.

At Tegerhy the four Europeans were still sickly. Hillman in fact was so weak that he had to be helped on and off his mule and his companions wondered whether they would have to leave him behind. They were most reluctant to do so but they knew that one of the hardest sections of their route lay immediately ahead of them and they wondered whether, in his weakened state, he was capable of marching from sunrise to dark for ten or twelve days on end. In the event however, this agonising decision did not have to be made because four days of rest improved the condition of the explorers so much that they all felt that they were fit to proceed.[4]

After replenishing its stock of dates, taking all that Tegerhy had to offer, the caravan set off again on December 13. Soon afterwards, at the wells of Omah, the travellers saw the first of the many human skeletons that they were to encounter along the route. Hillman, who was still weak and ill, was naturally much shaken by the spectacle. But worse was yet to come because, just as they reached the southern border of Fezzan, they

2. Ibid. p. 116.
3. H.R. Palmer, *Sudanese Memoirs*, III, p. 33.
4. Denham, I. pp. 119-20.

came upon much greater quantities of the human detritus that the slave trade had deposited.

> About sunset we halted near a well, within half a mile of Meshru. Round this spot were lying more than a hundred skeletons, some of them with the skin still remaining attached to the bones, not even a little sand thrown over them. The Arabs laughed heartily at my expression of horror and said 'they were only blacks, damn their fathers' and began knocking about the limbs with the butt end of their firelocks, saying 'This was a woman! This was a youngster!'[5]

Denham learned that they were the remains of captives who, having been taken in the Sultan of Fezzan's great raid on Baghirmi, had succumbed while being marched across the desert to slavery in North Africa.[6] On the following day there was another grisly encounter to report.

> One of the skeletons we passed today had a very fresh appearance: the beard was still hanging to the skin of the face and the features were still discernible. A merchant travelling with the caravan suddenly exclaimed 'That was my slave! I left him behind four months ago, near this spot'.
>
> 'Make haste! Take him to the market' said an Arab wag 'for fear anybody else should claim him.'[7]

But surprisingly enough there was life to be found as well as death and the same day one of the she-camels lay down in the path and, after only five minutes labour, was delivered of a fine little calf. The mother was then reloaded, the calf was slung across the back of another camel and the caravan moved on.[8]

The country here, though not sandy, was flat, monotonous and completely desiccated. The camels went eight days without water, Hillman became ill again and Dr. Oudney was so exhausted by the long marches that he lacked any strength to attend him. Moreover, as Tubus had been seen shadowing the caravan, there was reason to fear an attack. Strict orders were therefore given to keep in close order and avoid straggling.[9]

---

5. Ibid. pp. 125-7.
6. Ibid. p. 127. Denham said that the raid had taken place in the previous year 1821, but it was certainly earlier. Barth gave its date as 1818. (See *Travels,* Ch. VI p. 8, 10/8/52) but in fact, as Warrington in Tripoli knew of it in 1816, it cannot have been later than that.
7. Ibid. pp. 128-9.
8. Ibid. p. 128.
9. Ibid. pp. 129-30.

Because of the difficulties of the terrain and the lack of water, this section of the route, half way between Murzuk and Bilma, was a veritable graveyard.

> During the last two days we had passed, on an average, from sixty to eighty or ninety skeletons each day, but the numbers that lay about the wells of El-Hammar were countless. Those of two women, whose perfect and regular teeth bespoke them young, were particularly shocking. Their arms still remained clasped round each other, as they had expired, although the flesh had long since perished by being exposed to the burning rays of the sun and the blackened bones only left. The nails of the fingers and some of the sinews of the hand also remained and part of the tongue of one of them still appeared through the teeth.[10]

Denham, who as we shall see was by no means insensitive to feminine charm, was clearly touched by this spectacle. Soon afterwards his sensibility received another shock when his horse trampled on two skeletons while he was dozing in the saddle and kicked one of the skulls ahead of him like a football.

* * *

Christmas Day, 1822, was passed like any other. The morning was mild and sunny. The men filled their skins with water which though impregnated with sulphur was otherwise not disagreeable. At eight o'clock the caravan moved off and not until seven in the evening was a halt called. On New Year's Day, 1823, they reached Ikhbar, a valley in which there were patches of greenery, and they were glad of a day's rest. On the next march however, when twenty-four miles were covered, two of the camels foundered.

> On such occasions the Arabs wait in savage impatience in the rear, with their knives in their hands, ready on the signal of the owner to plunge them into the poor animal and tear off a portion of the flesh for their evening meal. . . . I attended the slaughter of one and, despatch being the order of the day, a knife is stuck in the camel's heart while his head is turned to the east and he dies almost in an instant. But before that instant expires, a dozen knives are thrust into different parts of the carcass in order to carry off the choicest parts of the flesh. The heart, considered the greatest delicacy, is torn out, the skin stripped from the breast and haunches, part of

---

10. Ibid. pp. 130-1.

the meat cut, or rather torn, from the bones and thrust into bags, and the remainder of the carcass is left for the crows, vultures and hyenas.[11]

On this same day exhaustion accounted for the poodle which had accompanied the Europeans all the way from Tripoli.

On January 5 the caravan reached Kisbi, a place where the westerly route to Agades and Katsina diverges from the easterly route to Bilma and Kuka. Here they were ordered to halt so that the ruler of the local Tubus could collect the tribute which he levied on all who crossed his territory. When he and his henchmen appeared however, they proved to be both dirty and dull-witted. Denham's attempt to engage their interest by displaying his watch and compass met with no success and even his musical box, the trump card of all early African explorers, failed to rouse them. But at least the Emir was conscious of not being as clean as he should have been because he afterwards took Denham aside to beg a piece of soap. By contrast the houses in the little town were neat and tidy. The inhabitants were mostly itinerant traders who, travelling north as far as Murzuk and south as far as Bornu, often spent eight months in the year away from home. They and their families lived in constant dread of the Tubus' enemies, the Tuaregs, who were very aggressive at this period.

The caravan now entered the region around Bilma where the water-table was high and the soil powerfully impregnated by saline deposits. After the monotony of the desert, the travellers were delighted to come upon two salt lakes, each about two miles in circumference, studded with islands, surrounded by palms and acacias and haunted by birds of the plover species. Soon afterwards they saw a herd of oxen and were exhilarated to think that they were again in a country that could afford fresh milk and wholesome food.[12] Near Dirki, another Tubu town, there were two natron lakes.

> ... Incrustations of pure, or almost pure, natron are found, sometimes extending several miles. The borders of these lakes have the same appearance: they are composed of a black mud which, almost as soon as exposed to the sun and air, becomes crisp like fresh-dug earth in a frosty morning. In the centre of each of these lakes is a solid body or island of natron which, the inhabitants say, increases in size annually. The one in the lake to the east is probably fourteen

11. Ibid. p. 137.
12. Ibid. pp. 142-3.

or fifteen feet in height and one hundred in circumference ... it breaks off in firm pieces but is easily reduced to powder.[13]

For this natron, hydrated sodium carbonate, there was a brisk demand in Bornu and Hausaland where it was compounded into medicines, used as an animal-lick and employed in the process of soap-making.

On January 12 the caravan reached Bilma, the place in the Kawar oasis which served the Chief as his capital. It lacked any of the attributes of a capital however, and its main importance lay in its being the centre of the salt and natron trade which formed the main support of the Tubus.

> The town stands in a hollow, and is surrounded by low mud walls which, with the houses within, are mean and miserable. About two miles north of the town are a few huts, and near them several lakes in which are great quantities of very pure crystallized salt; some was brought to us for sale in baskets, beautifully white, and of an excellent flavour. On visiting the two most productive lakes, which lay between low sand hills, I expressed my surprise at the difference between that which the Tubus were carrying away from the heaps by the side of the water and that which I had seen the day before; I however found that their time for gathering the salt was at the end of the dry season when it was taken in large masses from the borders of the lake. This transparent kind they put into bags and send to Bornu and Hausaland; a coarser sort is also formed into hard pillars for which a ready market is found. In Hausaland a single pillar weighing eleven pounds brings four or five dollars. The Tuaregs supply themselves with salt entirely from the wadis of the Tubus. Twenty thousand bags of salt were said to have been carried off during the last year by the Tuaregs alone. The Tubus say, 'It is hard to rob us, not only for their own consumption, but for the purposes of commerce too; and in consequence of paying nothing for the commodity, undersell us likewise in the market.'[14]

* * *

When the caravan left Bilma in mid-January, after a halt of only a few days, it entered upon one of the most difficult sections of the whole desert passage. Contrary to popular belief, the going over much of the Sahara is firm, often hard, but here the explorers encountered for the first time really deep sand and gigantic shifting dunes.

13. Ibid. p. 145.
14. Ibid. pp. 153-4.

> Our road lay over loose hills of fine sand, in which the camels sank nearly knee-deep. In passing these desert wilds, where hills disappear in a single night by the drifting of the sand and where all traces of the passage even of a large caravan sometimes vanish in a few hours, the Tubus have certain points in the dark sandstone ridges, which from time to time raise their heads in the midst of this dry ocean of sand and form the only variety, and by them they steer their course. From one of these landmarks we waded through sand formed into hills from twenty to sixty feet in height, with nearly perpendicular sides, the camels blundering and falling with their heavy loads. The greatest care is taken by the drivers in descending these banks; the Arabs hang with all their weight on the animal's tail, by which means they steady him in his descent. Without this precaution the camel generally falls forward and, of course, all he carries goes over his head.[15]

On traversing this section the caravan lost twenty-four of its camels through straying or foundering and it was only after nine days of exhausting travel that they reached the oasis of Aghadem.

When they set off again, after a day's rest, they met two couriers from Bornu carrying despatches to Murzuk, who said that they expected to complete their journey of a thousand miles in under forty days.

> The Tubus are the only people who will undertake this most arduous service and the chances are so much against both returning in safety that one is never sent alone. The two men we encountered were mounted on two superb *maherhies* and proceeding at the rate of about six miles an hour. A bag of parched corn and one or two skins for water, with a small brass basin and a wooden bowl out of which they ate and drank, were all their comforts. A little meat cut in strips and dried in the sun is sometimes added to the store. A bag is suspended under the tail of the *maherhy*, by which means the dung is preserved, and this serves as fuel on halting in the night. Without a caravan and a sufficient number of camels to carry such indispensables as wood and water, it is indeed a perilous journey.[16]

On January 27 the travellers saw the first signs that they were beginning to emerge from the desert. First clumps of coarse grass appeared, then mimosas, next a herd of more than a hundred gazelle and finally an ostrich. The caravan had, in fact, reached the extreme northern limit of the monsoon rain-belt and was entering the territory of Mina Tahr, the

15. Ibid. p. 155.
16. Ibid. pp. 163-4.

ruler of the Tubus of Gunda. Had it been weaker he would have extracted a stiff levy, up to half the goods it carried, before giving a safe-conduct. He was only a petty chieftain however, and he knew better than to try conclusions with so strong a party or to risk provoking the powerful rulers in the north whom they represented. He was therefore content to call on Bu-Khalum in his tent and receive from him presents consisting of a scarlet burnous and a silk kaftan.[17]

Denham noted at this time how the men's tastes adapted themselves to necessity. Six months ago, he said, camel's milk would have acted on them as an emetic but now they considered it a most refreshing and grateful cordial. But after long periods of privation it was necessary to exercise great restraint in the choice of rich food, particularly meat.

> Eating more than a very moderate quantity ever disorders the stomach which is often succeeded by fever, ague, and all its attendant evils. Although not gormandizers, some of us suffered from too great an indulgence in the luxuries of boiled mutton. Illness here should be the more avoided from its being altogether of a nature different from illness elsewhere: the attacks are sudden and render a person incapable of exertion, leaving him in a state of weakness and debility scarcely credible to those who have not been eye-witnesses to the fact.[18]

In the desert the explorers had thrown off the malaria and dysentery that had plagued them in Murzuk and had generally managed to maintain good health. But after their short stay in Bilma, due probably more to the flies than to an over-indulgence on their part, their dysentery returned.

> The wind and drifting sand were so violent that we were obliged to keep to our tents the whole day. Besides this, I was more disordered than I had been since leaving Murzuk. I found a loose shirt only the most convenient covering, as the sand could be shaken off as it made a lodgement which, with other articles of dress, could not be done, and the irritation it caused produced a soreness almost intolerable. A little oil or fat from the hand of a negress (all of whom are early taught the art of shampooing to perfection) rubbed well round the neck, loins, and back, is the best cure, and the greatest comfort, in cases of this kind. And although from my Christian belief I was deprived of the luxury of possessing half a dozen of these shampooing beauties, yet by marrying my negro Barka to one of the Pasha's

17. Ibid. pp. 164-5.
18. Ibid. 168-9.

> freed women slaves, as I had done at Sokna, I became to a certain degree also the master of Zerega, whose education in the castle had been of a superior kind, and she was of the greatest use to me on these occasions of fatigue or sickness. It is an undoubted fact, and in no case probably better exemplified than in my own, that man naturally longs for attentions and support from female hands, of whatever colour or country, so soon as debility or sickness comes upon him.[19]

The Gunda Tubus, who inhabited the semi-desert country between Bilma and Lake Chad, were ruled by a hereditary Sheikh, the seventh of his line, who owed allegiance neither to Murzuk nor Bornu and only loosely to Tripoli. They grew a little millet and, through brigandage or blackmail, exacted what they could from the caravans which traversed their territory. But their main wealth lay in their herds and their Sheikh boasted to Denham that the tribe had more than five thousand camels. For six months in the year they lived on practically nothing but camel's milk which they drank both sweet and sour. Corn being rare and precious, they even fed camel's milk to their horses which Denham found to be fat, handsome and in excellent condition.

The men of Gunda were of medium height, slim but well-built and had sharp intelligent faces, high foreheads, prominent eyes and copper coloured skin. But they lacked sophistication and not only went in fear of their enemies, the Tuaregs, but also held the Arabs in exaggerated awe.

> It is quite surprising with what terror these children of the desert view the Arabs and the idea they have of their invincibility, while they are smart active fellows themselves and both ride and move better and quicker. But the guns! the guns! are their dread, and five or six of them will go round and round a tree, where an Arab has laid down his gun for a minute, stepping on tiptoe, as if afraid of disturbing it, talking to each other in a whisper, as if the gun could understand their exclamations, and I dare say praying to it not to do them an injury as fervently as ever man Friday did to Robinson Crusoe's musket.[20]

Like the Tuaregs, the Gunda Tubus had a bad reputation for preying on travellers and small caravans[21] but the fault did not always lie with them. When the explorers reached Kanimani, for example, Bu-Khalum

19. Ibid. pp. 167-8.
20. Ibid. p. 170.
21. Ibid. p. 201.

decided to send two messengers ahead to El-Kanemi, the ruler of Bornu, to give him notice of their approach. Two days later one of the messengers was found tied to a tree by the road, stark naked and robbed of all his possessions including the despatches. He told how he and his companion had been waylaid by a party of eighteen men who had stripped them and taken their camels, saying that they cared nothing either for El-Kanemi or Bu-Khalum. The assailants were identified as being the Wandela, a small tribe of Tubus who had taken up brigandage as their way of life.

> Mina Tahr represented these people as the worst on the road in every sense of the word. 'They have no flocks,' said he, 'and have not more than three hundred camels, although their numbers are one thousand or more; they live by plunder and have no connexion with any other people. No considerable body of men can follow them; their tents are in the heart of the desert and there are no wells for four days in the line of their retreat. Giddy-ben-Agah is their chief and I alone would give fifty camels for his head. These are the people who often attack and murder travellers and small caravans and the Gundowy, who respect strangers, have the credit of it.'[22]

Even when the Wandala were not involved, however, it was clear that the fault did not always lie with the natives and that sometimes the provocation came from the other side. Such was clearly the case when the caravan's Arab escort got out of hand.

> Arabs are always on the look out for plunder—'Tis my vocation, Hal!' None are ashamed to acknowledge it, but they were on this occasion to act as an escort to oppose banditti, not play the part of one. Nevertheless, greatly dissatisfied were they at having come so far and done so little: they formed small parties for reconnoitring on each side of the road and were open-mounted for anything that might offer.
>
> One fellow on foot had traced the marks of a flock of sheep to a small village of tents to the east of our course and now gave notice of the discovery he had made, but added that the people had seen him and, he believed, struck their tents. I felt that I should be a check upon them in their plunderings, and Bu-Khalum, myself, and about a dozen horsemen (with each a footman behind him) instantly started for their retreat which lay over the hills to the east. On arriving at the spot, in a valley of considerable beauty where these flocks and tents had been observed, we found the place quite

22. Ibid. p. 177.

deserted. The poor frighted shepherds had moved off with their all, knowing too well what would be their treatment from the white people, as they call the Arabs. Their caution, however, was made the excuse for plundering them and a pursuit was instantly determined on. 'What! Not stay to sell their sheep, the rogues! We'll take them now without payment.'

We scoured two valleys, without discovering the fugitives, and I began to hope that the Tubus had eluded their pursuers when, after crossing a deep ravine and ascending the succeeding ridge, we came directly on about two hundred head of cattle and about twenty persons—men, women and children— with ten camels laden with their tents and other necessaries, all moving off. The extra Arabs instantly slipped from behind their leaders and, with a shout, rushed down the hill; part headed the cattle, to prevent their escape, and the most rapid plunder I could have conceived quickly commenced. The camels were instantly brought to the ground and every part of their load rifled. The poor women and girls lifted up their hands to me, stripped as they were to the skin, but I could do nothing for them beyond saving their lives. A sheikh and a maraboot assured me it was quite lawful (*halal*) to plunder those who left their tents instead of supplying travellers.

Bu-Khalum now came up and was petitioned. I saw he was ashamed of the paltry booty his followers had obtained, as well as moved by the tears of the sufferers. I seized the favourable moment and advised that the Arabs should give everything back and have a few sheep and an ox for a feast. He gave the order and the Arabs, from under their barracans, threw down the wrappers they had torn off the bodies of the Tubu women. And I was glad in my heart when, taking ten sheep and a fat bullock, we left these poor creatures to their fate as, had more Arabs arrived, they would most certainly have stripped them of everything.[23]

This was the first intimation that the explorers received that their Arab companions were growing restless.

Three days later there was a similar incident as the caravan was approaching Lake Chad. The local Tubus refused to provide the Arabs with milk and the high words which followed ended in the Arabs giving the Tubu sheikh a thrashing and driving off half his stock. Again Bu-Khalum, who as a Fezzaneer seemed to have had less false pride than the Arabs and a greater sense of justice, had to intervene to secure the return of the animals. This he did, with a caution to the Sheihk to be more

23. Ibid. pp. 174-6.

accommodating in future and the trouble seemed to have been smoothed over.[24] But these Traita Tubus, unlike the Gunda Tubus further north, acknowledged the suzerainty of Bornu and enjoyed its protection.[25] We may be sure, therefore, that the incident was reported in the capital before ever the caravan got there and it may well have created prejudice.

Later on the same day, 4 February 1823, the caravan reached the town of Lari. Here the explorers, with intense gratification, caught sight of the first of their objectives.

> The great Lake, Chad, glowing with the golden rays of the sun in its strength, appeared to be within a mile of the spot on which we stood. My heart bounded within me at the prospect, for I believed the lake to be the key to the great object of our search, and I could not refrain from silently imploring Heaven's continued protection...[26]

Apart from the unfortunate Hornemann, the explorers believed that they were the first Europeans ever to have looked upon the lake.[27]

24. Ibid. pp. 180-1.
25. Ibid. pp. 180 and 200-201.
26. Ibid. p. 182.
27. This belief was probably inaccurate. There is evidence that a Franciscan mission penetrated as far as Katsina in 1710. Fr. Carlo and Fr. Severino da Delesia, a Bohemian who spoke fluent Arabic travelled this same route from Tripoli through Fezzan. Travelling through Bornu, they eventually reached Katsina. In August 1711 both died in that city. No further penetration was attempted by the Franciscan Order until 1845. (Journal of African History VIII 3 (1967) pp. 383-393. *Christian Traces and a Franciscan Mission in the Central Sudan 1700-1711*, by Richard Gray).

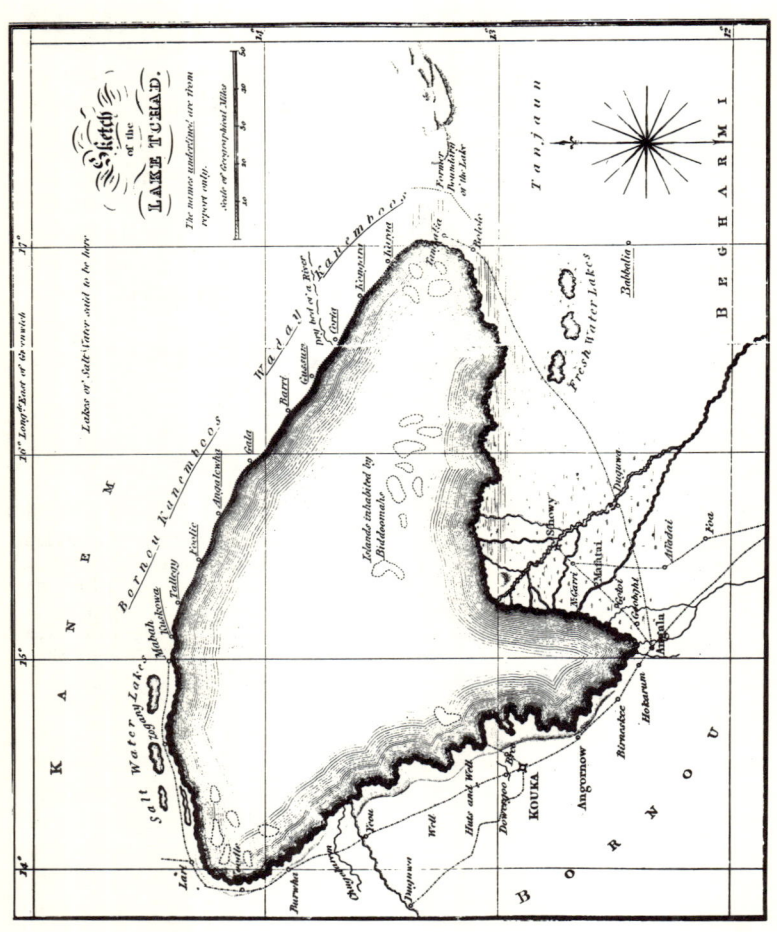

Denham's original map of the environs of Lake Chad.

III

Lake Chad

The people of Lari, when they first saw the caravan, thought that it was a raiding party come out of the desert and so they took to their heels and scattered in every direction.

> It was long before Bu-Khalum's best endeavours could restore confidence: the inhabitants had been plundered by the Tuaregs only the year before and four hundred of their people butchered and, but a few days before, a party of the same nation had again pillaged them, though partially. When at length these people were satisfied that no harm was intended them, the women came in numbers with baskets of millet, beans, fowls, and honey, which were purchased by small pieces of coral and amber, of the coarsest kind, and coloured beads. One merchant bought a fine lamb for two bits of amber worth, I should think, about twopence each in Europe. Two needles purchased a fowl and a handful of salt, four or five good sized fish from the lake. Lari is inhabited by the people of Kanem who are known by the name of Kanembu. The women are good-looking laughing negresses and all but naked. . . .[1]

Although the explorers had by now penetrated fifteen hundred miles into the continent, they had hitherto been moving in an environment which was an extension of the Maghreb and among people who, in the main, had Arab or Berber blood in them. In Lari they caught their first glimpse of the authentic Sub-Sahara. Even there, of course, the influence

1. Denham, I. pp. 182-3.

of the Maghreb was still felt but the watershed had now been crossed and the scene was unmistakably Black African.

> In the evening I visited the town of Lari: it stands on an eminence and may probably contain two thousand inhabitants. The huts are built of rush which grows by the sides of the lake, have conical tops, and look very like well-thatched stacks of corn in England. They have neat enclosures around them, made with fences of the same reed, and passages leading to them like labyrinths. In the enclosure is a goat or two, poultry, and sometimes a cow. The women were almost all spinning cotton, which grows well, though not abundantly, near the town and lake. The interior of the huts is neat: they are completely circular, with no admission for air or light except at the door, which has a mat hung up by way of safeguard. I entered one of the best appearance. In one corner stood the bed, a couch of rushes lashed together and supported by six poles fixed strongly in the ground. This was covered by the skins of the tiger-cat and wild-bull. Round the sides were hung the wooden bowls used for water and milk... The hut had a division of mat-work, one half being allotted to the female part of the family.[2]

At this time of the year, early February, the long dry-season of the Sudan was little more than half over and although no rain would have fallen since the previous September, equally none could be expected until the following May. The cold weather however would have been approaching its end and during the day the sun recovering its customary heat. Nevertheless the mornings would still have been crisp and bracing and the evenings pleasantly cool, perhaps even chilly. On such a day, Denham took his gun and went down to the Lakeside.

> By sunrise I was on the borders of the lake... Flocks of geese and wild ducks, of a most beautiful plumage, were quietly feeding at within half pistol shot of where I stood... As I moved towards them they only changed their places a little to the right or left and appeared to have no idea of the hostility of my intentions. All this was really so new that I hesitated to abuse the confidence with which they regarded me and very quietly sat down to contemplate the scene before me. Pelicans, cranes, four and five feet in height, grey variegated, and white, were scarcely so many yards from my side, and a bird between a snipe and a woodcock, resembling both and larger than either; immense spoonbills of a snowy whiteness,

---

2. Ibid. pp. 186-7. The animal Denham described as a wild-bull was no doubt a bush-cow.

widgeon, teal, yellow-legged plover, and a hundred species of (to me at least) unknown water fowl, were sporting before me, and it was long before I could disturb the tranquility of the dwellers on these waters by firing a gun.

The soil near the edges of the lake was a firm dark mud and, in proof of the great overflowings and recedings of the waters, even in this advanced dry season, the stalks of the millet of the preceding year were standing in the lake, more than forty yards from the shore. The water is sweet and pleasant, and abounds with fish which the natives have a curious way of catching. Some thirty or forty women go into the lake, with their wrappers brought up between their legs and tied round their middles ... and, forming a line at some distance in the water, fronting the land for it is very shallow near the edges, absolutely charge the fish before them so close that they are caught by the hand or leap upon the shore.[3]

While Denham was amusing himself by the lake, his horse freed itself from its bridle and trotted back to the camp. At the same time his burnous, which had been thrown over the saddle, fell to the ground where it was soon afterwards retrieved by one of the women of the party. Seeing first the riderless horse and then the abandoned burnous, Bu-Khalum jumped to the conclusion that Denham must have been carried off by a party of Buduma the buccaneers of the lake. These people, inhabiting inaccessible islands, preyed constantly upon the riparian population, subjecting them to murder, arson, kidnap, pillage, robbery and cattle lifting and frequently imposing a "danegeld" which the less warlike villagers were usually more than ready to pay. The dread in which the Buduma were held was surpassed only by that which the Tuaregs inspired. Bu-Khalum hastily organised a search-party of Arabs who arming themselves, mounted their horses and hurried down to the lake. There, after a long search, they at length found Denham, safe and sound but loaded with more birds than he could well carry.[4]

The solicitude that the Arabs showed here for Denham's safety probably contained an element of self-interest but there is no doubt, as will later appear, that they developed a genuine affection for him and he for them. The fact is that he had a way with him. After being educated at the Merchant Taylors' School, he had originally been destined for a solicitor's office, but was of far too adventurous a nature to settle down in such a prosaic career. In 1811, therefore, at the age of twenty-five,

3. Ibid. pp. 183-4. This method is still utilized, especially in Western Sokoto.
4. Ibid. pp. 185-6.

Denham had thrown his job and joined the army, which was then engaged in the Peninsular campaign. In the following year he had been commissioned into the Royal Welch Fusiliers and had seen active service in Portugal, Spain, and southern France. In 1813, as a 1st Lieutenant, he had distinguished himself at the battle of Toulouse by carrying Sir James Douglas out of the fire when Douglas had lost a leg. Later, after transferring to the 54th Foot, he had been with the reserve at Waterloo and assisted at the occupation of Paris.

Though in war his courage and enterprise had earned him the respect and affection of his brother officers, Denham lacked either the seniority or influence to maintain the momentum of his career in peace. In 1818 therefore, like hundreds of other officers, he had found himself relegated to half pay and had spent a year travelling in France and Italy. Later, it is true, he had succeeded in gaining a place at the Royal Military College but he must have felt that his prospects were limited because it was from there, after hearing of Ritchie's death in Murzuk, that he had volunteered to fill the vacancy. Now he was in his mid-thirties, and it is clear that ten years of soldiering and travel, coupled with a naturally extrovert temperament, had taught him how to get on with all manner of men.

Nor was it only with the Arabs that Denham made his friends. During the desert marches he had got onto equally good terms with the Africans, a fact which the Arabs, with their contempt for the negro races, found incomprehensible.

> A gratifying scene took place this morning in the departure of nearly thirty freed slaves, natives of Kanem, who here left us for their homes, three days' journey to the eastward. I had been applied to, the night before, to intercede with Bu-Khalum for this indulgence for, as he had heard that the Sheikh was at war with some of the chiefs of Kanem, he had determined on first taking them to Bornu for fear of their being plundered on the road of the little they had saved in slavery. These poor creatures had, however, found one or two of their countrymen at the market of Lari who assured them of their safety on the road between that place and their homes. The good man complied with evident reluctance on their own account and they took leave, kissing his hand with tears and blessings.
>
> They had most of them been in the service of the Pasha, some for a term of years, and were returning to die at home at last. One poor deaf and dumb woman, whom the rapacity of Mukni, the former Sultan of Fezzan who spared neither age, sex nor infirmity had induced him to march to Tripoli, had shed torrents of tears ever

since she had been made acquainted by signs that she was to go to Bornu. She had left two children behind her and the third, which was in her arms when she was taken by the Arabs, had been torn from her breast after the first ten days of her journey across the desert in order that she might keep up with the camels. Her expressive motions in describing the manner in which the child was forced from her and thrown on the sand, where it was left to perish, while whips were applied to her, lame and worn out as she was, to quicken her tottering steps, were highly eloquent and interesting.

They had all been my friends for more than five months, and to some I had rendered little services by carrying their bags of parched corn or salt. They were not ungrateful and our parting had something in it affecting, which, considering negroes in the degraded light they do, seemed greatly to astonish the Arabs.[5]

*   *   *

On February 6, after only one day of rest and relaxation, the caravan left Lari and, skirting the north-west corner of the lake, made its way to Wudi. The contrast with the desert, which had so recently been left behind, could hardly have been greater. The country was thickly wooded, the ground moist and game plentiful.

> On quitting Lari, we immediately plunged into a thickly-planted forest of acacias, with high underwood, and at the distance of only a few hundred yards from the town we came upon large heaps of elephants' dung, forming hillocks three and four feet in height, and marks of their footsteps. The tracks of these animals increased as we proceeded. Part of the day, our road lay along the banks of the Chad, and the elephants' footmarks, of an immense size and only a few hours old, were in abundance. Whole trees were broken down where they had fed and, where they had reposed their ponderous bodies, young trees, shrubs, and underwood, had been crushed beneath their weight.
>
> We also killed this day an enormous snake, a species of coluber; it was a most disgusting, horrible animal but not, however, venomous. It measured eighteen feet from the mouth to the tail; it was shot by five balls and was still moving off when two Arabs, with each a sword, nearly severed the head from the body. On opening the belly, several pounds of fat were found and carefully taken off by the two native guides who accompanied us. This they pronounced a

---

5. Ibid. pp. 187-9.

> sovereign remedy for sick and diseased cattle, and much prized amongst them.
> We bivouacked near a small parcel of huts, called Nyagami, in a beautiful spot so thick of wood that we could scarcely find a clear place for our encampment. While the tents were fixing, an alarm was given of wild boars; one of our party followed the scent and, on his return, said he had seen a lion and near him seven gazelles.[6]

At Wudi, Bu-Khalum received a message from El-Kanemi, the ruler of Bornu, saying that the caravan was not to approach any nearer until his pleasure was known. The Arabs, aware of the suspicion with which they were regarded in the Sudan, speculated gloomily about their chances of being admitted to the capital. Later on the following evening however, two more messengers arrived bearing letters in which El-Kanemi pressed Bu-Khalum to continue his march to Kuka and to bring all his people with him. This was regarded as a very great mark of confidence and favour, especially as the messengers were also authorised to promise that the caravan would be supplied with fifteen bullocks, six sheep and seventeen baskets of millet. Some of these provisions were furnished then and there while the remainder were to be provided at Yo, two days march to the south. As a personal present from El-Kanemi the messengers also brought baskets of cola-nuts which, then as now, were considered one of the greatest delicacies and which the explorers here tasted for the first time. 'They have a pleasant bitter taste' wrote Denham 'and are much esteemed by all the people of Tripoli. After eating these nuts, water has a grateful flavour, be it never so bad. The Arabs call them the coffee of the black country.'[7]

At Barua, which they reached next day, the explorers saw for the first time one of the great walls of sun-baked clay by which the towns Bornu and Hausaland were protected.

> The walls may be about thirteen or fourteen feet high and have a dry ditch which runs quite round them. The town probably covers an extent equal to three square miles and contains five or six thousand inhabitants. There is a covered-way from which the defenders lance their spears at the besiegers and instantly conceal themselves. There are but two gates, which are nearly East and West; and these being the most vulnerable parts for an enemy to attack, are defended by mounds of earth thrown up on each side

---

6. Ibid. pp. 189-190. The snake must have been a python, a species which is still fairly common in Bornu and Hausaland.
7. Ibid. pp. 194 and 198-9.

> and carried out at least twenty yards in front of the gate ... [with] nearly perpendicular faces. These advanced posts are always thickly manned, and they conceive them to be a great defence to their walls; they cannot, however, calculate upon their being abandoned, as an enemy once in possession of them would so completely command the town that from thence every part of it may be seen.[8]

The town had apparently been attacked from time to time by Tuareg marauders but never taken.

The country south of Barua was still full of game. The Arabs killed a wild hog on the road and in the evening, despite fires round the camp, a lion killed one of the camels. Hyenas later moved in to finish what he had left. On the following day, February 13, the caravan reached the Yobe, the principal river flowing into Lake Chad from the west. As the dry-season was far advanced, the stream was now only fifty yards wide but still deep enough for canoes to be needed at the crossing and with a current running at three and a half knots.

> The camels and horses swim with their heads made fast to the canoes. These canoes were of the rudest manufacture and were formed of planks, rudely shaped by a small hatchet and strongly fastened together by cords passed through holes bored in them, and a wisp of straw between, which they say effectually keeps out the water. They have high poops like the Grecian boats and would hold twenty or thirty persons. The air from a running stream of clear water, and the freshness it imparted to all around, was such a relief after a march through sandy deserts that both man and beast were in a manner renovated by its effects. The men, and even the women, bathed and washed and the negroes swam all the horses.[9]

Two days later, when the caravan was approaching Kuka, the capital of Bornu, a message was brought to Bu-Khalum requesting him to pitch camp as the huts which were being prepared for his men in the city were not yet ready. The Arabs now began to speculate on the kind of reception that they would receive. Their theories differed but all agreed that a large body of troops would turn out to meet them and that the purpose of such a demonstration would be more than just to pay the Pasha a compliment.

* * *

8. Ibid. pp. 199-200.
9. Ibid. p. 204. In its lower reaches the Yobe traverses such sandy country that, unlike most rivers, its volume of surface water, instead of increasing, actually diminishes. Near Chad it is a smaller river than are some of its main tributaries further up-stream.

At length, on 17 February 1823, the signal to advance was again given.

Notwithstanding all the difficulties that had presented themselves at the various stages of our journey, we were at last within a few short miles of our destination; were about to become acquainted with a people who had never seen, or scarcely heard of, a European; and to tread on ground, the knowledge and true situation of which had hitherto been wholly unknown...

Our accounts had been so contradictory of the state of this country that no opinion could be formed as to the real condition or the numbers of its inhabitants. We had been told that the Sheikh's soldiers were a few ragged negroes armed with spears who lived upon the plunder of the negro countries by which he was surrounded and which he was enabled to subdue by the assistance of a few Arabs who were in his service. And, again, we had been assured that his forces were not only numerous but to a certain degree well trained. The degree of credit which might be attached to these reports was nearly balanced in the scales of probability and we advanced towards the town of Kuka in a most interesting state of uncertainty, whether we should find its chief at the head of thousands or be received by him under a tree, surrounded by a few naked slaves.

These doubts, however, were quickly removed. I had ridden on a short distance in front of Bu-Khalum, with his train of Arabs all mounted and dressed out in their best apparel, and from the thickness of the trees soon lost sight of them. Fancying that the road could not be mistaken, I rode still onwards and, on approaching a spot less thickly planted, was not a little surprised to see in front of me a body of several thousand cavalry drawn up in line and extending right and left quite as far as I could see; and, checking my horse, I awaited the arrival of my party under the shade of a wide-spreading acacia. The Bornu troops remained quite steady, without noise or confusion, and a few horsemen who were moving about in front giving directions were the only persons out of the ranks.

On the Arabs appearing in sight, a shout or yell was given by the Sheik's people which rent the air; a blast was blown from their rude instruments of music, equally loud, and they moved on to meet Bu-Khalum and his Arabs. There was an appearance of tact and management in their movements which astonished me: three separate small bodies, from the centre of each flank, kept charging rapidly towards us, to within a few feet of our horses' heads, without checking the speed of their own until the moment of their halt, while the whole body moved onwards. These parties...

mounted on small very perfect horses . . . stopped and wheeled from their utmost speed with great precision and expertness, shaking their spears over their heads, exclaiming *'Barka! Barka!*—Blessing! Blessing! Sons of your country! Sons of your country!' and returning quickly to the front of the body in order to repeat the charge.

While all this was going on, they closed in their right and left flanks and surrounded the little body of Arab warriors so completely as to give the compliment of welcoming them very much the appearance of a declaration of their contempt for their weakness. I am sure this was premeditated: we were all so closely pressed as to be nearly smothered and in some danger from the crowding of the horses and clashing of the spears. Moving on was impossible and we therefore came to a full stop. Our chief was much enraged but it was all to no purpose. He was only answered by shrieks of 'Welcome!' and spears most unpleasantly rattled over our heads expressive of the same feeling. This annoyance was not however of long duration: Barka Gana, the Sheikh's first General, a negro of a noble aspect clothed in a figured silk gown and mounted on a beautiful Mandara horse, made his appearance and, after a little delay, the rear was cleared of those who had pressed in upon us and we moved on. . .

The Sheikh's negroes, as they were called, meaning the black chiefs and favourites, all raised to that rank by some deed of bravery, were habited in coats of mail composed of iron chain which covered them from the throat to the knees, dividing behind and coming on each side of the horse. Some of them had helmets, or rather skull-caps, of the same metal, with chin-pieces, all sufficiently strong to ward off the shock of a spear. Their horses' heads were also defended by plates of iron, brass, and silver, just leaving sufficient room for the eyes of the animal.

At length, on arriving at the gate of the town, ourselves, Bu-Khalum, and about a dozen of his followers, were alone allowed to enter the gates, and we proceeded along a wide street completely lined with spearmen on foot, with cavalry in front of them, to the door of the Sheikh's residence. Here the horsemen were formed up three deep, and we came to a stand. Some of the chief attendants came out, and after a great many 'Barka's! Barka's!' retired, when others performed the same ceremony.

We were now again left sitting on our horses in the sun. Bu-Khalum began to lose all patience and swore by the Pasha's head that he would return to the tents if he was not immediately admitted. He got, however, no satisfaction but a motion of the hand from one of the chiefs, meaning 'wait patiently', and I whispered to him the necessity of obeying as we were hemmed in on all sides and to retire without permission would have been as difficult as to advance. Barka Gana now appeared and made a sign that Bu-Khalum should dismount; we were about to follow his example when an intimation that Bu-Khalum was alone to be admitted again fixed us to our saddles.

Another half hour at least passed without any news from the interior of the building when the gates opened and the four Englishmen only were called for and we advanced to the entrance. Here we were stopped most unceremoniously by the black guards-in-waiting and were allowed, one by one only, to ascend a staircase at the top of which we were again brought to a stand by crossed spears and the open flat hand of a negro laid upon our breast. Bu-Khalum came from the inner chamber and asked 'If we were prepared to salute the Sheikh as we did the Pasha?'. We replied 'Certainly', which was merely an inclination of the head and laying the right hand on the heart. He advised our laying our hands also on our heads, but we replied 'the thing was impossible! we had but one manner of salutation for anybody, except our own sovereign'. Another parley now took place but in a minute or two he returned and we were ushered into the presence of the Sheikh of Spears.

We found him in a small dark room, sitting on a carpet, plainly dressed in a blue Hausa gown and a shawl turban. Two negroes were on each side of him, armed with pistols, and on his carpet lay a brace of these instruments. Fire-arms were hanging in different parts of the room, presents from the Pasha and Mustafa, the Sultan of Fezzan, which are here considered as invaluable. His personal appearance was prepossessing, apparently not more than forty-five or forty-six, with an expressive countenance and a benevolent smile.

We delivered our letter from the Pasha and, after he had read it, he enquired 'what was our object in coming?' We answered 'to see the country merely, and to give an account of its inhabitants, produce, and appearance, as our Sultan was desirous of knowing every part of the globe.' His reply was that 'we were welcome and whatever he could show us would give him pleasure'.[10]

After this brief audience, the explorers were conducted to the lodging that had been prepared for them.

10. Ibid, pp. 206-213.

IV

Bornu

The State of Bornu, into which the explorers had now been welcomed, was the rump of one of the ancient Empires of the Sudan.

The early history of Kanem-Bornu is obscure, but its roots almost certainly go back to the early Berber migrations from North Africa to the Sudan which probably took place first in the seventh and then again in the eleventh centuries. It seems likely that the immigrants, who had been displaced from their homes by the Arab invasions of the Maghreb and had then chosen or been compelled by circumstances to make the arduous passage of the desert, were predominantly men and that it was the unions that they formed with Sudanese women which produced first the Kanembu people of Kanem and then, at one remove, the Kanuri people of Bornu. *Barebari,* the name by which the Hausas know the Kanuri, reveals the old link with the Berbers of North Africa.[1]

The State of Kanem, situated north-east of Lake Chad, was the first to emerge. According to legend its rulers, the Sefawa dynasty, were descended from an Arab who in pre-Islamic times had been the Persian viceroy of the Yemen.[2] On the other hand the Sudanese historian Yakubi described them as Zaghawa and Leo Africanus as Libyans, both terms indicating that they were of Berber and not of Arab descent.[3] There may

---

1. H.A.S. Johnston, The Fulani Empire of Sokoto, London, 1967, pp. 3-5 and 73.
2. H.R. Palmer, Sudanese Memoirs, Lagos, 1928, I, pp. 4-6.
3. Ibid, p. 6.

be an element of truth in both versions because we know from the Arab historian El-Bekri that some of the Umayyads came to Kanem after the collapse of the dynasty in Damascus[4] and it is conceivable that, by intermarrying with the Berber ruling class, they gave rise to the legend of an Arabian origin.

Be that as it may, there is no doubt that the people of Kanem embraced Islam much sooner than their neighbours in Hausaland, perhaps as early as the twelfth century. At about the same time, under a vigorous ruler, they began the first phase of their expansion. Legends that they extended their authority from Egypt to the Niger are doubtless exaggerated but certainly Kanem then became a power in the Sudan. Its importance was founded on the great caravan route between Tripoli and Chad, the same that the explorers had just traversed. Their prosperity grew as they learnt to exploit it as a channel for exporting gold, ivory, and slaves and importing in exchange arms, horses, and the luxuries of the Mediterranean.[5]

In the thirteenth century the Kanembu began to spread around the northwestern corner of Lake Chad and down its western shore until they reached the river Yobe, a movement that brought them into collision with the indigenous pagan people. In the fighting which followed, the Kanembu were victorious and they thus gained control of the whole of northern Chad. But a generation or two later they were torn by a serious dynastic schism. As a result of it part of the ruling family broke away and established a new state named Gaoga in the region of Lake Fittri. By about A.D. 1385, Gaoga had become powerful enough to challenge and vanquish Kanem. The legitimate sultan was thereupon forced to abandon his capital to the usurping dynasty—who were now known as the Bulala—and to seek refuge in the settlements to the west of Lake Chad where the mingling of the blood of the Kanembu immigrants with that of the indigenous tribes was already in the process of producing a new and distinctive race, the Kanuri of Bornu.[6]

Despite their defeat and expulsion from Kanem, the legitimate branch of the Sefawa Dynasty retained the allegiance of the Kanuri in Bornu. Moreover, in a remarkably short space of time they succeeded in rebuilding their fortunes. In this task they were assisted not only by the loyal Kanuri but also by the Shuwa-Arab pastoralists who, after the destruction

4. Ibid, p. 6.
5. Johnston, pp. 73-4.
6. Ibid.

of the Christian kingdom of Nubia, had made their way from the Nile Valley to the central Sudan and had recently settled in substantial numbers round the southern shores of Lake Chad. Kanem now became a battle ground between the Sefawa and Bulala Dynasties. As it declined in importance, as inevitably was the case, so the centre of gravity shifted increasingly to Bornu.[7]

In the fourteenth and fifteenth centuries the prosperity of the Chad region was greatly enhanced by the reopening of the old caravan route from Egypt and later by its extension westwards to Gwanja and the gold-bearing regions of Ashanti. It was probably this second development that led, in about 1440 A.D., to Bornu's either conquering or else overawing the Hausa States. In 1488 A.D. its growing importance was marked by the construction on the River Yobe of a fine new capital, Ngazargamu and early in the following century Kanem itself was reconquered. The wheel had now come full circle and instead of Bornu being a province of Kanem, Kanem had become a tributary of Bornu. Moreover, with suzerainty over Kanem in the east and over all the Hausa States in the west, Bornu had emerged as a significant imperial power.[8]

In the turbulent conditions then prevailing in the Sudan, the Sultans of Bornu were never left for long in peace or to enjoy the fruits of their conquests. In the east, the war with Gaoga continued intermittently for several generations, reaching its peak of intensity in the period 1571-76.[9] Later, when the power of Gaoga began to decline, Baghirmi and Wadai continued to menace Bornu from this quarter. From the west the threats were no less serious. First, in the early sixteenth century, just when the Kanuri were preoccupied with the reconquest of Kanem, a Songhai army marched into Hausaland and annexed the principal Hausa States to the Songhai Empire. Then, very soon afterwards, the Hausa soldier of fortune, Muhammadu Kanta, defeated the armies of both Songhai and of Bornu and carved out an empire of his own at their expense. Next, as Kanta's empire began to disintegrate, a new threat appeared in the south, namely that of the Jukun of Kwararafa. For the whole of the seventeenth century the Jukun, from the seat of their power on the Benue River, disputed with Bornu the suzerainty of the Hausa States. By the early eighteenth century, however, their strength was on the ebb and in 1734 Bornu was able to reassert its suzerainty over Hausaland.[10] The empires

7. Ibid.
8. Ibid.
9. Palmer, I, pp. 14-72.
10. Johnston, p. 75.

of Ghana, Mali and Songhai having long since passed away, Bornu was now the most powerful state in the Sudan.

But, though the Kanuri did not realise it, a new danger to their hegemony had already begun to form. Throughout this period, by imperceptible degrees, the Fulani had been infiltrating the central Sudan from the west. They probably reached Hausaland in the twelfth century and Bornu soon afterwards. A few passed on eastward into Baghirmi and Wadai but the majority, finding the country congenial and suitable for the cattle which were their mainstay either stayed in Hausaland or Bornu or else turned south into what later came to be known as Bauchi and Adamawa. By the beginning of the nineteenth century they had become an important minority in all the Hausa States—perhaps a fifth of the total population—and were also well established in Bornu.[11]

* * *

The Fulani are one of the great enigmas of Africa. Unlike the Kanuri and the Hausas, they are not products of unions between Berbers and Sudanic peoples, nor are they of Arab descent. The structure of their language, Fulfulde, suggested that they originated in Senegambia but this evidence is not conclusive and their own legends assert that they came originally from Palestine. Their physical characteristics—copper-coloured skin, straight hair, narrow nose, thin lips and slight but wiry frames—bear out their claim that they are of Asiatic and not African origin and the fact that they speak a language that is classified as African can be explained by their having sojourned long enough in Senegambia to have discarded their own earlier language and picked up a local one.[12]

Whatever their origins, the Fulani are unquestionably a most talented people. Physically they are extremely tough and courageous. Intellectually they combine considerable natural gifts with a deep veneration for all learning and a particular aptitude for theology and law. Spiritually they are proud and uncompromising. By the time they reached Hausaland and Bornu the great majority of them were already Moslems and a substantial number were ready to relinquish their nomadic existence. Certainly with the passage of years, their way of life became more sedentary. They clung to their cattle, of course, but some took to farming and others to letters. In relation to their numbers, they produced a high proportion of divines and jurists. Nevertheless, though latterly they were

11. Ibid, pp. 24-5 and 75.
12. Johnston, p. 262.

living in close contact with the indigenous peoples, they seldom intermarried with them but remained a race apart. As Moslems, moreover, they were generally much stricter than the more genial and worldly Hausas and Kanuri.[13]

In the latter part of the eighteenth century a young Fulani teacher began to attract attention as a religious reformer in Gobir one of the leading Hausa States. His name was Othman d'an Fodiyo but to history he is generally known as Shehu Usman. At first the Chief of Gobir and his courtiers treated him with marked deference, but later, when they discovered that he was absolutely uncompromising in exposing oppression, denouncing corruption and insisting on the strict observance of Moslem law, their attitude changed. By this time however, he had attracted such a large following among the Hausa peasants as well as the Fulani pastoralists that they did not dare to molest him personally but instead began to persecute his adherents. At length in 1804, after a period of acute tension, he fled to the west with his closest followers and there, in a remote camp in the bush, he formally renounced his allegiance and declared a *jihad,* or holy war. Yunfa, the Chief of Gobir responded by leading an army against him with the object of crushing the movement once and for all. But, against all the odds, it was the reformers who emerged as the victors from the ensuing battle.[14]

After this victory, the Shehu wrote to the other Chiefs of Hausaland to explain why he had raised his banner against Sarkin Gobir. He was fighting for truth against falsehood, he explained, and called on them to join him in the struggle. But the Hausa ruling classes regarded the reformers with suspicion and accordingly they began to close their ranks and to take measures against the Fulani and the religious zealots within their own borders. The war therefore spread to all the other Hausa States.[15]

As the suzerain of Hausaland, Bornu ought to have assisted the Hausa Chiefs in suppressing the revolts with which they were now faced. In the event however, the Kanuri found that they were fully occupied in trying to contain the risings of their own Fulani, with the result that Bornu was unable to offer any reinforcements. Even so the Hausa Chiefs should have been capable of asserting their authority but, though they mobilized their feudal levies, they failed to obtain any support from their own peasantry

13. Ibid, p. 17-26.
14. Ibid, p. 35-46.
15. Ibid, p. 47-48.

who in the main remained passive.[16] On the other hand the Fulani, who everywhere formed the core of the reformers' movement, fought with fanatical courage and an unquenchable faith in an ultimate victory. One by one, therefore, the Hausa dynasties were toppled. Kebbi fell in 1804, Zazzau in 1805, Katsina in the dry-season of 1806-07, and Kano a year later in 1807-08.[17]

In Bornu the main concentrations of Fulani were in the west and south and it was there that the war first flared up. In the west the Galadima, who ruled the marches from the walled town of Nguru, was defeated and killed and the principalities of Auyo, Bedde, Shira and Tashena were overrun and remoulded into the Fulani Emirates of Hadejia and Katagum. In the south the pagan lands in the bend of the Gongola, which had hitherto been within Bornu's sphere of influence, were annexed and converted into the new Emirate of Gombe. Finally, having established bases in the south and west, the Fulani felt strong enough to attack the heart of Bornu. Their assault was completely successful and on 12 March 1808 they put the Sultan to flight and occupied Ngazargamu, the capital of the Empire.

In the *jihad*, for so it was pronounced by Shehu Usman, the stiffest resistance offered to the predominantly Fulani reformers came from their prime adversaries, the Gobirawa. In the autumn of 1808 however, their capital at Alkalawa was at last stormed and with its fall the war in Hausaland was brought to a close. The Shehu, was now the ruler of a very considerable empire. In the north, it covered the whole of Hausaland and most of Bornu and in the south it already included Bauchi and Adamawa and was still being advanced on a broad front.

After the series of defeats that the Kanuri had suffered, it seemed in 1808 that the Bornu Empire had been irretrievably shattered and even that the kingdom might disintegrate. But at this point the fugitive Sultan, Muhammadu Lefiami, summoned the assistance of Sheikh Muhammad el-Amin el-Kanemi, then still a comparatively young man and noted only for his piety and learning. El-Kanemi had great influence with his fellow Kanembu however, who were renowned as pikemen and he was also successful in mobilising in the Sultan's cause the majority of the Shuwa Arabs. By bringing in these reinforcements and rallying the demoralised Kanuri, he turned the tide of the war.

The triumphs which the Fulani had everywhere enjoyed had perhaps

16. Ibid, pp. 95-102 and 266.
17. Ibid, 47-72.

made them over-confident. At any rate, when El-Kanemi delivered his counter-stroke in the autumn of 1809, they were not prepared for it. Gwani Muktar, who had established himself in the old capital as Emir of a new Fulani Emirate comprising all of central Bornu, was killed in the fighting and his followers were driven out. The Kanuri then reoccupied Ngazargamu, only to lose it again in the dry-season of 1811-12 when the Fulani recaptured it for the second time. At length, after further inconclusive fighting, both sides seem to have realised that the sandy plains of central Bornu were not worth the price in blood. The Fulani therefore consolidated their gains in the west while the Kanuri fell back on Lake Chad in the east. No formal peace was made but, with the contestants now separated by an extensive no-mans-land, the fighting gradually petered out.[18]

From first to last the war had lasted nearly ten years. By the end of it the Fulani Empire, which now became established as the Caliphate of Sokoto and its fifteen attendant Emirates[19] was still expanding southwards in the direction of the Niger and Benue Rivers and had displaced Bornu as the leading power in the Sudan. Indeed it had emerged as the greatest power that the Sudan had seen since 1591 when the Songhai Empire had been overthrown by a Moroccan army. Bornu, by contrast, stood shorn of all its possessions except Kanem and Damagaram. Nevertheless, though now little more than a kingdom, it was still a potentially powerful one.

Long before the end of the war, effective authority in Bornu had passed from the Mai, as the Sultan of Bornu was known, to Sheikh El-Kanemi. In 1811 El-Kanemi proved this beyond question by deposing Mai Muhammadu Lefiami and then, in 1814, restoring him again. Three years later, as we shall see, Lefiami was killed when leading an expedition against Baghirmi. He was succeeded as Mai by Ibrahim who secured El-Kanemi's nomination by promising to resign to him all power and patronage. Under this arrangement El-Kanemi, though not the titular ruler, was the undisputed master of Bornu. Such was the position at the time when the explorers arrived.

* * *

18. Ibid, pp. 73-80.
19. The fifteen Emirates already in being were Kano, Katsina, Zaria, Bauchi, Adamawa, Daura, Hadeija, Katagum, Gombe, Kazaure, Aïr, Yauri, Gurma, Keffi and Jema'a. Gwandu is not included in the list because it had not yet been severed from Sokoto. Similarly Nupe, Lapai, Agaie, Lafiagi, Pategi and Ilorin had not yet been brought within the Empire and Misau, Lafia, Nassarawa, Jama'are, Muri and Kontagora had not yet been forged into separate Emirates.

68 | DENHAM IN BORNU

What sort of country was it that they had now reached? Among them, Denham during the next eighteen months was to take great pains to ingratiate himself with the people, the humble as well as the mighty and to study their history, environment, and customs. Having to contend with difficulties of language, and lacking as he did the means of verifying his information, he was sometimes led into error, it is true, but on the whole his account of Bornu and the Kanuri people is as faithful and realistic as it is interesting.

In addition to the descriptions which were woven into his narrative of experiences, Denham added a retrospective chapter to his book to supplement and draw together the scattered impressions he had already recorded. Though written as a summing-up, it also provides an excellent survey of the Bornu scene and is worthy of being quoted at some length.

> Bornu, a kingdom of central Africa, is comprehended, in its present state, between the 15th and 10th parallel northern latitude, and the 12th and 18th of east longitude.[20] It is bounded on the north by part of Kanem and the desert; on the east by the Lake Chad, which covers several thousand miles of country and contains many inhabited islands; on the south-east by the kingdom of Logone and the river Shari which divides Bornu from the kingdom of Baghirmi and loses itself in the waters of the Chad; on the south by Mandara, an independent kingdom situated at the foot of an extensive range of primitive mountains; and on the west by Hausaland.
>
> The heat is excessive but not uniform, from March to the end of June being the period when the sun has most power. At this season, about two hours after noon, the thermometer will rise sometimes to 105° and 107°, and suffocating and scorching winds from the south and south-east prevail.[21] The nights are dreadfully oppressive, the thermometer not falling much below 100° until a few hours before day-light when 86° or 88° denote comparative freshness.
>
> Towards the middle of May, Bornu is visited by violent tempests of thunder, lightning, and rain. Yet in such a dry state is the earth at this time, and so quickly is the water absorbed, that the inhabitants scarcely feel the inconvenience of the season. Considerable damage is done to the cattle and the people by the lightning. They now

20. Denham exaggerated the extent of Bornu's dominion to the east of Lake Chad. At this time it hardly went beyond 15°E.
21. Here Denham under-estimated the intensity of the heat in the hot season. Temperatures normally go up to 110-112°F and even higher figures have been recorded.

BORNU

prepare the ground for their corn and it is all in the earth before the end of June when the lakes and rivers begin to overflow. From the extreme flatness of the country, tracts of many miles are quickly converted into large lakes of water. Nearly constant rains now deluge the land with cloudy, damp, sultry weather. The winds are hot and violent and generally from the east and south.

In October the winter season commences: the rains are less frequent and the harvest near the towns is got in. The air is milder and more fresh, the weather serene; breezes blow from the north-west and with a clearer atmosphere. Towards December and in the beginning of January, Bornu is colder than from its situation might be expected. The thermometer will at no part of the day mount higher than 74° or 75°, and in the morning descends to 58° and 60°.

It is these cold fresh winds from the north and north-west that restore health and strength to the inhabitants, who suffer during the damp weather from dreadful attacks of fever and ague which carry off great numbers every year. The inhabitants are numerous; the principal towns or cities are thirteen. Ten different languages, or dialects of the same language, are spoken in the Empire.

The Bornu people, or Kanuri as they are called, have mouths of great dimensions, with good teeth, and high foreheads. They are peaceable, quiet, and civil: they salute each other with courteousness and warmth and there is a remarkable good-natured heaviness about them which is interesting. They are no warriors, but revengeful, and the best of them given to commit petty larcenies on every opportunity that offers.

As their country produces little beside grain, mostly from a want of industry in the people, so are they nearly without foreign trade. In their manner of living, they are simple in the extreme. Flour made into a paste, sweetened with honey, and fat poured over it, is a dish for a Sultan. The use of bread is not known; therefore but little wheat is grown. Indeed it is found only in the houses of the great. Barley is also scarce: a little is sown between the wheat and is used, when bruised, to take off the brackish taste of the water.

The grain most in use amongst the people of all classes, and upon which also animals are fed, is a species of millet called *gussub*. This grain is produced in great quantities, and with scarcely any trouble. The poorer people will eat it raw, or parched in the sun, and be satisfied without any other nourishment for several days together. Bruised and steeped in water, it forms the travelling stock of all pilgrims and soldiers. Four kinds of beans are raised in great quantities . . . and are eaten by the slaves and poorer people. A paste made from these and fish was the only eatable we could find in the towns near the river. Salt they scarcely knew the use of. Rice might have been cultivated in Bornu before it became the scene of such constant warfare as has for the last fifteen years defaced the country. It is now brought from Hausaland. Indian corn, cotton, and indigo, are the most valuable productions of the soil... The indigo is of a superior quality and forms a dye which is used in colouring gowns (the only dress the people wear) dark blue, which probably is not excelled in quality in any part of the world.

The only implement of husbandry they possess is an ill-shaped hoe, made from the iron found in the Mandara mountains, and the labours of their wretched agriculture devolve, almost entirely, on women. Most of their grain is reaped within two or three months of its being scattered on the earth (for it can scarcely be called sowing) and probably there is no spot of land between the tropics, not absolutely desert, so destitute of either fruit or vegetable as the kingdom of Bornu. Mangoes are only found growing in the neighbourhood of Mandara and to the west; and, with the exception of two or three lemon, or rather lime trees, and as many fig trees, in the garden of the Sheikh at Kuka, raised on a spot of ground watched by himself, the care and culture of which give employment to about fifty negroes, not a fruit of any description can be found in the whole kingdom. Date trees there are none south of Wudi, four days north of Kuka, where they are sickly and produce but an indifferent fruit. Onions are to be procured near the great towns only but no other vegetable.

The people indeed have nothing beyond the bare necessities of life and are rich only in slaves, bullocks, and horses. Their dress consists of one, two or three gowns, or large shirts, according to the means of the wearer. A cap of dark blue is worn on the head by persons of rank. Others, indeed generally all, go bare-headed, the head being kept constantly free from hair, as well as every other part of the body. They carry an immense club, three or four feet in length, with a round head to it, which they put to the ground at every step and walk with great solemnity, followed by two or three slaves. They have what we should call a rolling gait. Red caps are brought by the Tripoli and Mesurata merchants but are only purchased by the chiefs and their immediate attendants. They are Moslems and very particular in performing their prayers and ablutions five times a day. They are less tolerant than the Arabs and I have known a Bornuese refuse to eat with an Arab because he had not washed and prayed at the preceding appointed hour.

In the Bornu towns are many *Hajis* who have made the pilgrimage to Mecca and excel in writing the Arabic characters, as well as teaching the art to others. However strange it may appear, each caravan leaving Bornu for Fezzan (the only road now open) carries several copies of the Koran, written by the Bornu clerks, which will sell in Barbary or Egypt for forty or fifty dollars each. The Arabic characters are also used by them to express their own language: every chief has one of these clerks attached to him who writes despatches from his dictation with great facility.

They seldom take more than from two to three wives at a time, even the rich, and divorce them as often as they please by paying their dower. The poorer class are contented with one. The women are particularly cleanly but not good-looking: they have large mouths, very thick lips, and high foreheads. Their manner of dressing the hair is also less becoming than that of any other negro nation I have seen: it is brought over the top of the head in three thick rolls, one large one in the centre and two smaller on each side, just over the ears, joining in front on the forehead in a point, and plastered thickly with indigo and bees' wax. Behind the point it is wiry, very finely plaited, and turned up like a drake's tail.

The tattoos, which are common to all negro nations in these latitudes and by which their country is instantly known, are here particularly unbecoming. The Bornuese have twenty cuts or lines on each side of the face, which are drawn from the corners of the mouth towards the angles of the lower jaw and the cheekbone, and it is quite distressing to witness the torture the poor little children undergo who are thus marked, enduring not only the heat but the attacks of millions of flies. They also have one cut on the forehead in the centre, six on each arm, six on each leg and thigh, four on each breast, and nine on each side, just above the hips. They are, however, the most humble of females, never approaching their husbands except on their knees or speaking to any of the male sex otherwise than with the head and face covered and kneeling. When summoned to the matrimonial bed, they invariably enter at the foot.

Previous to marriage, there appears to be more jealousy than after. When two candidates declare themselves for one lady and are allowed to pay their visits (which, however, never extend beyond the inner court, when the solicited lady turns her back and the lover talks to the mother) each watches the motions of the other, but by stealth for such proceeding is considered very ill-bred. To be correct, one lover should enter while the other is urging his suit, unconscious of his intrusion: both affect great surprise at the appearance of a rival and the daggers, which they carry on the left

Kanuri women tired as described by Denham in 1823. Photos 1960. Denham's observations appear extremely harsh!

arm, are instantly unsheathed. Sometimes, after a parley, one of them declares his affection goes not so far as to fight for his mistress, in which case the bolder gallant turns him quickly out of the court. It oftener happens that they both fight desperately for a few minutes and the victor, of course, wins the day and the lady.

Adultery is not common. The punishment is very severe: if caught in the fact and secured on the spot, and this is the only evidence on which conviction is granted, the guilty couple are bound hand and foot, cast on the ground, and their brains dashed out by the club of the injured husband and his male relations.

Girls rarely marry until they are fourteen or fifteen, often not so young. The age of puberty does not arrive here at so early a period as in Barbary; females there not unfrequently becoming mothers at the age of twelve, and even eleven. In Bornu, such circumstance is unknown. For a woman to have twins is extremely rare, and to make them believe that more were ever brought into the world at one time, in any country, would be difficult.

The domestic animals are dogs, sheep, goats, cows, and herds of oxen beyond all calculation. The Shuwas on the banks of lake Chad have probably 20,000 near their different villages, while the shores of the great river Shari could furnish double than number. They also breed multitudes of horses with which they furnish the Hausa market where this animal is very inferior.

The domestic fowl is common and is the cheapest animal food that can be purchased: a dollar will purchase forty. They are small but well flavoured. The bees are so numerous as in some places to obstruct the passage of travellers. The honey is but partially collected. That buzzing, noisy insect, the locust, is also a frequent visitor. Clouds of them appear in the air and the natives, by screams and various noises, endeavour to prevent their descending to the earth. In the district where they pitch, every particle of vegetation is quickly devoured. The natives eat them with avidity, both roasted and boiled and formed into balls as a paste.

Game is abundant and consists of antelopes, gazelles, hares, an animal about the size of a red deer with annulated horns called *Kouorigum,* partridges very large, small grouse, wild ducks, geese, snipe, and the ostrich, the flesh of which is much esteemed. Pelicans, spoonbills, the Balearic crane in great numbers, with a variety of other large birds of the crane species, are also found in the marshes. The woods abound with guinea-fowl.

The wild animals are the lion, which in the wet season approaches to the walls of the towns, panthers, and a species of tiger-cat in great numbers in the neighbourhood of Mandara, the leopard, the hyena, the jackal, the civet cat, the fox, hosts of monkeys, black, grey and brown, and the elephant, the latter so numerous as to be seen near Lake Chad in herds of from fifty to four hundred. This noble animal they hunt and kill for the sake of his flesh as well as the ivory of his tusk. The buffalo, the flesh of which is a delicacy, has a high game flavour. The crocodile and the hippopotamus are also numerous, and the flesh of both is eaten. That of the crocodile is extremely fine: it has a green firm fat, resembling the turtle, and the callipee has the colour, firmness, and flavour of the finest veal. The giraffe is seen and killed by the buffalo hunters in the woods and marshy grounds near Chad. Reptiles are numerous; they consist of scorpions, centipedes, and disgusting large toads, serpents of several kinds, and a snake said to be harmless, of the congo kind, sometimes measuring fourteen and sixteen feet in length.

The beasts of burden used by the inhabitants are the bullock and the ass. A very fine breed of the latter is found in the Mandara valleys. Strangers and chiefs in the service of the Sheikh or Sultan alone possess camels. The bullock is the bearer of all the grain and other articles to and from the markets. A small saddle of plaited rushes is laid on him, when sacks made of goat-skins, and filled with corn, are lashed on his broad and able back. A leather thong is passed through the cartilage of his nose and serves as a bridle, while on the top of the load is mounted the owner, his wife, or his slave. Sometimes the daughter or the wife of a rich Shuwa will be mounted on her particular bullock and precede the loaded animals, extravagantly adorned with amber, silver rings, coral, and all sorts of finery, her hair streaming with fat, a black rim of *kohl*, at least an inch wide, round each of her eyes, and I may say arrayed for conquest at the crowded market. Carpets or gowns are then spread on her clumsy palfrey; she sits astride and, with considerable grace, guides her animal by his nose. Notwithstanding the peaceableness of his nature, her vanity still enables her to torture him into something like caperings and curvetings. The price of a good bullock is from three dollars to three dollars and a half.

The Bornu laws are arbitary and the punishment summary. Murder is punished by death: the culprit, on conviction, is handed over to the relations of the deceased who revenge his death with their clubs. Repeated thefts by the loss of a hand or by burying the young Spartan, if he be a beginner, with only his head above ground, well buttered or honeyed, and so exposing him for twelve or eighteen hours to the torture of a burning sun and innumerable flies and mosquitoes who all feast on him undisturbed. These punishments are, however, commuted for others of a more lenient kind. Even the judge himself has a strong fellow-feeling for a culprit of this description.

When a man refuses to pay his debts and has the means, on a creditor pushing his claims, the *Kadi* takes possession of the debtor's property, pays the demand, and takes a handsome percentage for his trouble. It is necessary, however, that the debtor should give his consent, but this is not long withheld as he is pinioned and laid on his back until it is given, for all which trouble and restiveness he pays handsomely to the *Kadi,* and they seldom find that a man gets into a scrape of this kind twice. On the other hand should a man be in debt, and unable to pay, on clearly proving his poverty he is at liberty. The judge then says, 'God send you the means'—the bystanders say 'Amen'—and the insolvent has full liberty to trade where he pleases. But if at any future time his creditors catch him with even two gowns on, or a red cap, on taking him before the *Kadi,* all superfluous habiliments are stripped off and given towards payment of his debts.

Appeals from the decisions of the *Kadi* may be made to the Sheikh in person by the meanest of his subjects and the question argued in full divan. His court is simple, though numerously attended. On certain days of the week, until the hour of mid-day prayer, he sits in the court-yard, outside his private apartments, and all his subjects have access to his presence and liberty to state their grievances. The governors of the different provinces sit immediately before him and introduce the case of their own people to his notice in their own language; he listens to the different witnesses without speaking and decides promptly and with judgement. A wave of the hand passes for a sentence of death, which is instantly executed, and a whisper decides a question of property which is, the moment after, placed in the possession of him who has the verdict in his favour.

The Sheikh is most anxious to encourage marriage and to curb licentiousness and looseness of morals amongst his people. The population of Bornu has, from the sacrifice of lives since he became ruler, greatly decreased, although beginning to recover itself. El-Kanemi's shrewdness has discovered that the Shuwas, who confine themselves wholly to their own women and generally to one wife, far exceed the blacks in fruitfulness and that the immorality of the latter is the probable cause of this falling off. The excessive severity of this Chief to the failings of the *beau-sexe* has only this excuse: a general looseness of manner has engendered extravagance amongst the fair which, though as yet not carried to an extent comprehensible to the ladies of the West, yet is nevertheless prejudicial to the welfare of the Bornu state and a regulation of marriage portions became necessary for the lower orders of society. During my stay a case of this kind was brought before the council and a man was imprisoned and all but bastinadoed, for having given two blue wrappers, or kerchiefs, their substitute for a chemise, as a wedding gift when one was considered equal to the apparent means and rank of the lady, notwithstanding he declared that she would not consent to a smaller settlement. Madame, however, did not escape without a lecture on the extravagance of her ideas, and was threatened with the disgraceful punishment of having her head shaved if any further complaints were heard against her on that score.

There is considerable form observed in their marriage ceremony which is esteemed a solemn contract: the bride as well as the bridegroom name a *wakil*, or representative, who is referred to on any disagreement taking place and sees justice done to both. For, although the husband has the power of divorcing his wife at pleasure, without giving any reason so that he pays the dower, yet the lady can also demand freedom under certain circumstances. For instance, should a husband sleep two nights together with another wife, the neglected one has a right of appeal. Her delicacy is however spared this explanation before the judge; she enters the justice-room veiled and turns her shoe with the sole uppermost: this is considered as sufficient to explain the nature of the charge and the *Kadi* forthwith examines into the case without asking a question. When these domestic misfortunes occur, they are usually attributed to fate and the ommission of certain charms which should always be performed on marriages: the sprinkling of warm salt water should never be omitted in every direction near the dwelling to prevent the approach of any evil spirit for, should such a one get between the new married couple, *his* strength might be taken away in an instant or *her* fruitfullness changed to dreary barrenness.

The husband, also, must never omit, on entering his wife's appartment after marriage, to look over the door, as the bride's friends constantly hide a shoe there, in order that he may pass under her foot, as they say. And, should he enter without finding it, her foot has been on his head and she rules the roost.

The towns generally are large and well built: they have walls thirty-five and forty feet in height and nearly twenty feet in thickness. They have four entrances, with three gates to each, made of solid planks eight or ten inches thick and fastened together with heavy clamps of iron. The houses consist of several court-yards, between four walls, with apartments leading out of them for slaves; then a passage and an inner court leading to the habitations of the different wives who have each a square space to themselves, enclosed by walls, and a handsome thatched hut. From thence also you ascend a wide stair-case of five or six steps, leading to the apartments of the owner which consist of two buildings like towers or turrets with a castellated window. The walls are made of reddish clay, as smooth as stucco, and the roofs most tastefully arched on the inside with branches and thatched on the out with grass. . . . The horns of the gazelle and antelope serve as a substitute for nails or pegs. These are fixed in different parts of the walls and on them hang the quivers, bows, spears, and shields of the chief. A man of consequence will sometimes have four of these terraces and eight turrets, forming the faces of his mansion or domain, with all the apartments of his women within the space below. Not only those *en activité* (as the French would say) but those on the superannuated list are allowed habitations. Horses and other animals are usually allowed an enclosure near one of the court-yards forming the entrance. Dwellings, however, of this description are not common...

Our dwellings were called *bongos* and were about eight feet in diameter inside, the shape of a hay-stack, and with a hole at the bottom, about two feet and a half high, which we used to creep in and out at. Air or light holes we were obliged to dispense with as they admitted both flies and mosquitoes which were worse than darkness.

Their utensils are few and consist of earthen pots for cooking, which they make beautifully, and wooden bowls for dishes. Water, which is their only beverage, is drunk from a large calabash . . . after being cooled in earthen jars. They sleep on mats covered with the skins of animals. Married women are extremely superstitious, in having their beds covered with the skins of particular animals when their husbands visit them, and never fail to predict the fate and fortune of a child in consequence of these arrangements. A panther or a leopard's skin is sure to produce a boy or nothing. Should the father be a soldier and a chief, the boy will be a warrior, bold but bloody. A lion's skin is said to prevent child-bearing altogether, yet exceptions to this rule sometimes occur. It is then always a boy and a wonderful one. He puts his foot on the necks of all the world and is alike brave, generous, and fortunate. Leather cushions of various colours, and fancifully ornamented, are brought from Hausaland and are used as pillows by persons of superior rank who also have a small Turkey carpet on which they sit or sleep and the price of which is a young female slave.

The amusements of the people consist in meeting together in the evenings, either in the courtyard of one of the houses of the great or under the shades formed with mats which are in the open places of the town ... Here they talk and sometimes play a game, resembling chess, with beans and twelve holes made in the sand. The Arabs have a game similar to this, which they play with camel's dung in the desert, but the Bornuese are far more skilful.

Like the birds, their day finishes when the sun goes down ... very few, even of the great people, indulge in the luxury of a lamp which is made of iron and filled with bullock's fat. They have no oil ... Soap is also an article they are greatly in want of. An oily juice, which exudes from the stem of a thorny tree called *Kadinya*,[22] resembling a gum, enables the people of Hausaland to make a coarse soap by mixing it with bullock's fat and natron. It is something like soft soap and has a pleasant smell. This is brought in small wooden boxes, holding less than half a pound, which sell for seven *rottala*[23] each, two-thirds of a dollar ... This tree is not found in Bornu.

The skin of their sheep is covered with a long hair; wool therefore they have none. Brass and copper are brought in small quantities from Barbary. A large copper kettle will sell for a slave. The brass is worked into leglets and worn by the women.

A small brass basin, tinned, is a present for a Sultan and is used to drink out of. Four or five dollars, or a Hausa gown, will scarcely purchase one. Gold is neither found in the country nor is it brought into it. The Tuaregs are almost the only merchants visiting Hausaland who trade in that metal which they carry to Barbary and Egypt. It is said the Sheikh has a store which is brought him directly from the Hausa States.

Iron is procured in the Mandara mountains, but it is not brought in large quantities and is coarse. The best iron comes from Hausaland, worked up in that country into good pots and kettles. The money of Bornu is the manufacture of the country. Strips of cotton, about three inches wide and a yard in length, are called *gubbuk,* and three, four, and five of these, according to their texture, go to a *rottala.* Ten *rottala* are now equal to a dollar.

Of the climate, it may be reckoned quite as healthy as any other country of the torrid zone, and far preferable to many. It is dreaded

22. This is the shea-butter tree, called in Hausa *Kadanya.*
23. *Rottala* is a corruption of *rotl*, a pound of copper, an early form of currency in Bornu which was already dying out in Denham's day and which Barth, a generation later, described as completely obsolete. See Barth's *Travels,* chapter xxx.

by the Arabs, particularly in the rainy season, and not without reason, but they allow that Hausaland is still more sickly. There appears to be a succession of the hot, the dry, and the humid, which tempers the climate. The whole country is flat and by far the greater part is covered with thick underwood and high coarse grass . . . [24]

---

24. Denham, II, pp. 157-176.

V

Kuka And New Birni

The town of Kuka, in which the explorers now found themselves, was the seat of the Sheikh, not of the Sultan, and as such was the administrative but not the ceremonial capital of Bornu. It had been built by El-Kanemi in the previous decade, after he had abandoned the idea of recapturing the western part of the Sultanate and had decided to consolidate his strength round Lake Chad and was therefore of recent origin when the explorers knew it.

Denham's plan shows that it was laid out on a roughly quadrangular plan. As is customary in Bornu towns, there was a long open space, the *dendal,* in front of the palace. This was intended primarily as a ceremonial parade ground but at that time it also served as a market. The northern wards were inhabited mainly by Kanuri, while the Kanembu lived in the south-west and the Shuwas in the south-east. The whole was enclosed by a wall, pierced by four gates and in area was just under a square mile.[1]

The quarters prepared for the explorers and their Arab companions were in open ground to the north of the market and at no great distance from the palace. They had been divided into separate compounds by fences or partitions made of *zanas,* the mats woven from tall grass which were and indeed still are a feature of life in the Sudan. In each compound

---

1. Denham, I, p. 263. When the explorer Barth came to Kuka in 1851, nearly a generation later, the town had grown to three times the size and the market had been moved to a site outside the walls.

there was a cluster of huts, little round buildings shaped like beehives with mud walls and thatched roofs.[2]

So far their reception had been reasonably friendly but the Europeans realized that the success of their mission and indeed their own comfort and safety, depended ultimately upon the all-powerful Sheikh. If they could win his trust and friendship, everything else would be added unto them. If, on the other hand, they aroused his suspicion or animosity, they might find themselves under constraint, even in danger, and it would certainly be impossible for them to accomplish what they had come to do. They must therefore have looked forward with a mixture of hope and trepidation to their first meeting with this remarkable man about whose character and exploits they had already heard so much.

> Born in Fezzan of Kanem parents, though on his father's side descended from a Moor, El-Kanemi had, after visiting Egypt, proceeded to Kanem ... where he was greatly beloved and respected on account of the extreme correctness of his life and benevolence of his disposition, while the miracles and cures which he performed by writing charms were the theme of all the country round.
>
> Soon after the conquest of Bornu [by the Fulani], El-Kanemi formed a plan for delivering that country from the bondage into which it had fallen. Stirring up the Kanembu to assist him by a well-planned tale of having been called by a vision to this undertaking, he made his first campaign with scarcely 400 followers and defeated an army of the Fulani nearly 8,000 strong. He followed up this victory with great promptitude and resolution and, in less than ten months, had been the conqueror in forty different battles.[3]
>
> Nature had bestowed on him all the qualifications of a great commander: an enterprising genius, sound judgement, features engaging with a demeanour gentle and conciliating: and so little of vanity was there mixed with his ambition that he refused the offer of being made Sultan and, placing Muhammad, the brother of Sultan Ahmed, on the throne, he first doing homage himself, insisted on the whole army following his example ... [4]

---

2. Ibid, p. 213.
3. Denham is here repeating the Bornu version of these events. It would be more accurate to say that the many victories that the Fulani had won over the Kanuri during the *jihad* had made them over-confident so that El-Kanemi's counter-attack caught them off their guard. The exaggeration of the Bornu version is a good specimen of a legend or myth in the making.
4. There was more political calculation in El-Kanemi's actions than Denham supposed. The Sultan Muhammad, to whom he thus did homage in 1811, was a

> The whole population now flocked to his standard and appeared willing to invest him with superior power and a force to support it.... He now raised the green flag, the standard of the Prophet, refused all titles but that of the 'Servant of God', and after clearing the country of the Fulani, he proceeded to punish all those nations who had given them assistance, and with slaves—the produce of these wars—rewarded his faithful Kanembu and other followers for their fidelity and attachment....
>
> If he has impressed his followers with a belief that supernatural powers are vested in their leader, much good policy as well as superstition may have influenced his conduct. No one could have used greater endeavours to substitute laws of reason for practices of barbarity and, though feared, he is loved and respected.... Compared to all around him, he is an angel and has subdued more by his generosity, mildness, and benevolent disposition than by the force of his arms. He is completely the winner of his own honour and reputation and assumes to himself the title of Liberator.... His highest ambition is to restore the Empire of Bornu to its former splendour and vast extent. His life, however, will most likely be too short for this work unless his means for carrying on offensive war should be surprisingly increased....
>
> At the present moment there is but one power in central Africa to be at all compared to the Sheikh of Bornu in importance—that of Bello, the Fulani chieftain. From the sensation created throughout the neighbourhood of Kano and Katsina on his late defeat of the Baghirmi force, I imagine he would find but little difficulty in extending his empire in that direction....[5]

Four years later, in 1827, El-Kanemi did in fact invade Hausaland but with none of the success that Denham had predicted.

On the day following their arrival, after Bu-Khalum had delivered the presents which the Pasha of Tripoli had sent by his hand, the explorers were summoned to the Palace so that they too could pay their respects to the Sheikh.

> We proceeded to the palace, preceded by our negroes, bearing the articles destined for the Sheikh by our Government, consisting of a double-barrelled gun by Wilkinson with a box and all the apparatus

puppet appointed by himself. Three years later, however, he changed his mind, deposed Muhammad, and restored Lefiami. If he refused the title for himself, it was because he preferred to exercise power from behind the throne rather than to risk usurping the throne itself.

5. Denham, II, pp. 179-182 and 186.

complete, a pair of excellent pistols in a case, two pieces of superfine broad cloth, red and blue, to which we added a set of china and two bundles of spices.

The ceremony of getting into the presence was ridiculous enough, although nothing could be more plain and devoid of pretension than the appearance of the Sheikh himself. We passed through passages lined with attendants and when we advanced too quickly we were suddenly arrested by these fellows, who caught forcibly hold of us by the legs and, had not the crowd prevented our falling, we should most infallibly have become prostrate before arriving in the presence. Previous to entering into the open court, in which we were received, our papouches or slippers were whipped off by these active though sedentary gentlemen of the chamber and we were seated on some clean sand on each side of a raised bench of earth, covered with a carpet, on which the Sheikh was reclining. We laid the gun and the pistols together before him and explained to him the locks, turnscrews, and steel shot-cases holding two charges each, with all of which he seemed exceedingly well pleased. The powder-flask and the manner in which the charge is divided from the body of powder did not escape his observation. The other articles were taken off by the slaves, almost as soon as they were laid before him.

Again we were questioned as to the object of our visit. The Sheikh, however, showed evident satisfaction at our assurance that the king of England had heard of Bornu and himself and, immediately turning to his counsellor, said 'This is in consequence of our defeating the Baghirmis'. Upon which the chief who had most distinguished himself in front of us, demanded, 'Did he ever hear of me?' The immediate reply of 'Certainly' did wonders for our cause. Exclamations were general and, 'Ah then, your king must be a great man' was re-echoed from every side. We had nothing offered us by way of refreshment and took our leave.[6]

But at their lodgings the travellers had no cause to complain of El-Kanemi's generosity. Morning and evening, wheat, rice and fish arrived by the camel-load together with five or six wooden bowls containing cooked rice and meat or a savoury paste made with barley flour, skins of butter, jars of honey, not to mention honey in the comb and sweetmeats made of honey and curds.[7]

* * *

6. Ibid, I, pp. 214-6.
7. Ibid, p. 216.

84 | DENHAM IN BORNU

In the Sudan, more than in any other part of Africa, markets are part of the way of life. People attend them not merely to buy or sell but to meet their friends and relations, to exchange news, and to listen to gossip and rumour. For this pleasure they will cheerfully walk fifteen or even twenty miles in a day. Each great market had its appointed day of the week, sometimes two days, and these are arranged so as not to interfere with one another. During the mornings the market-places gradually fill up; from noon until about three in the afternoon they fairly pullulate with life, like disturbed anthills and in the evenings they slowly empty. Courtiers and grandees do not deign to attend them, of course, nor are wives in purdah and lepers permitted to do so, but every other class rubs shoulders there—merchants, brokers, traders, money-changers, peddlers, pastoralists with their cattle, peasants with their produce, drovers with their donkeys, craftsmen of every kind with their wares and, until the present century, masters with their slaves.

In Kuka the explorers had their first sight of one of these major markets:

> Slaves, sheep, and bullocks, the latter in great numbers, were the principal livestock for sale. There were at least fifteen thousand persons gathered together, some of them coming from places two and three days distant. Wheat, rice, and millet were abundant: tamarinds in the pod, ground-nuts, ban beans, ochra, and indigo. The latter is very good and in great use amongst the natives to dye their gowns and linen, stripes of deep indigo colour, or stripes of it alternately with white, being highly esteemed by most of the Bornu women. The leaves are moistened and pounded up altogether when they are formed into lumps and so brought to market. Of vegetables there was a great scarcity—onions, bastard tomatoes, alone were offered for sale; and of fruits not any: a few limes, which the Sheikh had sent us from his garden, being the only fruit we had seen in Bornu. Leather was in great quantities; and the skins of the large snake, and pieces of the skin of the crocodile, used as an ornament for the scabbards of their daggers, were also brought to me for sale; and butter, sour milk, honey, and wooden bowls, from Hausaland.
>
> The variety in costume amongst the ladies consists entirely in the head ornaments; the only difference in the scanty covering which is bestowed on the other parts of the person lies in the choice of the wearer who either ties the piece of linen, blue or white, under the arms and across the breasts or fastens it rather fantastically on one shoulder, leaving one breast naked. The Kanembu women have small plaits of hair hanging down all around the head, quite to the

poll of the neck, with a roll of leather or string of little brass beads in front, hanging down from the centre on each side of the face which has by no means an unbecoming appearance. They have sometimes strings of silver rings instead of the brass and a large round silver ornament in front of their foreheads. . . .

The principal slaves are generally entrusted with the sale of such produce as the owner of them may have to dispose of and, if they come from any distance, the whole is brought on bullocks which are harnessed after the fashion of the country by a string of iron run through the cartilage of the nose. . . . The masters not infrequently attend the market with their spears and loiter about without interfering. Purchases are mostly made by exchange of one commodity for another or paid for by small beads, pieces of coral and amber, or the coarse linen manufactured by all the people and sold at forty yards for a dollar.

Amongst other articles offered to me for sale by the people (who, if I stood still for an instant, crowded round me) was a young lion and a monkey. . . . The lion walked about with great unconcern, confined merely by a small rope round his neck held by the negro who had caught him when he was not two months old and, having had him for a period of three months, now wished to part with him. He was about the size of a donkey colt, with very large limbs, and the people seemed to go very close to him without much alarm, notwithstanding he struck with his foot the leg of one man who stood in his way and made the blood flow copiously. They opened the ring which was formed round this noble animal as I approached . . . . He fixed his eye upon me in a way that excited sensations I cannot describe, from which I was awakened by the fellow calling me to come nearer, at the same time laying his hand on the animal's back. A moment's recollection convinced me that there could be no more danger nearer than where I was so I stepped boldly up beside the negro and I believe should have laid my hand on the lion the next moment but, after looking carelessly at me, he brushed past my legs, broke the ring, and pulled his conductor away with him, overturning several who stood before him, and bounded off to another part where there were fewer people[8]

* * *

On February 27 the explorers had their second audience of El-Kanemi. He received them very affably, asked a great number of questions and showed an interest in their maps, which they had to explain to him.

8. Ibid, pp. 216-220.

One of the difficulties that all the early African explorers had to contend with was suspicion. The people in whose midst they suddenly appeared found it almost impossible to believe that they should have travelled so far and endured so many privations simply to satisfy their own or their ruler's curiosity. There must, they thought, be some hidden purpose. The Arab and Fezzan merchants, intent on preserving their monopoly of the Sudan trade, were always ready to fan these fears by hints and innuendoes which gave rise to wild rumours. In Kuka, for example, word got abroad that the explorers intended to build ships and this was soon blown up into a report that they were going to embark on the lake, sail home, and then return with an army to destroy Bornu. Even El-Kanemi was not immune to certain suspicions and he intimated to Bu-Khalum that, while the Europeans were welcome to see any part of his dominion, he would not at present permit them to travel beyond it. Bu-Khalum, in passing on this news, advised the travellers to be satisfied with this offer and not, for the present, disclose their more ambitious plans. When therefore at the audience they were asked by El-Kanemi what they wished to see, they mentioned only Lake Chad, the River Shari, and Ngazargamu, the old capital.[9]

The conversation then turned to the technique and tactics of war:

> He asked many questions about our manner of attacking a walled town and, on our explaining to him that we had guns which carried ball of 24 and 32 pounds weight with which we breached the wall and then carried the place by assault, his large eyes sparkled again as he exclaimed 'Wonderful! Wonderful!' He enquired whether we had anything with us like wild-fire, which could be thrown into a place and burn it, and was greatly disappointed on our answering in the negative....
>
> We promised at night to show him two rockets and we had scarcely eaten our dinner when Karouash, one of his chiefs, came to say the Sheikh was impatient. There were in the town several of the hostile Shuwas, a dangerous race of Arab origin who occupy the frontiers of his Kingdom, and he was anxious that they should see the effect of these terrible fire-engines. Mr. Clapperton fixed them on a rest of three spears in front of the Sheikh's residence, before a crowd of persons and the shrieks of the people, both there assembled and in their huts, were heard for some seconds after the rockets had ascended.[10]

9. Ibid, pp. 221-5.
10. Ibid, pp. 225-6.

Back in the town, the explorers had to endure not only the heat but also the inquisitiveness of the visitors who thronged their quarters and pestered them with questions and requests for favours. Lyon's sketchbook, in particular, seemed to have a strange fascination for them.

> ... The numbers of persons who crowded my hut, from morning to night, were greater, and consequently their visits more pestering than common. Every little thing, from the compass to the pen and ink, from the watch to the tin cup out of which I drank, excited their curiosity. And, as they now became bolder, they seized hold of everything which they formerly only eyed at a distance. It was not, however, their curiosity alone that was excited—the possession was coveted, either for themselves or the Sheikh, of every article: a looking-glass and a small lantern I rescued out of the hands of at least a dozen a dozen times.
>
> A copy of Captain Lyon's book, the fame of which had preceded us in consequence of Doctor Oudney's having shown it to some merchants at Murzuk, was demanded twenty times a day and it required all my patience to go over and explain the pictures as often as they required. It produced very different effects, but in all astonishment and in most suspicion. The Sheikh had heard of it, and one of his slaves borrowed it for him of one of my servants, by stealth, as he did not wish it to be known that he had a desire to see it. For three days after this I was again and again applied to by all his chief people to see what I had drawn. ... I repeatedly assured them that those in the book were not mine, that the person who wrote them was far away. It would not do: they shook their heads and said I was cunning and would not show them. They then changed their tone and very seriously begged that I would not ... *draw* their portraits; that they did not like it; that it was a sin.[11]

Within a fortnight of the expedition's arrival in Kuka, a quarrel flared up among the Arabs which revealed to the Europeans for the first time how dangerous a divergence there was between the peaceful aims of the merchants and the warlike ambitions of the escort.

> March I. ... A meeting took place this morning at daybreak under a large tree in front of the Sheikh's residence, and in his presence, between the Arab chieftains and Bu-Khalum. The Arabs had appealed to him as their umpire and, although he appeared not to take any part in their disputes, yet I thought a disposition was very

---

11. Ibid, pp. 238-9.

apparent in him to increase the feud.... He offered to mount one hundred of the Arabs and send one of his chiefs, under Bu-Khalum's orders, to Baghirmi with fifteen hundred or two thousand horsemen; and a great part of the produce of this expedition was to be sent as a present to the Pasha. Nothing could be more distressing than Bu-Khalum's situation: he knew the disposition of his master too well not to feel what his fate would be if he refused such an opportunity of taking him at least two thousand slaves [but] his own inclinations led him to proceed to Hausaland [and] he was still anxious to avoid becoming the scourge of one people to gratify the revenge of another. The Arabs were also divided. The people of Baghirmi had, on the last expedition, nearly foiled their invaders by abandoning their towns, driving off their flocks and cattle, and obliging the Sheikh's people to subsist entirely, for twenty-five days, on a little prepared paste, made of flour and curd which they always take with them to the field. This the mounted Arabs dreaded a repetition of, while the more adventurous infantry, who had nothing to trade with but their guns and consequently to lose but their lives, exclaimed loudly for the raid.[12]

This dispute, as we shall see, was to have dire consequences.

* * *

Though the Sheikh was the real ruler of Bornu, and the Sultan no more than a figurehead, protocol clearly required that the explorers should not delay unduly in going to the ceremonial capital to pay their respects.

By this time Sultan Dunama Lefiami, whom El-Kanemi had first deposed and then restored, was dead. He had been killed during the Baghirmi wars, as we shall hear, in circumstances that were unusual enough to arouse some speculation, at any rate in Court circles. His successor, Ibrahim, had been hardly more than a boy when first appointed and had therefore been even more dependent than his predecessor on El-Kanemi's favour. Now, at the time of the explorers' visit, he was still only in his early twenties.[13]

New Birni, the capital that El-Kanemi had built for the Sultan after the abandonment of Ngazargamu, was situated sixteen miles from Kuka. When the explorers travelled there in early March, accompanied by Bu-Khalum, they found that it was a walled town with a population of

12. Ibid, pp. 228-9.
13. Ibid, II, p. 184.

about 10,000. Accommodation had been arranged for the whole party and for their evening meal seventy dishes, each enough to satisfy six people with normal appetites, were sent down from the Palace.

Early on the following morning they were summoned to attend the Sultan.

> He received us in an open space in front of the royal residence. We were kept at a considerable distance while his people approached to within about 100 yards, passing first on horseback and, after dismounting and prostrating themselves before him, they took their places on the ground in front, but with their backs to the royal person which is the custom of the country. He was seated in a sort of cage of cane or wood, near the door of his garden, on a seat which at the distance appeared to be covered with silk or satin, and through the railings looked upon the assembly before him who formed a sort of semi-circle extending from his seat to nearly where we were waiting.
>
> Nothing could be more absurd and grotesque than some, nay all, of the figures who formed this court. Here was all the outward show of pomp and grandeur without one particle of the staple commodity, power, to plead its excuse. He reigns and governs by the sufferance of the Sheikh who, to make himself more popular with all parties, amuses the Sultan by suffering him to indulge in all the folly and bigotry of the ancient negro sovereigns. Large bellies and large heads are indispensable for those who serve the court of Bornu and those who unfortunately possess not the former by nature, or on whom lustiness will not be forced by cramming, make up the deficiency of protuberance by a wadding which, as they sit on the horse, gives the belly the curious appearance of hanging over the pummel of the saddle. The eight, ten, and twelve shirts of different colours that they wear one over the other help a little to increase this greatness of person. The head is enveloped in folds of muslin or linen of various colours, though mostly white, so as to deform it as much as possible.... Besides this they are hung all over with charms, enclosed in little red leather parcels, strung together; the horse also has them round his neck, in front of his head, and about the saddle.
>
> When these courtiers, to the number of about two hundred and sixty or three hundred, had taken their seats in front of the Sultan, we were allowed to approach to within about a pistol-shot of the spot where he was sitting and desired to sit down ourselves when the ugliest black that can be imagined, his chief eunuch, the only person who approached the Sultan's seat, asked for the presents.

> Bu-Khalum's were produced, enclosed in a large shawl, and were carried unopened to the presence. Our glimpse was but a faint one of the Sultan, through the lattice-work of his pavilion, sufficient however to see that his turban was larger than any of his subjects' and that his face, from the nose downwards, was completely covered. A little to our left, and nearly in front of the Sultan, was an extempore declaimer shouting forth the praises of his master, with his pedigree, and near him one who bore the long wooden horn on which he ever and anon blew a blast, loud and unmusical. Nothing could be more ridiculous than the appearance of these people ... tottering under the weight and magnitude of their turbans and their bellies.[14]

By a careless oversight, the explorers had failed to bring with them from Kuka their presents for the Sultan but, if this lapse caused any offence, no mention was made of it.

The dynasty, in all its effete splendour, was destined to survive for two more decades. In 1846, however, when El-Kanemi was dead and his son Umar had succeeded him as chief minister, this same Sultan Ibrahim entered into a conspiracy with the Chief of Wadai to repossess himself of the power that the Sultans had lost to the Sheikhs. But, when it came to the crunch, his allies failed him and first he and then his son, Ali Dalatumi, were defeated and killed by Sheikh Umar. With that, this very ancient line was finally extinguished and the descendants of El-Kanemi became the titular as well as the real rulers of Bornu.

14. Ibid, I, pp. 231-3.

VI

Excursions In Bornu

After visiting the Sultan at New Birni, the explorers went on to Ngornu, then the most populous town in Bornu. As it was also the most important commercial centre, the Tripoli and Fezzan merchants who had accompanied the caravan had already left Kuka and installed themselves there so that they could better pursue their trading.

Denham described Ngornu as a sprawling place, lacking a city wall, and he estimated its population at 30,000. He did not see the principal market, which was held on Wednesdays, but noted that even the lesser markets that took place in the evenings on other days were well attended and provided an abundance of fish, flesh and fowl. His informants assured him that, in times of peace, the Wednesday markets were attended by 80,000-100,000 people. This was almost certainly an exaggeration but the number may well have been 30,000-40,000.[1]

The mercantile community, Denham found, employed a variety of different currencies. The Maria-Theresa silver dollar, which was familiar in all the principal towns of the Sudan, was of course accepted but amber and coral were more eagerly sought. A large piece of amber had the same purchasing power as four dollars in cash and a good string of coral as eighty. Brass and copper were also much prized. For the rest, imported merchandise was bartered against slaves or locally made gowns.[2] But, for some reason which has not yet been explained, the cowry-shells that

1. Denham. I, pp. 233-4.
2. Ibid, p. 235.

provided the rest of the Sudan with a servicable, if bulky, currency, had not yet gained acceptance in Bornu.[3] The Sheikh recognized that the lack of a good currency was a serious handicap and later discussed with Denham the question of having coins minted.

> Probably the strong desire of the Sheikh to improve the state of his country and the habits of its people cannot be better exemplified than in his having given me the designs for three coins which he entreated might be laid before the King of England with his request to have the stamp and apparatus for striking money so that he might introduce a more convenient medium of exchange than the one at present in use amongst them. One of these pieces of money he intended should be of gold, a second of silver, and a third of iron.[4]

The possibility of developing profitable trade between Bornu and Europe, especially of course with Great Britain, was always present in Denham's mind. In accordance with the theories of the day, he saw in this the best hope of killing the slave trade and drawing the country into the main stream of civilization. Later, in the supplementary chapter of his book, he dealt with the subject at some length.

> The articles most in request among the negro nations are:
> Writing paper, on which the profit is enormous,
> Coral barelled and imitation coral,
> Printed cottons of all kinds with a great deal of red and yellow in the pattern,
> Coloured silks in pieces for large shirts and shifts, of the most gaudy patterns,
> Imitations of damask, worked with gold thread and flowers,
> Common red cloth,
> Common green cloth,
> White barracans, purchased in Tripoli,
> Small looking-glasses,
> White burnouses, purchased in Tripoli,
> Small carpets, five or six feet long, purchased in Tripoli; English carpets of the same size would sell better and might be bought at one third of the price of Turkish ones,
> Ornamented cheap pistols with long barrels,
> Common razors,

---

3. A generation later Barth observed that cowries had been only recently introduced and were still not in general use. See *Travels and Discoveries*, Chapter XXX.

4. Denham, II, pp. 195-6.

Red caps, purchased in Tripoli,
Turbans of all descriptions,
Large amber for the Kanembu women and the Shuwas,
Common china basins, much esteemed,
Coffee cups,
Brass basins, tinned in the inside,
Red breeches, made up,
Cotton caftans, striped, made up,
Pieces of striped cotton,
Handkerchiefs and coarse white muslin,
Large shirts, or gowns, ready made of striped cottons and white calico,
Fine white calico, much esteemed,
Frankincense, Ottaria, Spices, purchased of the Jews in Tripoli or Leghorn,
The beads most in demand, indeed the only ones that they will purchase, are:-
White glass beads with a flower,
mock coral,
white sand beads,
small black beads with yellow stripes,
ant's head beads with black stripes,
red and white,
the Pasha's sash,
red pebble from Trieste,
long beads,
Arab's nose, a large red bead.
Arms of all descriptions, of an inferior quality, will always meet with a ready sale, as well as balls of lead and what we call swan-shot . . .[5]

Arab or Moorish merchants, the only ones who have hitherto ventured amongst them, are encouraged and treated with great liberality. Several of them are known to have returned, after a residence of less than nine years, with fortunes of fifteen and twenty thousand dollars, which might perhaps by a more intelligent trader have been doubled, as the commodities with which they barter are mostly European produce purchased at Tripoli at prices full two hundred and fifty percent above their prime cost.

The usual calculation of a Moorish merchant is that a camel load of merchandize, bought at Murzuk for 150 dollars, will make a

---

5. Ibid, 189.

return, in trading with Bornu, of 500 dollars after paying all expenses. Persons in Fezzan will send three camel loads in charge of one man and, after paying all the expenses out of the profits, give him a third of the remainder for his labour.

For the circumstances, however, of there being no direct trade from this country [Great Britain] with Tripoli, or I believe with any of the ports of Barbary, English goods, the demand for which is daily increasing amongst a population of not less than five million within six hundred miles of the coast, are sold at enormous prices, although frequently of the very worst description . . .[6]

Already the desire of exchanging whatever their country produces for the manufactures of the more enlightened nations of the north exists in no small degree amongst them. A taste for luxury, and a desire of imitating such strangers as visit them, are very observable and the man of rank is ever distinguished by some part of his dress being of foreign materials, though sometimes of the most trifling kind. It is true that these propensities are not yet fully developed but they exist and give unequivocal proof of a tendency to civilisation and the desire of cultivating an intercourse with foreigners . . .[7]

The return which European traders might in the first instance obtain would not, probably, be sufficient to employ large capitals but that would annually improve and the great profits would in some measure compensate for the deficiency. The propensity of the natives to war upon and plunder their neighbours, from the profit arising from such a system, would gradually subside when other more profitable occupations were encouraged amongst them.

The Kanembu who inhabit the northern and eastern borders of Lake Chad are a bold and hardy people, extremely expert with the spear, swift of foot, and practised hunters. The tusk of the elephant, the horn of the buffalo, both of which may be obtained at a very low price and in exchange for English goods, are eagerly bought even at Tripoli and at all the European ports in the Mediterranean at high prices. The cultivation of indigo, also of a very superior kind, might be carried to any extent as it now grows wild, as well as henna, in many parts of the country. The musk from the civet cat is also to be procured, about two hundred per cent lower than it will sell for in Tripoli.

The following are the prices in Bornu of some of those articles which would be most esteemed in Europe:

6. Ibid, pp. 188-9.
7. Ibid, p. 192.

> Ostrich skins, from three to six dollars each,
> Elephants' teeth, two dollars the 100 lbs,
> Raw hides may also be purchased at about two dollars for 100 skins.[8]

In his analysis of the overland slave trade, Denham was inclined to exculpate the Africans and place all the blame on the Moors.

> Until introduced by the Moors, the trading in slaves was little known amongst them. The prisoners taken in battle served them, and were given as portions to their children on their marriage for the same duties, but they were seldom sold. Even now the greater part of the household of a man of rank are free with the exception of the women who often die in the service of the master of their youth. They are treated always like the children of the house and corporal punishment is a rare occurrence amongst them.... In short, it is to the pernicious principles of the Moorish traders, whose avaricious brutality is beyond all belief, that the traffic for slaves in the interior of Africa not only owes its origin but its continuance. They refuse all other modes of payment for the articles which they bring with them; they well know the eagerness with which these articles are sought after and, by offering what appears to the natives an amazing price, tempt them to sell their brethren to the most inhuman of all human beings while they gain, in Fezzan, Benghazi and Egypt, sometimes a profit of 500 per cent. I am not, however, without hopes that a more extended intercourse with Barbary might detach even the proverbially unfeeling Moor from dealing in human flesh and it was with feelings of the highest satisfaction that I listen to some of the most respectable of the merchants when they declared that, were any other system of trading adopted, they would gladly embrace it in preference to dealing in slaves.[9]

The loss of territory that Bornu had suffered at the hands of the Fulani had deprived the Kanuri ruling classes of most of the preserves where they had previously enjoyed exclusive rights of slave raiding. Having lost most of their vested interest in the traffic, they were the more ready (to the slightly naive satisfaction of the explorers) to applaud schemes for supplanting it.

> Bornu is scarcely anything more than a mart or rendezvous of caravans from Hausaland. These unhappy victims are handed over to

8. Ibid, pp. 194-5.
9. Ibid, pp. 197-9.

the Tripoli and Fezzan traders who are waiting with their northern produce to tempt the cupidity of the Hausa slave merchants. I think I may say that neither the Sheikh himself nor the Bornu people carry on this traffic without feelings of disgust which even habit cannot conquer. . . . Let the words of the Sheikh himself, addressed to us in the hearing of his people, speak the sentiments that have already found a place in his bosom: 'You say true—we are all sons of one father. You say also that the sons of Adam should not sell one another, and you know everything. God has given you all great talents, but what are we to do? The Arabs who come here will have nothing else but slaves: why don't you send us your merchants? You know us now. And let them bring their women with them, and live amongst us, and teach us what you talk to me about so often, to build houses and boats and make rockets'. The reader will conceive with what exulting hearts we heard these words from the lips of a ruler in the centre of Africa.[10]

It was natural that the explorers should have been gratified at hearing El-Kanemi echoing these fine sentiments, even though the mention of rockets suggested that his motives were slightly less altruistic than he would have them believe. But what they did not realise, at any rate until much later, was how alarming and unwelcome these proposals sounded to the Arabs who wished neither for interference with the slave trade, about which they at least had no qualms of conscience, nor for any competition in ordinary commerce.

* * *

When the explorers returned to Kuka from the excursion to New Birni and Ngornu, they made oblique enquiries to find out whether the Sheikh would allow them to travel to Hausaland. But Bu-Khalum, who put the proposal to El-Kanemi, reported that he would not hear of it. The Pasha's dispatch, said the Sheikh, had made no mention of that being the King of England's wish.[11]

This was a serious setback. All along the plan had been to get to Bornu first and then, by splitting up, to explore as much of the central Sudan as possible. Now it appeared that the Sheikh would not allow anyone to

---

10. Ibid, pp. 190-1 and 193-4. There, for once, Denham was being unrealistic. The overland slave trade had been passing through Bornu for centuries and there is no other evidence to suggest that the consciences of rulers or people were troubled by the taint on the profits that it brought them.

11. Ibid, p. 240.

proceed beyond his boundaries. Though the fact is not specifically mentioned in Denham's narrative, it seems almost certain that, when this decision was conveyed to him, Oudney lost no time in sending off a letter to Warrington in Tripoli asking him to intervene. Certainly in about August, for no other obvious reason, the Pasha wrote again to the Sheikh and specifically asked him to arrange for the party to visit Hausaland. [12]

Meanwhile the explorers were beginning to think that, even in Bornu, they were making little headway. They had now been in the country for nearly a month but had seen El-Kanemi only three times. Moreover their audiences had been of a formal character and, though the Sheikh had seemed affable enough, they had felt that, in spite of the boxes made by Hillman in response to his request and of a second demonstration of rockets intended to intimidate the recalcitrant Shuwas, they had not made much progress in gaining either his intimacy or his confidence.

From this predicament they were rescued by their musical box.

> March 11—Doctor Oudney was still confined to his bed and I received a summons from the Sheikh to whom a report had been made of a musical box of mine which played or stopped merely by my holding up my finger. The messenger declared he was dying to see it and I must make haste. The wild exclamations of wonder and screams of pleasure that this piece of mechanism drew from the generality of my visitors were curiously contrasted in the person of the intelligent Sheikh: he at first was greatly astonished, and asked several questions exclaiming 'Wonderful! wonderful' but the sweetness of the Swiss *Ranz-des-Vaches* which it played at last overcame every other feeling. He covered his face with his hand and listened in silence and, on one man near him breaking the charm by a loud exclamation, he struck him a blow which made all his followers tremble. He instantly asked, 'if one twice as large would not be better?' I said 'Yes; but it would be twice as dear'. 'By God!' said he 'if one thousand dollars would purchase it, it would be cheap'. Who will deny that nature has given us all a taste for luxuries?
>
> During this short conversation we became better friends than we had ever been before during our three former visits. To his surprise, he now found that I spoke intelligible Arabic and he begged to see me whenever I chose. These were just the terms upon which I wished to be with him and, thinking this a favourable moment for adding strength to his present impressions, I could not help begging he would keep the box. He was the more delighted as I had refused

12. Ibid, II, pp. 420-422.

it before to Karouash when he had requested it in the Sheikh's name.[13]

On the following day El-Kanemi received Denham and his musical box again, this time in his garden. The only other people present were the courtier Karouash and Barka Gana, the Sheikh's leading General. After another session with the *Ranz-des-Vaches,* relations had become so cordial that, when Denham sought permission to visit Lake Chad on the following day, El-Kanemi readily agreed and ordered the General to make the necessary arrangements.

Early next morning Denham set off with the two guides who had been commissioned to look after him, a Kanemma called Fajah and a halfcaste Fulani called Marami. They rode north-eastward to the village of Bree where the Headman, when he heard the Sheikh's orders, invited Denham to return for the night and promised that a hut, a meal, and a troop of dancing girls would be ready for him. But Denham sternly declined this offer and affirmed that he had brought his blanket and would sleep by the lake. Riding on eastward for another five miles they came to open water.

> I had seen no part of the lake so unencumbered by trees as this and there were evident proofs of its overflowings and recedings near the shores; but beyond was an uninterrupted expanse of waters, as far as the eye could reach east and southeast. A fine grass grew abundantly along the marshy shores and thousands of cattle belonging to the Sheikh, the produce of his last expedition to Baghirmi, were grazing and in beautiful condition.
>
> The sun was not at its greatest power and, spreading my mat under the shade of a clump of mimosa trees, I was just preparing a repast of some bread and honey when two or three black boys, who had accompanied us from Bree and whom I had seen rushing about in the water, brought me five or six fine fish, resembling a mullet, which they had driven into the shallow water almost in as many minutes. A fire was quickly made and they roasted them so well and expeditiously that their manner of cooking deserves to be noticed. A stick is run through the mouth of the fish and quite along the belly to the tail; this stick is then stuck in the ground, with the head of the fish downwards, and inclined towards the fire...
>
> I told my satellites that here would be my quarters for the night. They assured me that the mosquitoes were both so numerous and so large that I should find it impossible to remain and that the horses

---

13. Ibid, pp. 241-3.

would be miserable. They advised our retiring with the cattle to a short distance from the water and sleeping near them, by which means the attention of these insects would be taken off the quadrupeds. Englishman-like, I was obstinate and, very soon falling asleep, although daylight, I was so bitten by mosquitoes, in size equalling a large fly, that I was glad, on awakening, to take the advice of my more experienced guides.

Towards the evening we mounted our horses and chased some very beautiful antelopes and saw a herd of elephants at a distance, exceeding forty in number. Two buffaloes also stood boldly grazing, nearly up to their bodies in water. On our approaching them they quickly took to the lake: one of them was a monstrous animal, at least fourteen feet in length from the tail to the head...

The tamarind and locust-trees[14] were here abundant and loaded with fruit; the former of a rich and fine flavour. The horses now became so irritated by the shoals of insects that attacked them, the white one of Fajah being literally covered with blood, that we determined on seeking the cattle herd and taking up our quarters for the night with them. A vacant square was left in the centre and ourselves and the horses were admitted. Mats were spread, and about thirty basket jars of sweet milk were set before me with another of honey; this, in addition to some rice which I had brought with me, made a sumptuous repast. And although previous to leaving the lake my face, hands, and back of the neck resembled those of a child with smallpox from the insects, yet here I slept most comfortably without being annoyed by a single mosquito.

Denham, himself a keen shot, made some interesting observations on the techniques that the Kanuri and Shuwa Arabs employed in their hunting.

Ostriches were hunted regularly because the feathers were always in demand for export to North Africa. If a hunter found a nest, he would dig a hole nearby and, concealing himself, watch for the return of the bird. An arrow through the head then secured the quarry without injuring the plumage. Alternatively, if young birds were seen, they were pursued until they could be run down and taken alive. In captivity they became as tame as domestic fowls. 'Ostriches' Denham noted 'have a most extraordi-

14. This tree is usually called the locust-bean. It is a fine species found all over Bornu and Hausaland and is much prized for its economic value. It usually grows singly in farmland or fallow and when mature, has an immense spread. Its seeds, crushed and fermented, are made into *daddawa*, a relish, and the empty pods are pounded up to make a protective plaster, *makuba*, for strengthening clay walls and floors.

nary aversion, from nature, to a pregnant woman and a sensibility in discovering when such a person is near them quite astonishing: they will make directly towards her and, with lifted feet and menaces, oblige her to withdraw. I have even known them single out a woman so situated in the street and, following her to her own door, beat her with their long beaks, the whole time hissing with the greatest agitation and anger.'[15]

Despite their lack of firearms, the local hunters were not afraid to tackle big game. The bush-cow, for example, one of Africa's most dangerous animals, was hunted with spears from horseback.

> Their manner of killing these animals is curious and rather perilous—they chase them in the swamps, where they now feed in preference to nearer the lake, and as their horses are trained so as to go quite close to them as they run, the rider is enabled to get his foot well fixed on the buffalo's back. With singular skill he then strikes just behind the animal's shoulder, one or two spears if he can place them. Pierced with these, the animal is able to run but a short distance. Then, with the assistance of his companions, but frequently alone, he dismounts, and despatches his prey. It sometimes happens that the buffalo, by quickly turning his head before they strike, oversets both horse and rider. A Shuwa friend of mine has his horse completely ripped open and killed on the spot only a few days since by the sudden twist the animal gave his head, catching the horse with his pointed horn.[16]

Here, next, is Denham's description of how the people of Kabshari trapped and killed a lion which had turned man-eater.

> The skin of a noble lion was sent me by the Sheikh which had been taken near Kabshari, measuring from the tail to the nose fourteen feet two inches. He had devoured four slaves and was at last taken by the following stratagem: the inhabitants assembled together and, with loud cries and noises, drove him from the place where he had last feasted. They then dug a very deep *blaka,* or circular hole armed with sharp-pointed stakes. This they most cunningly covered over with stalks of millet. A bundle of straw, enveloped in a gown, was laid over the spot, to which a gentle motion, like that of a man turning in his sleep, was occasionally given by means of a line carried to some distance. On their quitting the spot, and the noise ceasing, the lion returned to his haunt and was observed watching

15. Ibid, p. 195.
16. Ibid, I, pp. 411-412.

his trap for seven or eight hours—by degrees approaching closer and closer—and at length he made a dreadful spring on his supposed prey and was precipitated to the bottom of the pit. The Kabsharians now rushed to the spot and, before he could recover himself, despatched him with their spears.[17]

After his comfortable night in the middle of the herd of cattle, Denham awoke to find that there had been a very heavy dew and that the burnous which had covered him was wet right through. He felt no ill-effect, however, and set out for the lake to shoot water-fowl while Marami went off on horseback in search of elephant. Soon afterwards, Marami came galloping back with the news that he had found a small herd not far away, grazing by the lake.

> When we came within a few hundred yards of them, all the persons on foot, and my servant on a mule, were ordered to halt while four of us, who were mounted, rode up to these stupendous animals. The Sheikh's people began screeching violently and, although at first they appeared to treat our approach with great contempt, yet after a little they moved off, erecting their ears which had until then hung flat on their shoulders, and giving a roar that shook the ground underneath us. One was an immense fellow, I should suppose sixteen feet high; the other two were females and moved away rather quickly, while the male kept in the rear, as if to guard their retreat. We wheeled swiftly round him and, Marami casting a spear at him which struck him just under the tail and seemed to give him about as much pain as when we pricked our finger with a pin, the huge beast threw up his proboscis in the air with a loud roar and from it cast such a volume of sand that, unprepared as I was for such an event, nearly blinded me. The elephant rarely, if ever, attacks and it is only when irritated that he is dangerous. But he will sometimes rush upon a man and horse, after choking them with dust, and destroy them in an instant.
>
> As we had cut him off from following his companions, he took the direction leading to where we had left the mule and footman. They quickly fled in all directions and my man Columbus (the mule not being inclined to increase its pace) was so alarmed that he did not get the better of it for the whole day. We pressed the elephant now very close, riding before, behind and on each side of him, and his look sometimes as he turned his head, had the effect of checking instantly the speed of my horse—his pace never exceeded a clumsy rolling walk but was sufficient to keep our horses at a short gallop. I

---

17. Ibid, pp. 419-20.

gave him a ball from each barrel of my gun, at about fifty yards' distance, and the second which struck his ear, seemed to give him a moment's uneasiness only but the first, which struck him on the body, failed in making the least impression. After giving him another spear, which flew off his tough hide without exciting the least sensation, we left him to his fate... A number of the birds, here called *tuda,* were perched on the backs of the elephants; these resemble a thrush in shape and note and were represented to me as being extremely useful to the elephant in picking off the vermin from those parts which it is not in his power to reach.[18]

This elephant got away but later, during the dry season, Denham witnessed a kill.

About noon, a messenger came to our huts saying that, after hunting an enormous male elephant for five hours, they had at length brought him to a stand near Bree, about ten miles north-east of Kuka. Accompanied by a Shuwa guide, we arrived at the spot where he had fallen just as he breathed his last.

Although not more than twenty-five years old, his tusk measuring barely four feet six inches, he was an immense fellow. His dimensions were as follows:

	ft.	in.
Length from the proboscis to the tail	25	6
Proboscis	7	6
Small teeth	2	10
Foot longitudinally	1	7
Eye		2 by 1½
From the foot to the hip-bone	9	6
From the hip-bone to the back	3	0
Ear	2	2 x 2ft. 6 ins.

I had seen much larger elephants than this alive when on my last expedition to Chad, some I should have guessed sixteen feet in height and with a tusk probably exceeding six feet in length. The one before me, which was the first I had seen dead, was however considered as of more than common bulk and stature, and it was not until the Kanembu of the town of Bree came out and, by attracting his attention with their yells and teasing him by hurling spears at his more tender parts, that the Shuwa dared to dismount when, by ham-stringing the poor animal, they brought him to the

---

18. Ibid, pp. 247-250.

ground and eventually despatched him by repeated wounds in the abdomen and proboscis. Five leaden balls had struck him about the haunches in the course of the chase but they had merely penetrated a few inches into his flesh and appeared to give him but little uneasiness.

The whole of the next day the road leading to the spot where he lay was like a fair from the numbers who repaired thither for the sake of bringing off a part of the flesh which is esteemed by all and even eaten in secret by the first people about the Sheikh. It looks coarse but it is better flavoured than any beef I found in the country. Whole families put themselves in motion, with their daughters mounted on bullocks.

The eyes of this noble animal were, though so extremely small in proportion to his body, languid and expressive even in death. His head, which was brought to the town, I had an opportunity of seeing the next day, when I had it opened, and the smallness of the brain is a direct contradiction to the hypothesis that the size of this organ is in proportion to the sagaciousness of the animal. His skin was a full inch and a half in thickness, and a dark gray or nearly black, hard and wrinkled.

In Africa they are scarcely ever taken alive but hunted as a sport, for the sake of their flesh and also in order to obtain their teeth which, however, as they are generally small, are sold to the merchants for a very trifling profit. The manner of hunting the elephant is simply this: from ten to twenty horseman single out one of these ponderous animals and, separating him from the flock by screaming and hallooing, force him to fly with all his speed. After wounding him under the tail, if they can there place a spear, the animal becomes enraged. One horseman then rides in front, whom he pursues with earnestness and fury, regardless of those who press on his rear, notwithstanding the wounds they inflict on him. He is seldom drawn from this first object of his pursuit and at last, wearied and transfixed with spears his blood deluging the ground, he breathes his last under the knife of some more venturesome hunter than the rest, who buries his dagger in the vulnerable part near the abdomen: for this purpose he will creep between the animal's hinder legs and apparently expose himself to the greatest danger. When this cannot be accomplished, one or two will hamstring him, while he is baited in the front, and this giant quadruped then becomes comparatively an easy prey to his persecutors.[19]

* * *

---

19. Ibid, pp. 463-6.

A few miles south-east of Bree, where the second elephant was killed, stands the little town of Kauwa and there, after his inconclusive encounter with the first elephant, Denham made an unheralded appearance.

> When I appeared in the town, the curiosity and alarm which my hands and face excited almost inclined me to doubt whether they had not been changed in the night. One little girl was in such agonies of tears and fright at the sight of me that nothing could console her, not even a string of beads which I offered her—nor would she put out her hand to take them. I must, however, do the sex the justice to say that those more advanced in years were not afflicted with such exceeding diffidence—at the sight of the beads they quickly made up to me and, seeing me take from the pocket of a very loose pair of Turkish trousers a few strings, which were soon distributed, some one exclaimed: 'Oh! those trousers are full of beads, only he won't give them to us'. This piece of news was followed by a shout and they all approached so fully determined to ascertain the fact that, although I did not until afterwards understand what had been said, Fajah, my guide, thought it right to keep the ladies at a distance by what I thought rather ungentle means.... [20]

Next day, tired from his exertions in the great heat but gratified by the success of his brief excursion, Denham returned to Kuka. But there was bad news awaiting him.

> The horse that had carried me from Tripoli to Murzuk and back again, and on which I had ridden the whole journey from Tripoli to Bornu, had died a very few hours after my departure for the lake. There are situations in a man's life in which losses of this nature are felt most keenly and this was one of them. It was not grief, but it was something very nearly approaching to it and, though I felt ashamed of the degree of derangement which I suffered from it, yet it was several days before I could get over the loss. Let it be remembered, however, that the poor animal had been my support and comfort—may I not say companion?—through many a dreary day and night; had endured both hunger and thirst in my service with the utmost patience; was so docile, though an Arab, that he would stand still for hours in the desert while I slept between his legs, his body affording me the only shelter that could be obtained from the powerful influence of a noon-day sun. He was yet the fleetest of the fleet and ever foremost in the race.

20. Denham, I, pp. 244-251.

My negro lad opened his head, and found a considerable quantity of matter formed on the brain. Three horses at the Arab tents had died with similar appearances and there can be little doubt that it was the effect of climate, the scarcity and badness of the water, and the severe exposure to the sun which we had all undergone.[21]

Soon afterwards Clapperton's horse died in exactly the same way.

But the explorers had other troubles besides these. On March 18 Oudney, whose health had temporarily improved, waited on El-Kanemi to ask him a second time for permission to leave Bornu and pay a visit to Hausaland. Once again, however, he met with a firm refusal. In the event, this proved to be a blessing in disguise, because ten days later he suffered a severe relapse and became so weak that he could hardly move from one hut in the compound to another. His cough had become very violent and he was treating it by applying a blister to his chest.[22]

Denham, meanwhile, was receiving disquieting reports from Dris-Abu, the Shuwa Arab with whom he had become friendly. Dris, a man of some consequence, had previously been a subject of the Emir of Wadai but had recently transferred his allegiance to Bornu. He could afford to be more frank than any of the Kanuri and from him Denham got an inkling of the suspicion with which the explorers were still regarded in Kuka. The Sheikh, he said, was unwilling for the Europeans to see any of the country beyond the Shari and had given orders that they were not to be allowed to cross the river. On his next visit, which was at night, Dris was at pains to ensure that no-one should see him. 'Do not mention my coming to you' he said. 'Everybody who visits your hut is a spy on your actions. Everything you say is repeated to the Sheikh'.[23]

This was disturbing enough but what was more serious still was the high tension that now existed in the Arab camp.

---

21. Ibid, pp. 252-3. Probably a case of "African glanders" (Epizöotic lymphangitis) a still prevalent disease.
22. Ibid, pp. 254-6.
23. Ibid, The news that he and his companions were under surveillance evidently surprised Denham. There was nothing remarkable about it, however, and any contemporary African ruler would have taken similar precautions with influential strangers.

VII

Quarrels Among The Arabs

From the quarrel which had broken out among the Arabs soon after the caravan's arrival in Bornu, the explorers knew that the interests of the Bedouin who formed the escort were in sharp conflict with those of Bu-Khalum and the merchants who had come to Bornu in his company.

The merchants, having plenty of trade goods to sell or barter, had no ambitions but to pursue their commerce peacefully and then, when they had done, to return to Murzuk and Tripoli. The profits of the trans-Saharan trade being as high as the risks they knew that, if it pleased God to restore them to their homes and families, they would not be poor. Among them Bu-Khalum, with the greatest stake in the caravan, had the strongest interest in pursuing this policy and avoiding any unnecessary adventure that might put his life or his capital at risk.

But the Bedouin of the escort had aims that were diametrically opposed to these. Not only had they no capital or merchandise but the very idea of earning their living through trade was abhorrent to them. Riches that were not won by force of arms, they said, were not worth having. As a breed they were fierce, touchy, boastful, quarrelsome and intensely proud. For Africans and others whom they regarded as their inferiors, they had a contempt which they took no pains to conceal. Even with their own leaders they were stiff-necked and contumacious.

And yet there were unexpected paradoxes in their characters. Though cherishing their independence and chafing against any form of discipline, they were the slaves of a rigid code of honour. Any man who transgressed against it suffered agonies of shame and became a moral outcast. Similarly, for all their martial virtues, they had a sentimental streak in them and were by no means devoid of imagination, wit and sensibility. They loved to hear their traditional ballads recited and listened with almost equal enjoyment to the extemporary verses with which, sometimes for an hour on end, the poets and singers among them would relieve a tedious journey.[1]

In many of their qualities, and perhaps particularly in the panache which enabled paupers to carry themselves like lords, these North African Bedouin resembled the Highlanders of the Stuart era. Denham's description of them is very fair. Though their attractive qualities clearly appealed strongly to him, he did not close his eyes to their failings.

> The fondness of an Arab for traditional history of the most distinguished actions of their remote ancestors is proverbial. Professed story-tellers are ever the appendages to a man of rank: his friends will assemble before his tent, or on the platforms with which the houses of the Moorish Arabs are roofed and there listen, night after night, to a continued history for sixty or sometimes one hundred nights together. It is a great exercise of genius and a pecular gift, held in high estimation amongst them. They have a quickness and clearness of delivery, with a perfect command of words, surprising to a European ear. They never hesitate, are never at a loss; their descriptions are highly poetical and their relations exemplified by figure and metaphor, the most striking and appropriate. Their extemporary songs are also full of fire and possess many beautiful and happy similies. Certain tribes are celebrated for this gift of extemporary singing and speaking. The chiefs cultivate the propensity in their children and it is often possessed, to an astonishing degree, by men who are unable either to read or write.
>
> Arabic songs go to the heart and excite greatly the passions. I have seen a circle of Arabs straining their eyes with a fixed attention at one moment and bursting with loud laughter; at the next, melting into tears and clasping their hands in all the ecstacy of grief and sympathy.
>
> Their attachment to the pastoral life is ever favourable to love. Many of these children of the desert possess intelligence and feeling, which belong not to the savage, accompanied by an heroic courage and a thorough contempt of every mode of gaining their livelihood except by the sword and gun. An Arab values himself

---

1. Denham, 1 pp. 52-63.

chiefly on his expertness in arms and horsemanship and on hospitality.

Hospitality was ever habitual to them. At this day, the greatest reproach to an Arab tribe is 'That none of their men have the heart to give, nor their women to deny'. Nor does this feeling of liberality alone extend to the chiefs or Arabs of high birth: I have known the poor and wandering Bedouin to practise a degree of charity and hospitality far beyond his means, from a sense of duty alone...

Cowardice is ever visited in an Arab by the most disgraceful punishments: he is often bound and led through the huts of the whole tribe with the bowels and offal of a bullock, or some other animal, tied round his head. And, amongst a people who only desire to be rich in order to increase the number of their wives, probably the greatest punishment of all is that, could even any woman be found who would receive him as a husband, which would be an extraordinary circumstance, no Arab would allow him to enter into his family with such a stain on his character as cowardice.

The *amor patriae* discoverable in even the wildest inhabitant of the most barren rock is not felt by the wandering Arab or the Moor. He wanders from pasture to pasture, from district to district, without any local attachment and his sole delight is a roving, irregular, but martial life...

Arabs have always been commended by the ancients for the fidelity of their attachments, and they are still scrupulously exact to their words and respectful to their kindred. They have been universally celebrated for their quickness of apprehension and penetration and the vivacity of their wit. Their language is certainly one of the most ancient in the world but it has many dialects. The Arabs, however, have their vices and their defects: they are naturally addicted to war, bloodshed, and cruelty, and so malicious as scarcely ever to forget an injury.

Their frequent robberies committed on traders and travellers have rendered the name of an Arab almost infamous in Europe. Amongst themselves, however, they are most honest and true to the rites of hospitality. And towards those whom they receive as friends into their camp, everything is open and nothing ever known to be stolen: enter but once into the tent of an Arab and by the pressure of his hand he ensures you protection, at the hazard of his life. An Arab is ever true to his bread and salt: once eat with him and a knot of friendship is tied which cannot easily be loosened.[2]

* * *

---

2. Ibid, pp. 57-8 and 61-2.

QUARRELS AMONG THE ARABS

The leader of the largest contingent in the escort was Sheikh Abdi Smud of the M'Garha tribe. He used to boast of his father's prowess in having killed a hundred men in battle with his own hand and would then add piously that, please God, he would yet surpass him for he was but thirty-five years of age and had already accounted for forty. It was not he, however, but another chieftain, Sheikh Abdullah Bugil, who emerged as the leader of the dissident faction and the chief opponent of Bu-Khalum. His pride was that his ancestors scorned to tend flocks but were ever foremost in the fight and that both his father and grandfather had been killed in battle because they would not save themselves by flight.[3]

In February, soon after their arrival in Kuka, the Arabs were thrown into a state of great expectancy by a report that the Sultan of Baghirmi was advancing on Bornu with a large army. It will be remembered that during the past seven or eight years, the Baghirmis had replaced the Fulani as the principal enemies of the Kanuri. Initially, by calling in the help of the Sultan of Fezzan, El-Kanemi had inflicted a very severe defeat on them. He had also got the better of subsequent encounters but, though their country had been repeatedly ravaged, the Baghirmis had shown extraordinary resilience and were known to be thirsting for revenge. For a few days therefore, the Arabs had happy visions of themselves helping to defend Bornu and reaping a rich reward for their pains in slaves and booty.

> All the Arabs, who had formed our escort, were in great glee by the report of the approach of the Sultan of Baghirmi with a large force to within four days of Kuka.
>
> The Sheikh El-Kanemi had in former expeditions laid waste his whole country, each time driving the Sultan from Kernuk the capital. On the last occasion he had destroyed by fire the towns which the natives had deserted and had remained nearly three months in the country. The Sultan, with all his family and slaves, had as before retired to the other side of a large river to the south of his dominions, inhabited by savages who nevertheless always afforded him shelter and protection. This people were described as resembling the sands of the desert in number and they had now accompanied him to revenge himself on the Sheikh of Bornu.
>
> The prospect of plunder and making slaves, which these reports held out to the Arabs, raised their spirits to such a degree that they passed half the night in debating how their booty was to be conveyed across the desert without remembering that their enemies

---

3. Ibid, pp. 52-55.

> were first to be conquered. A gun being merely presented they all declared sufficient to drive away a thousand negroes. Could these poor creatures but once be made to understand the real state of an Arab's pouch, with seldom more than one or two loads of bad powder, and the little dependence to be placed in his firelock, a miserable French piece of the original value of about twelve shillings that misses fire at least every other time, how much more justly would they estimate the Arabs' strength.[4]

But the hopes of the Arabs were soon disappointed because the Sultan of Baghirmi, when he heard of their presence in Kuka, immediately abandoned his expedition.

Shortly afterwards however, it was rumoured that El-Kanemi was planning to send an expedition into Baghirmi to take reprisals against the Sultan for his presumption. Unfortunately, at just about the same time Bu-Khalum announced his intention of going on to Hausaland to sell the rest of his merchandize and demanded that some at least of the Arabs should accompany him. This move finally brought to a head the difference in the Arab camp between the merchants and the Bedouin.

> There was a disturbance in the camp this morning that nearly approached to direct mutiny amongst Bu-Khalum's Arabs. He had brought with him a very large assortment of valuable merchandize, for which there was but little sale at either Kuka or Ngornu, and he was anxious to proceed to Hausaland. The infantry refused to accompany him: they said the Pasha had ordered them to come thus far with the English, that Hausaland was distant, and go they would not. Someone had hinted to them that the Sheikh wished to send a *Ghrazzie* (marauding expedition) to Baghirmi and that Bu-Khalum had opposed such wish as not consistent with his orders: and, their profit being greater by an expedition of plunder and cruelty than by one of peace and commerce, they preferred the east to the west. Bu-Khalum certainly had refused to proceed on one of these marauding expeditions, much to the credit of his humanity...[5]

All through March the rift between the two factions grew wider. El-Kanemi, being just as suspicious of the Arabs as of the Europeans, made no attempt to reconcile them. On the contrary, he was clearly relieved that his powerful guests, who would have been a dangerous force if they had been tempted into any intrigue against him, were divided among

4. Ibid, pp. 222-3.
5. Ibid, p. 226.

themselves and, if anything, he played on their dissensions. By the beginning of April there was an open breach.

> The disputes between the Arabs had arrived at such a height that all idea of an amicable arrangement between them seemed at an end. Abdullah Bugil had obtained the support of most of the Sheikh's people and was therefore favoured by the Sheikh himself. He succeeded in getting away nearly half of the Arabs from Bu-Khalum and they pitched their tents at a few miles' distance from the town.
>
> The chiefs, however, were in Kuka every day, always with loaded pistols under their barracans, fearing assassination from the intrigues of each other. Abdullah Bugil charged Bu-Khalum with wasting his time in Kuka, for the purpose of disposing of his merchandize, while the Arabs were starving and might have been employed in a marauding expedition for the benefit of the Pasha. Bu-Khalum very boldly, and with great truth, accused Abdullah of mutinous and disorderly conduct in opposing him on all occasions—taking the part of those refractory Arabs whom he had thought it right to punish on the road for robbery and seducing them from under his command where the Pasha had placed both them and himself. He most properly declared that they came as an escort to the English and he as a merchant—that if a raid was advisable, he was to judge when the proper time would be for undertaking it.
>
> The Sheikh, however, without lessening his attentions to Bu-Khalum, whom he now promised to send with his own people to the country beyond Mandara, encouraged Abdullah to pursue his plan of quitting Bu-Khalum.[6]

So serious a quarrel between the Arabs placed the explorers in a most awkward position. Though their sympathies were with Bu-Khalum, they felt that they were powerless to intervene effectively and that consequently it was best to stand aloof. But this was not easy because Abdullah Bugil, mindful no doubt of having to justify his conduct to the Pasha at a later date, tried to enlist their support.

> Bugil had been repeatedly to my hut and endeavoured to convince me of the uprightness of his conduct and his great love for the English. 'Only say, my lord captain, where you will go and I will bring you a hundred men who will accompany you and die by your side'. I told him 'I had no occasion for such an escort and no money to reward them; that he had better return to the tents be

---

6. Ibid, pp. 257-8.

reconciled to Bu-Khalum and, as he had left Tripoli with him, return with him and then make his complaint to the Pasha'. He said 'No: Bu-Khalum had once damned his father and his faith, that it was deep in his heart, and he could never forgive him. But would I write to the Pasha and the consul at Tripoli and say that he had always been my friend?' I replied 'Certainly not. That if I wrote at all, it would be to say that he was decidedly wrong in everything that he had done'.[7]

At this stage Denham's journal becomes less explicit than it might have been. It is evident, however, that the feeling among the Bedouins was so strong that Bu-Khalum was forced to put off his projected trading expedition to Hausaland and instead to use all his influence in persuading El-Kanemi to arrange a raid in which the Arabs would get the chance they craved of enriching themselves. But even this *volte face* did not suffice to bring about a reconciliation between him and Abdullah Bugil. In the end therefore, after Bu-Khalum had threatened to dismiss the most extreme of his opponents, two expeditions had to be arranged and it was settled that Bu-Khalum and his followers should head south, for a destination that was still kept secret, while Abdullah Bugil and his adherents went to Kanem. Both parties left Kuka during the second week of April.[8]

7. Ibid, p. 259.
8. Ibid, pp. 259-260.

VIII

South To Mandara

The hot weather had now set in and the temperature in the explorer's huts had reached 106°. Oudney and Clapperton were still not strong enough for any strenuous exertion but Denham, who thus far had enjoyed easily the best health in the party, was fit and active. As a soldier, he had always had a strong hankering to accompany a military expedition and see for himself how Sudanese warfare was conducted. Consequently, as soon as he heard about the raids that were being considered, he begged Bu-Khalum to obtain the Sheikh's permission for him to accompany the expedition to Mandara.[1]

When Bu-Khalum set out from Kuka without taking leave of him Denham was bitterly disappointed for he assumed, rightly, that his application to accompany the expedition had been refused. On April 10, however, he and his companions were unexpectedly summoned to the Palace and informed by El-Kanemi that their request to visit the Shari was granted. This gave Denham fresh hope and, knowing that Bu-Khalum was still at Ngornu, waiting for the accompanying Bornu force to muster, he succeeded in obtaining another audience and again asked El-Kanemi for permission to accompany the expedition.

> I had an interview with the Sheikh when he said 'I must refuse because I know not how to ensure your safety. Still, I wish that I could comply with your request. The application by Bu-Khalum for all your party to go was out of the question: your King could not

1. Denham, I, p. 258.

wish that a mission sent out so far should run such risks—it was an imprudent request and the Pasha would never have forgiven me if I had complied with it. You are differently situated: your Sultan expressly orders you to accompany any military expeditions. But, although you are a soldier, you will scarcely know how to take care of yourself in an expedition of this nature, should Bu-Khalum meet with a repulse, and on this account alone I cannot sanction your departure'. I replied, 'that I could not be otherwise than sensible of the anxiety he evinced for our safety but that the orders of my Sultan must be obeyed if possible; that, although he refused his approbation, I trusted he would not prevent my accompanying Bu-Khalum. Indeed' added I smiling 'if that is your intention, I given you notice that the irons had better be on—I shall certainly go for I dare not lose such an opportunity of seeing the country'.[2]

To Denham himself, El-Kanemi still did not give a direct answer but he arranged for Marami, the half-Fulani slave who had been one of his guides on the trip to Lake Chad, to accompany him again, ostensibly on his visit to the Shari. But he told Marami privately that, if Denham insisted on joining the expedition, he was to conduct him straight to Barka Gana, the commanding General and hand him over with every possible injunction about ensuring his personal safety.[3]

In the very early hours of the following morning Denham and his little party left Kuka for Ngornu. Denham was mounted on a small but powerful grey given to him by the Sheikh a few days earlier in exchange for the second of the two horses which he had brought from Tripoli. His negro servant followed on a mule and a camel easily carried their baggage which consisted of a small Egyptian tent, a bag of rice and canteens containing a few delicacies such as coffee.[4]

On the way, Marami allowed Denham to discover what his secret instructions were and Denham without hesitation decided to take advantage of the latitude allowed him. At Ngornu, however, they discovered that the expedition had already left. Staying the night, therefore, they set off again in the early hours of the following morning and, after resting during the heat of the day, caught up with the column in the evening at Marte.

Marami now told me 'that the Sheikh wished I should put myself under the protection of Barka Gana, that Bu-Khalum's

2. Ibid, pp. 264-5.
3. Ibid, pp. 267-8.
4. Ibid, pp. 265-6.

responsibility ceased on arriving at Bornu, that *he* was now bound to provide for my safety, and that with his people he wished me to remain'. I should have been better pleased to have pitched my tent closer to that of my tried friend and amongst my old companions the Arabs but, as Marami assured me the Sheikh would be highly displeased, I instantly gave up the idea.

Barka Gana received me with a great deal of civility in his tent, although he kept me several minutes waiting outside until he had summoned his charm-writer—an indispensable person—and one or two of his chiefs to attend him. 'If it was the will of God' he said 'I should come to no harm and he would do all in his power for my convenience'. A spot was appointed for my tent near his own and I took my leave in order to visit the Arabs. The cheers they all gave me, and the hearty shake of the hand of Bu-Khalum, made me regret that I was not to be amongst them, in spite of all their bad qualities. Bu-Khalum repeatedly exclaimed 'I knew you would come—I said you would by some means or other join us'.

One of Barka Gana's people now brought word that we should move on by daybreak. I retired to my tent, after making Bu-Khalum acquainted with the Sheikh's arrangements, first to write to Doctor Oudney of my proceedings and then to sleep off my fatigue. Sleep, however, was my only refreshment, I was as it were between two stools; one of my friends did not think it necessary, and the other never intended, to send me any supper.[5]

* * *

Barka Gana, the General into whose charge Denham had been entrusted, was a Hausa slave who enjoyed the privileges of a favourite freedman. He had been born in Sankara, a town situated forty miles north-east of Kano, but seventeen years earlier, during the *jihad,* he had been captured by the Kanuri and taken to Bornu as a slave where he had entered the Sheikh's household. His history shows just how hazardous and yet unpredictable life in the central Sudan could be. Barka Gana the boy could count himself most unfortunate to have been enslaved at all. Being Hausas, his family were unlikely to have thrown in their lot with the militant reformers, most of whom were Fulani, and in any case a boy of nine could hardly have been considered a serious combatant. Furthermore, even if he had been taken in arms, he was still a Moslem and Islamic law laid down that he could be captured but not enslaved. Those were turbulent times, however, and it was common after a siege or battle

5. Ibid, pp. 271-2.

for the victors, hungry for booty, to round up prisoners without taking much trouble to ascertain whether they were all enemies. As for the inconvenient point of law, it was the general practice of both sides to circumvent it by describing their opponents as apostates or heretics who, having forsaken the brotherhood of Islam, no longer enjoyed immunity from enslavement.

But, paradoxically enough, the wrong suffered by Barka Gana the boy proved to be the making of Barka Gana the man. The Shiekh not only perceived his talents but also became very attached to him. First he was given virtual freedom, next he was raised to the first rank of feudatories by being entrusted with a fief which comprised Ngala and other towns along the River Shari, and finally he was appointed *Kachalla* or commander-in-chief. Now, at the age of twenty-six, he was one of the foremost men in the kingdom. According to Denham's description, he had a powerful frame, a fine presence, refined and pleasing manners, an alert eye and a keen intelligence. Though a devout Moslem, he was yet superstitious enough to believe that a charm which he treasured made him invulnerable to both bullets and arrows.[6]

The Bornu troops mustered for this expedition were about 2,000 strong. On the morning of April 18, with Barka Gana at their head and Denham riding in his train, they set off again and, with a noonday halt, covered the twenty-five miles between Marte and Dikwa.[7] Dikwa, which seventy years later was to become the capital of Rabeh, the usurping conquerer of Bornu, was already one of the leading centres of the kingdom. Denham described it as a walled town with a population of about 30,000, the same as Ngornu's. As the expedition camped there, an unusually early thunderstorm, broke over them. The rain was heavy enough to penetrate Denham's light tent and give him an uncomfortable night.

Next morning they broke camp before it was light, crossed the dry water-course of the river Yedseram, and soon found themselves in closer country where mimosas and other thorns overhung and pressed in upon the path. Riding in the General's train, Denham was able to note the state he kept.

> Chiefs in this part of Africa are accompanied by as many personal followers as they think proper to maintain ... Barka Gana

6. Ibid, p. 272.
7. Denham, who was inclined to pitch his linear estimates too high, put the distance at 34 miles. But in the heat of April, when the last few miles always drag intolerably, such a mistake is very understandable.

had five mounted . . . behind him, three of whom carried a sort of drum, which hung round their necks, and beat time while they sang extemporary songs; one carried a small pipe made of a reed; and the other blew on a buffalo's horn loud and deep-toned blasts, as we moved through the wood.

But by far the most entertaining and useful were the running footmen who preceded the General and acted as pioneers. They were twelve in number and carried long forked poles with which they, with great dexterity, kept back the branches as they moved on at a quick pace, constantly keeping open a path, which would without them really have been scarcely passable. They, besides this, were constantly crying aloud something about the road or the expedition, as they went on. For example: 'Take care of the holes!—Avoid the branches! Here is the road! Take care of the mimosa! Its branches are like spears! Worse than spears! Keep off the branches!'

'For whom?'

'Barka Gana!'

'Who in battle is like the rolling thunder?'

'Barka Gana!'

'Here is the watercourse, but no water'.

'God be praised!'

'In battle, who spreads terror round him like a buffalo in his rage?'

'Barka Gana!'

This sort of question and answer, at once useful and exhilarating, is kept up until the time of halting.[8]

After a short march of only seven miles the column halted at Afaye. This had once formed part of a pagan principality called Dagwamba but, after its conquest by the Kanuri, it had been annexed to Bornu and its people converted to Islam. Denham put the population of the town and the surrounding villages at not less than 20,000. Food was plentiful and the whole force was supplied with bullocks and sheep.

Having hardly eaten since leaving Ngornu, sixty miles back, Denham was glad to receive an invitation to join Barka Gana at the evening meal where he found five or six members of the staff already assembled.

> Half a roasted sheep was laid on green boughs placed on the sand before us; the black chiefs then stripped off the dark blue shirt, their only covering; the sharpest dagger in the party was searched for and, being given to one who acted as carver, large slices of the

8. Ibid, pp. 274-6.

flesh were cut, distributed about, and quickly devoured without either bread or salt; when we arrived at the bones, another side shared the same fate, and our repast closed by huge draughts from a large wooden bowl of rice water, honey, tamarinds, and red pepper.[9]

* * *

Until now, the fact that the explorers were Christians had caused no difficulties. In Tripoli and Murzuk, as they were known to be under the Pasha's protection, none had presumed to challenge or question them. Later, during the passage of the desert, they had been insulated from embarrassing curiosity by the Arab escort, Moslems to a man, while in Kuka El-Kanemi's favour had been enough to save them from prying familiarities. But here, separated as he now was from the more tolerant Arabs and far removed from El-Kanemi's protective mantle, Denham found that his immunity was at an end.

The General's charm-writer, Mallam Chadili, had always eyed me with a look of suspicion and had once said, when the whole army halted at dawn, 'Do you wash and pray?'

'Yes' said I.

'Where?' rejoined the Mallam.

'In my tent', I replied.

This Mallam, who continued throughout my mortal enemy and annoyance, now asked Bu-Khalum 'what these English were? were they Hanafi or Maliki?' still believing that, as we appeared a little better than the pagans, we must be Moslem in some way or other. Bu-Khalum answered, with some hesitation, 'No: that we were unfortunate; that we believed not in "the Book", the title always given to the Koran; that we were not circumcised; that we had a Book of our own, which did not mention the Prophet Muhammad, and that, blind as we were, we believed in it. 'But Inshallah' added he 'they will see their error and die Moslems, for they are beautiful people, very beautiful'. This account was followed by a general groan and the Mallam clasped his hands, looked thoughtful, and then said 'Why does not the great Pasha of Tripoli make them all Moslems?'

This question made Bu-Khalum smile.

'Why' replied Bu-Khalum 'that he could not very well do, great as he is. These people are powerful, very powerful, and an affront to even one of these might cost the Pasha his kingdom. They are also rich, very rich'.

9. Ibid, p. 276.

'May it please the Lord quickly to send all their riches into the hands of true Moslems' said the Mallam, to which the whole assembly echoed 'Amen'.

'However', continued Bu-Khalum, 'there are a great many Christians in the world but the English are the best of any. They worship no images, they believe in one God, and are almost Moslem'. This was as much as he could say, although it raised me but little in the Mallam's estimation. And as he decided, so every body was obliged to think.

Our rice-water-and honey was always brought in a brass basin, tinned on the inside, such as are only used by Sultans and persons of rank, wooden bowls being always drunk out of by the people, and out of this basin Barka Gana and myself only were allowed to drink. To-night, while I was drinking, the Mallam made some remark. What I left in the bowl was instantly thrown away and soon after a separate vessel was assigned to me.[10]

* * *

In the Sudan the latter part of the dry-season is the hottest and most oppressive season of the year. Denham recorded that on one afternoon, although the sky was overcast, the temperature in his tent reached 109°. At the noonday halt on the following day, as his camel was slow in coming up, he had no tent to pitch and was forced to rest in the best shade he could find. There his thermometer registered 113°. To preserve his body moisture, he resorted to the Arab practice of wrapping himself up in his woollen burnous and covering his head with a cloth. Even so, he felt himself to be on the brink of exhaustion. In the evening however, after another march, he was cheered to find that the expedition had now entered Mandara and to catch his first glimpse of mountains to the south.

Next day the march was continued and a noble chain of hills came into view. Having been reinforced from time to time by contingents of Shuwa Arabs, the column was now 3,000 strong. Apart from the Maghreb Arabs, about eighty of whom still had to go on foot because they lacked horses, all were mounted. As they approached Mora, the capital of Mandara, which was situated in a fertile valley overlooked by hills studded with pagan villages, they were met by the Sultan.

> We saw before us the Sultan of Mandara, surrounded by about five hundred horsemen, posted on a rising ground ready to receive us, when Barka Gana instantly commanded a halt.

10. Ibid, pp. 278-280.

> Different parties now charged up to the front of our line and, wheeling suddenly round, charged back again to the Sultan. These people were finely dressed in Hausa gowns of different colours ... [and] burnouses of coarse scarlet cloth, with large turbans of white or dark coloured cotton. Their horses were really beautiful, larger and more powerful than anything found in Bornu, and they managed them with great skill. The Sultan's guard was composed of thirty of his sons, all mounted on very superior horses, clothed in striped gowns, and the skin of the tiger-cat and leopard forming their shabracks which hung fully over their horses' haunches.
>
> After these had returned to their station in front of the Sultan, we approached at full speed in our turn, halting with the guard between us and the royal presence. The parley then commenced and, the object of Bu-Khalum's visit having been explained, we retired again to the place we had left, while the Sultan returned to the town, preceded by several men blowing long pipes, not unlike clarionets ornamented with shells, and two immense trumpets from twelve to fourteen feet long, borne by men on horseback...[11]

The visitors pitched their camp a short distance from the town. After covering over 160 miles in just over a week at the height of the hot weather, Denham at least was thankful to call a halt. But, though there was a chance to rest, there was to be little relaxation for him. The heat was insufferable and for several hours a day the thermometer in his tent remained at 113°. His face, and particularly his eyes, were sore and swollen from the myriads of insects that had attacked him on the march. Now too, the flies gave him no rest and during the day he could only escape from them by wrapping himself in his blankets. To cap everything, Mallam Chadili continued to plague him. At one of their evening meals, when Denham had as usual plunged his right hand into the common dish, he ostentatiously took himself off to another bowl and then, when reproved by Barka Gana for his rudeness, stumped out of the tent in a huff.[12]

11. Ibid, pp. 281-2.
12. Ibid, p. 287.

IX

Mandara

To give him his due, Bu-Khalum had come to the Sudan for purely commercial reasons. If he had been left to himself, he would no doubt have completed his trading and departed without injuring anybody. As we have seen, however, the Arabs of the escort had brought such pressure to bear on him that in the end he had been forced to yield and beg El-Kanemi to arrange a foray in which the Arabs would have the opportunity of enriching themselves.

Bu-Khalum's request must have put El-Kanemi in a quandary. Before the rise of the Fulani, it would have presented little difficulty because until then the pagan areas to the south of Bornu had been regarded as lying within Bornu's sphere of influence. Their primitive peoples had then been treated by the Kanuri as a conveniently placed reservoir of slaves that could be drawn upon at will. But, with the establishment of the Fulani Emirates of Adamawa, Gombe, and Bauchi, Bornu had been cut off from its main sources of supply. The pagans were still raided, of course, but now the raiders were Fulani and the captive slaves were either sent to Sokoto as tribute or to Kano as merchandize. The preserves no longer belonged to Bornu.

Nor were there any other equally tempting targets. Had the Arabs been more numerous, El-Kanemi would probably have been disposed to try another full-scale invasion of Baghirmi and repeat the success which he had achieved in 1815-16 with the help of the Sultan of Fezzan. As it was, however, he doubtless concluded that their force was not strong enough to guarantee success, especially as nearly half of them were unmounted.

A decade or two earlier, Mandara might have served as an alternative but now an attack on it was out of the question because not only had the ruling classes been converted to Islam but the Sultan had made an alliance with El-Kanemi which had been cemented by marriage.[1] There remained only the pagan tribes in the south-west, like the Bolawa and the Kerikeri, who inhabited the no-man's-land between the Bornu and Sokoto Empires.[2] They did not constitute much of a prize however and El-Kanemi was probably unwilling to let the Arabs even see how limited his preserves now were, much less to invite them in. And yet he did not wish to offend them. From this predicament he extricated himself very adroitly by packing the Arabs off to Mandara with a request to the Sultan, who was very much the junior partner in the alliance with Bornu, that he would provide them with a suitable target.

Bu-Khalum must have been tempted to evade his own problem in the same way and send his hot-heads off on the Mandara expedition while he himself pursued his trading enterprises. If he ever seriously entertained such an idea however, reflection would have convinced him that it was out of the question. Had he failed to put himself at their head, he would soon have forfeited the confidence of those who were still loyal to him. Furthermore, if the raid had been successful, his enemies would have been in a position to take rich presents of slaves and booty back to the Pasha of Tripoli and the Sultan of Murzuk while he, whose presents should have been the richest of all, would have had nothing to offer. In short, if he had hung back he would have made himself fatally vulnerable to the accusation that he had been more intent on enriching himself than on serving his masters, a charge that would certainly have cost him all favour at court. Once the Mandara expedition had been decided upon, therefore, he had to make a virtue of necessity and throw himself into it with an appearance of enthusiasm.

Arrived in Mora, Bu-Khalum told Denham that 'he should make the Sultan handsome presents and that he was quite sure a pagan town full of people would be given him to plunder'. Though an essentially kindly man, he apparently felt no compunction or sense of guilt in hatching these plans.[3]

1. Denham, 1 p. 290.
2. C.K. Meek, *The Northern Tribes of Nigeria*, London, 1925, map at the end of vol. 1.
3. Denham, 1, p. 283. Mungo Park, on his first journey, encountered a similar paradox when Karfa Taura, a slave trader, showed the greatest kindness in nursing him through an almost fatal illness.

As for the rank and file, they were thirsting for action.

The Arabs were all eagerness. They eyed the pagan huts, which were now visible on the sides of the mountains before us, with longing eyes and, contrasting their own ragged and almost naked state with the appearance of the Sultan of Mandara's people in their silk gowns, not only thought but said 'if Buk-Khalum pleased, they would go no further: this would do'.

Bu-Khalum and the Arab sheikhs had repeatedly exclaimed, when urging El-Kanemi to send them to some country for slaves, 'Never mind their numbers! Arrows are nothing! And ten thousand spears are of no importance. We have guns! guns!', exclaiming with their favourite imprecations 'We'll eat them, the dogs! Why, they are negroes all!' I fancied I could see the keen features of El-Kanemi curl to these contemptuous expressions, which equally applied to his own people, and certainly nothing could be more galling than for him to hear them from such a handful of Arabs...

Towards the evening, Barka Gana sent to desire me to mount for the purpose of visiting the Sultan. We entered the town ... and at the farther end of a large square was the Sultan's palace. As is usual, on approaching or visiting a great man, we galloped up to the entrance at full speed, almost entering the gates. This is a perilous sort of salutation, but nothing must stop you, and it is seldom made except at the expense of one or more lives. On this occasion a man and horse, which stood in our way, were ridden over in an instant, the horses leg broke, and the man killed on the spot.

The trumpets sounded as we dismounted at the palace gate; our papouches, or outward slippers, were quickly pulled off; and we proceeded through a wide entrance into a large court where, under a dark blue Hausa tent, sat the Sultan on a mud bench, covered however with a handsome carpet and silk pillows. He was surrounded by about two hundred persons, all handsomely dressed in gowns of silk and coloured cotton, with his five eunuchs, the principal men of the country, sitting in front but all with their backs turned towards him.

The manner of saluting is curious: Barka Gana, as the Sheikh's representative, approached to a space in front of the eunuchs, his eyes fixed on the ground; he then sat down, with his eyes still fixed on the earth, with his back to the Sultan and, clapping his hand together, exclaimed 'May you live for ever! God send you a happy old age! How is it with you? Blessing! Blessing!' These words were repeated nearly by the Sultan and then sung out by all the court. The *fatah* was then said and they proceeded to business. Bu-Khalum produced some presents which were carried off by the eunuchs unopened. The Sultan then expressed his wish to serve him, said he would consider his request, and in a day or two give him his decision.

The Sultan, whose name was Muhammad Bukr, was an intelligent little man of about fifty with a beard dyed of a most beautiful sky-blue. He had been eyeing me for some time, as I sat between Bu-Khalum and Barka Gana, and first asking Bu-Khalum my name, enquired who I was? The answer that I was a native of a very distant and powerful nation, friends of the Pasha of Tripoli and the Sheik, who came to see the country, did not appear much to surprise him and he looked gracious as he said 'But what does he want to see?' A fatal question however followed and the answer appeared to petrify the whole assembly: 'Are they Moslem?'

'No! No!'

Every eye, which had before been turned towards me, was now hastily withdrawn and, looking round, I really felt myself in a critical situation. 'Has the great Pasha unbelieving friends?' said the Sultan. The explanation which followed was of little use: they knew no distinctions. Christians they had merely heard of as the worst people in the world and probably, until they saw us, scarcely believed them to be human. We shortly after returned to our camp and I never afterwards was invited to enter the Sultan of Mandara's presence.[4]

* * *

The population of Mandara at this time was very mixed. The ruling classes, who evidently had an infusion of Arab or Berber blood, had recently been converted, or perhaps reclaimed, to Islam. They inhabited towns situated in the valleys and, by the standards of the Sudan, were prosperous and fairly sophisticated. Certainly their houses were well built while their arms, accoutrements, and horses were all first-rate. Though they carried on some legitimate commerce with the outside world—working iron, for example and exporting hoes to Bornu—the real source of their wealth was the capture of and traffic in slaves.

In appearance, Denham found them much more handsome than the Kanuri of Bornu. The men had flashing eyes, noses inclining to the aquiline and high, flat foreheads; the women small hands and feet, good features and beautiful figures. Having plenty of slaves to do the hard work on their farms, they were able to devote themselves to other occupations. While the middle-classes were content with following their crafts or with the pursuit of trade or learning, the courtiers and their

4. Ibid, pp. 283-6.

numerous henchmen preferred to exploit the advantages of their situation, asserting their authority from time to time with a slave-raid or a punitive expedition.

But, unlike Bornu and the great majority of the Hausa States Mandara seems to have had little or no native peasantry. The other part of its population consisted of pagan tribes who were racially quite distinct from the upper and middle classes. Having been exposed for generations to the raids of stronger and more advanced neighbours, they had long since sought refuge in the hills. There, in remote and scarcely accessible villages, they lived according to their primitive lights, cultivating their patches of ground, propitiating their spirits, brewing the beer that they loved to drink and troubling as little about clothes as about learning, politics, or religion. Between the pagans in the hills and the ruling classes in the towns, there was little traffic. It was understood that, provided the pagans paid their tribute and refrained from making forays into the plains, they were free to go their own ways and would not normally be molested. Equally, however, it was accepted that failure to observe these conditions gave the Sultan the right to mount punitive expeditions or, what was much the same thing, slave-raids. In normal circumstances, the ruling classes adhered to these conventions but, as the stronger party, they tacitly reserved the right to abrogate them whenever they chose to do so. Such a relationship between Moslem rulers and pagan tributaries was not peculiar to Mandara. Elsewhere it had long been known in the semi-Hausa States of Yauri and Gurma and it had recently had been reproduced in the Fulani Emirates of Adamawa and Bauchi.

Now some years before the arrival of the European explorers, the Sultan of Mandara, in order to set the seal on his treaty of friendship with Bornu and make what he regarded as a fitting settlement on the daughter whom he had given in marriage to El-Kanemi, had invoked his reserved rights, suspended the normal relationship between himself and his pagans and presented a very large draft on his slave-bank.

> This treaty of alliance was confirmed by the Sheikh's receiving in marriage the daughter of the Sultan of Mandara, and the marriage portion was to be the produce of an immediate expedition into the pagan country called Musgau to the south-east of Mandara, by the united forces of the Sheikh and the Sultan. The results were as favourable as the most savage confederacy could have anticipated three thousand unfortunate wretches were dragged from their native wilds and sold to perpetual slavery, while probably double that number were sacrificed to obtain them. These nuptials are said to

have been celebrated with great rejoicing and much barbarian splendour.[5]

The Arabs, when they reached Mora, were hoping that a similar dispensation would be arranged for their benefit. On the other side the pagans, seeing the expedition arrive, naturally assumed that another raid had been planned and were at once thrown into a ferment.

> The dread in which they hold the Sultan has been considerably increased by his close alliance with the Sheikh and the appearance of such a force as that which accompanied Barka Gana, bivouacked in the valley, was a most appalling sight to those who occupied the overhanging heights. They were fully aware that for one purpose alone would such a force visit their country, and which of them were to be the victims must have been the cause of most anxious inquietude and alarm to the whole. By the assistance of a good telescope, I could discover those who, from the terms on which they were with Mandara, had the greatest dread, stealing off into the heart of the mountains, while others came towards Mora bearing leopard skins, honey, and slaves, plundered from a neighbouring town, as peace-offerings, also asses and goats with which their mountains abound. These were not, however, on this occasion destined to suffer.
>
> The people of Musgau, whose country it was at first reported (although without foundation) that the Arabs were to plunder, sent two hundred head of their fellow-creatures, besides other presents, to the Sultan with more than fifty horses. Between twenty and thirty horsemen, mounted on small, fiery, and very well formed steeds of about fourteen hands ... were the bearers of these gifts—and a most extraordinary appearance they made. I saw them on their leaving the Sultan's palace and, both then and on their entrance, they threw themselves on the ground, pouring sand on their heads and uttering the most piteous cries. The horsemen, who were chiefs, were covered only by the skin of a goat or leopard, so contrived as to hang over the left shoulder with the head of the animal on the breast... On their heads, which were covered with long wooly, or rather bristly, hair, coming quite over their eyes, they wore a cap of the skin of the goat and some foxlike animal. Round their arms, and in their ears, were rings of what to me appeared to be bone. And round the necks of each were from one to six strings of what I was assured were the teeth of the enemies they had slain in battle. Teeth and pieces of bone were also pendant

---

5. Ibid, p. 290.

from the clotted locks of their hair and, with the red patches with which their bodies were marked in different places and of which colour also their teeth were stained, they really had a most strikingly wild and truly savage appearance.[6]

The Sultan of Mandara was just as well aware of the hopes of the Arabs as of the fears of the pagans, but it was only his own interests that he consulted. For this there was perhaps some excuse because the fact was that El-Kanemi's diversion of the Arabs to Mandara had placed him in a position of some delicacy. If he was too open-handed, his uninvited guests would simply ravage his preserves and carry off the spoils. On the other hand, if he was too tight-fisted, they might complain about him to El-Kanemi and the Pasha and perhaps bring reprisals down on his head. In short, he had an extremely difficult hand to play. As a man he emerges from Denham's narrative in a singularly unattractive light; nevertheless, considered as a politician, one cannot help admiring the machiavellian finesse that he brought to the game. The Arabs, for all their bombast and the scorn that they professed for Africans generally, were to be out-manoeuvred at every point and in the end reduced to humiliating impotence.

The Sultan of Mandara had given no intimation whatever of his intentions with regard to Bu-Khalum's destination and in consequence the impatience and discontent of the latter were extreme. Offerings poured in from all the pagan tribes and the Sultan excused himself to Bu-Khalum for the delay on account of the extreme tractability of the people around him who, he said, were becoming Moslems without force. Again Musgau was mentioned, adding that the warlike arm of the Arabs, bearing the sword of the Prophet, might turn their hearts. This hypocrisy, however, Bu-Khalum inveighed against most loudly to me declaring that the conversion of the pagans would lose him (the Sultan) thousands of slaves, as their constant wars with each other afforded them the means of supplying him abundantly.[7]

* * *

While the Arabs were waiting impatiently for the Sultan to make up his mind, Denham determined to undertake an excursion into the neighbouring hills. His request for permission to do so was passed on from one dignitary to another until it reached the Sultan's chief eunuch. After

6. Ibid, pp. 292-4.
7. Ibid, p. 295.

being kept waiting for nearly an hour, Denham was at length received into this august presence and questioned about his motives.

> I was conducted into the presence of the chief eunuch; he desired me to stop within about twelve yards of him and then said 'The Sultan could not imagine what I wanted at the hills. Did I wish to catch the pagans alone:—that I had better buy them—he would sell me as many as I pleased.' He then made some remark which was not interpreted and which created a loud laugh in all the bystanders; the joke was evidently at my expense although I was not aware of its point. I assured him 'that I did not wish to go at all to the hills if the Sultan had the slightest objection, that it was purely curiosity, and that as to catching pagans I would not take them if given to me.' This put us all to rights; I gave him some powder, and he was as civil as he could be to such an unbeliever as myself.[8]

After this interview, an escort was provided and Denham set off on his horse to explore the nearer foothills. In the course of a tiring and not very profitable morning he saw a number of naked pagans, who made off with great agility as he approached, and collected a few geological specimens. His guides assured him that the mountains extended southward over the span of more than two months journey—a very fair estimate as we now know—and that they were inhabited by many different pagan tribes. A few venturesome freedmen travelled there to trade gowns and beads for slaves and pelts but otherwise there were no communications. They affirmed—again perfectly correctly as scientific surveys were later to confirm—that apart from iron no metals were to be found in the hills.[9]

The chief eunuch had evidently found it difficult to believe that nothing but curiosity had taken Denham to the hills. When he heard from the guides of Denham's having picked up pebbles and brought them back, his suspicions were again aroused. He therefore called on Barka Gana to make further enquiries and Denham was summoned to account for his actions.

> Nothing can be more solemn than these interviews: not an eye is raised, or a smile seen, or a word spoken, beyond 'Long life to you! A happy old age! Blessing! Blessing! May you trample on your enemies! Please God! Please God!' Then the *fatah*, which is seldom or never omitted.

8. Ibid, p. 297.
9. Ibid, p. 298.

> The great man first inquired 'why I went to the hills and what I wanted with the stones I had picked up and put in a bag which I carried near my saddle?' Barka Gana applied to me for information and the bag was sent for. My specimens were not more than fifteen in number and the eunuch, laying his hand on two pieces of fine grained granite and some quartz, asked 'how many dollars they would bring in my country?' I smiled and told him 'Not one—that I had no object in taking them beyond curiosity—that we had as much in England as would cover his whole country—and that I was pleased to find similar natural productions here. Assure the Sultan' added I to Barka Gana 'that to take anything from any of the inhabitants of these countries is not the wish of the English king. The Shiekh knows our intentions which are rather to make them acquainted with European produce and, if useful to them, send more into their country.'[10]

This speech led naturally to the question of what presents Denham had brought for the Sultan and again he found himself in the awkward predicament of being inadequately provided. Back in Kuka the explorers had with them cases of merchandise, purchased especially to be given away as presents, but unfortunately because of the haste and uncertainty that had attended his start, Denham had none of them with him. Obviously something had to be found, however, and so he sent for his trunk and selected from his personal belongings a razor, a pair of scissors, and two red shawls of French manufacture. It was hardly a princely present but the Sultan did not spurn it. Moreover, in the course of the following day, no fewer than fifteen of his sons called on Denham in the hope of picking up knives, scissors, or gunpowder. But apart from two silk handkerchiefs and a pair of cotton socks, the cupboard was now bare and so most of them departed in sulky discontent.[11]

To occupy the time, Denham next tried to make some sketches of Mora but this only aroused further suspicion and led to another brush with Mallam Chadili.

> I this morning ventured to make two attempts at sketching, but my apparatus and myself were carried off without ceremony to the Sultan. My pencils marking without ink created great astonishment and the facility with which its traces were effaced by India rubber seemed still more astonishing.

10. Ibid, pp. 300-301.
11. Ibid, p. 301.

My old antagonist, Mallam Chadili, was there and affected to treat me with great complaisance: he talked a great deal about me and my country, which made his hearers repeatedly cry out 'Y-e-o-o-o!', but what the purport of his observations was I could not make out. I endeavoured, however, to forget all his former rudeness, took everything in good part, and appeared quite upon as good terms with him as he evidently wished to appear to be with me. Several words were written, both by him and the others, which the rubber left no remains of. At length he wrote *Bismillahi rahamani rahim* (in the name of the great and most merciful God)[12] in large Arabic characters. He made so deep an impression on the paper that, after using the India rubber, the words still appeared legible. 'This will not quite disappear' said I.

'No, No' exclaimed the Mallam exulting 'they are the words of God, delivered to our Prophet. I defy you to erase them.'

'Probably so' said I. 'Then it will be in vain to try'.

He showed the paper to the Sultan, and then around him, with great satisfaction. They all exclaimed 'Y-e-o-o-o! *La illah il Allah Muhammad ras'ul Allah*', cast looks at me expressive of mingled pity and contempt, and I was well pleased when allowed to take my departure.

The whole of this scene was repeated to Barka Gana in his tent in the evening and they all exclaimed 'Wonderful! Wonderful! ... As I did not contradict any part of his account, the Mallam thus addressed me: '*Rais,* you have seen a miracle. I will show you hundreds, performed alone by the words of the wonderful book.
You have a book also, you say, but it must be false. Why? Because it says nothing of Muhammad the Prophet. That is enough. Turn! Turn! Say 'God is God and Muhammad is his Prophet'. Wash, pray, and become clean, and paradise is open to you. Without this, what can save you from eternal fire? Nothing. Oh! I shall see you while sitting in the third heaven, in the midst of the flames, crying out to your friend Barka Gana and myself, give me a drink or a drop of water, but the gulf will be between us and then it will be too late.' The Mallam's tears flowed in abundance during this harangue and everybody appeared affected by his eloquence.[13]

I felt myself at this period extremely uncomfortable and Barka Gana, who saw my distress, called me into the inner tent where

---

12. More correctly 'In the name of God, the Merciful and Compassionate'.

13. Among Moslem preachers, the ability to shed tears on such occasions is regarded as a sign of fervour and sincerity, if not of grace, and is revered accordingly.

nobody accompanied him except by invitation. 'The Mallam' said he 'is a clever man'.

'Very likely' said I 'but he might surely leave me to my own belief, as I leave him to his'.

'God forbid!' said he. 'Do not compare them'.

'I do not' said I. 'God knows, but you, Kachalla, should protect me from such repeated annoyance'.

'No' replied Barka. 'In this I cannot interfere. The Mallam is a holy man. Please God you will be enlightened, and I know the Sheikh wishes it: he likes you and would you stay amongst us he would give you fifty slaves of great beauty, build you a house like his son's, and give you wives from the families of any of his subjects you choose.'

'Were you to return to England with me, Kachalla, as you sometimes talk about, with the Sheikh's permission, would it not be disgraceful for you to turn Christian, and remain? Were I to do as you would have me, How should I answer to my Sultan who sent me?'

'God forbid!' said he. 'You are comparing our faiths again. I propose to you eternal paradise, while you would bring me to. . . .'

'Not a word more' said I. 'Good night'.

'Peace be with you! I hope we shall always be friends' said he.

'Please God!' returned I.

'Amen!' said the Kachalla.[14]

* * *

There was to be no respite for Denham on this expedition. During the ensuing night a storm came up which he described as the most violent he had ever experienced: a nearby tree was torn up by the roots, masses of stone thundered down the hillsides, and the lightning made the night as bright as day. Worse still, the pole of the tent snapped off, the top was carried away by the gale and Denham had to take refuge in the tent used by Barka Gana's guards. Though drenched to the skin, he soon fell asleep again but awoke in the morning with sore limbs and an aching head.[15]

The storm also completed the discomfiture of the Arabs and reduced them to a state of hungry and exasperated frustration. Rather than endure any further delay, they were now ready to fall in with almost any plan of action. This, of course, was precisely the goal towards which the Sultan of Mandara had been working from the start.

14. Denham, 1 pp. 301-4.
15. Ibid, p. 305.

The Arabs, also, were full of complaints and extremely dissatisfied with their situation. They loudly exclaimed against their delay. They had for days eaten nothing but a little flour and water without fat. The Sultan of Mandara would grant them no supply and they demanded of Bu-Khalum to go on or turn back.

The rain again fell in torrents, which is an Arab's greatest dread, and they assembled round Bu-Khalum's tent, almost in a state of mutiny. Bu-Khalum himself was excessively ill, more I believe from vexation than sickness. He had a long interview with the Sultan and returned very much irritated. He merely told me, as he passed, 'that we should move in the evening', and when I asked 'if every thing went well?' he merely answered, *'Inshallah'* [Please God]. The Arabs, from whom he kept his destination a secret, received him with cheers. Whom they were going against they cared but little, so long as there was a prospect of plunder, and the whole camp became a busy scene of preparation.[16]

On the same afternoon, April 26th, a combined force, consisting of Barka Gana's column, the Arabs and a Mandara contingent led by the Sultan in person, marched out of Mora and headed south.

16. Ibid, pp. 305-6.

A Disastrous Raid

After the barren rigours of the Sahara and the parched monotony of the Chad plain, Denham was delighted with the fertility of the hill country through which the expedition now made its way.

We commenced our march through a beautiful valley to the east of Mora, winding round the hills which overhang the town and penetrating into the heart of the mass of mountains nearly to the south of it. About sunset we halted in a very picturesque spot, called Hairi, surrounded by a superb amphitheatre of hills. Barka Gana's tent was pitched under the shade of one side of an immense tree, much resembling a fig-tree although wanting its delicious fruit, and the remnants of my tent, which had been mended by his people and now stood about three feet from the ground, were placed on the opposite side. The trunks of these trees commonly measure ten and twelve yards in circumference near the root and I have seen them covering more than half an acre of ground with their wide-spreading branches.

Soon after our arrival, the Sultan's trumpets announced his approach, and he took up his station, at no great distance, under a tree of the same kind. He never used a tent, but slept in an open space surrounded by his eunuchs.

At Hairi are the remains of a Mandara town, long since destroyed by the Fulani. Parts of the mud walls were still standing and under shelter of these the troops bivouacked. The scorpions, however, made their appearance in the course of the night in great numbers and several men were stung by them. On hearing the disturbance, and learning the cause, I called my negro and, striking a light, we killed three in my tent. One of them was full six inches in length, of the black kind exactly resembling those I had seen in Tripoli.[1]

It was only now, when they were on the march towards their objective, that the Arabs learned that it was not to be a group of pagan settlements, as they had supposed, but two Fulani towns. Had the proposal been put to them when they first reached Mora, they would probably have rejected it angrily, but now they had become so frustrated and impatient that they acquiesced without demur. The Sultan, by his delaying tactics, had therefore extricated himself most adroitly from the predicament in which his ally El-Kanemi had placed him. His plan now was simply to use the Arabs as a battering-ram against the adversaries he most feared, the Fulani. If they succeeded, the gain would be all his. If, on the other hand, they failed and were broken, he intended to take good care not to share their fate. It was simple yet masterly.

On the following day, April 27, the march was resumed.

> In consequence of Bu-Khalum's illness, it was after daylight when we broke up from our encampment... The mountain scenery by which we were surrounded could scarcely be exceeded in beauty and richness. On all sides the apparently interminable chain of hills closed upon our view: in rugged magnificence and gigantic grandeur, though not to be compared with the Higher Alps, the Apennines, the Jura, or even the Sierra Morena in magnitude, yet by none of these were they surpassed in picturesque interest. Horza, exceeding any of her sister hills in height as well as in beauty, appeared before us to the south, with its chasm or break through which we were to pass, and the winding rugged path we were about to tread was discernible in the distance. The valley had an elevation superior to that of any part of the kingdom of Bornu, for we had gradually ascended ever since quitting Kuka.
>
> On proceeding through the pass of Horza, where the ascent continued, its perpendicular sides, exceeding two thousand five hundred feet in height, hung over our heads with a projection almost frightful. The width of the valley did not exceed five hundred yards. It was long after mid-day when we came to the mountain stream and it afforded an indescribable relief to our almost famished horses and ourselves. The road, after quitting the

---

1. Denham, 1, pp. 306-7. Though the black scorpions are much larger, and look much more formidable, than the little sand scorpions, their stings are in fact no worse.

135 | A DISASTROUS RAID

Horza pass, had been through an extensive and thickly-planted valley where the *gubberah* tree, the tamarind, a gigantic wild fig, and the mango flourished in great numbers and beauty. This was the first spot I had seen in Africa where Nature seemed at all to have revelled in giving life to the vegetable kingdom. The ground had frequent irregularities and broken masses of granite, ten and twelve feet in height, were lying in several places, but nearly obscured by the thick underwood growing round them and by the trees, which had sprung up out of their crevices. The nearest part of the hills to which these blocks could have originally belonged was distant nearly two miles.

When the animals had drunk we again moved on and, after eighteen miles of equally verdant country, more thickly wooded, we came after sunset to another stream near some low hills, called Makeri, where we were to halt for a few hours to refresh and then move again so as to commence an attack on the Fulani, who were said to be only sixteen miles distant, with the morning sun.

Our supper this night, which indeed was also our breakfast, consisted of a little parched corn pounded and mixed with water, the only food we had seen since leaving Mora. Nothing could look more like fighting than the preparations of these Bornu warriors, although nothing could well be more unlike it than the proof they gave on the morrow. The closely-linked iron jackets of the chiefs were all put on and the sound of their clumsy and ill-shapen hammers, heard at intervals during the night, told the employment of the greater part of their followers.

About midnight, the signal was given to advance. The moon, which was in her third quarter, afforded us a clear and beautiful light while we moved on silently and in good order, the Sultan of Mandara's force marching in parallel columns to our own and on our right. At dawn, the whole army halted to pray: my own faith also taught me a morning prayer, as well as that of a Moslem, though but too often neglected.

As the day broke on the morning of the 28 April, a most interesting scene presented itself. The Sultan of Mandara was close on our flank, mounted on a very beautiful cream-coloured horse with several large red marks about him and followed by his six favourite eunuchs and thirty of his sons, all being finely dressed and mounted on really superb horses, besides which they had each from five to six others, led by as many negroes. The Sultan had at least twelve. Barka Gana's people all wore their red scarfs, or burnouses, over their steel jackets, and the whole had a very fine effect. I took my position at his right hand and, at a spot called Duggur, we entered a very thick wood in two columns, at the end of which it was said we were to find the enemy.

During the latter part of the night we had started several animals of the leopard species who ran from us so swiftly, twisting their long tails in the air, as to prevent our getting near them. We, however, now started one of a larger kind, which Marami assured me was so satiated with the blood of a negro, whose carcass we found lying in the wood, that he would be easily killed. I rode up to the spot just as a Shuwa had planted the first spear in him, which passed through the neck a little above the shoulder and came down between the animal's legs. He rolled over, broke the spear, and bounded off with the lower half in his body. Another Shuwa galloped up within two arms' length and thrust a second through his loins; and the savage animal, with a woeful howl, was in the act of springing on his pursuer when an Arab shot him through the head with a ball which killed him on the spot. It was a male panther of very large size and measured, from the point of the tail to the nose, eight feet two inches. The skin was yellow and beautifully marked with orbicular spots on the upper part of the body, while underneath and at the throat the spots were oblong and irregular, intermixed with white. These animals were found in great numbers in the woods bordering on Mandara; there are also leopards, the skins of which I saw, but not in great numbers.[2]

* * *

The Fulani towns which the expedition was now approaching were the most northerly outposts of the Emirate of Adamawa, the south-eastern bastion of the Empire of Sokoto. In shape Adamawa is long and narrow and even then, though it had not yet grown to its full stature, it probably measured 400 miles from top to toe. Certainly the capital, which was then Gurin, was 200 miles south of the two towns that were now being threatened.

On emerging from the wood, the large Fulani town of Dirkulla was perceivable and the Arabs were formed in front, headed by Bu-Khalum. They were flanked on each side by a large body of cavalry and, as they moved on shouting the Arab war-cry which is very inspiring, I thought I could perceive a smile pass between Barka Gana and his chiefs at Bu-Khalum's expense. Dirkulla was quickly burnt, and another smaller town near it, and the few inhabitants that were found in them, who were chiefly infants and aged persons

2. Ibid, pp. 307-312.

A DISASTROUS RAID

Bornu horsemen accoutered in a manner strikingly similar to that described by Denham in 1823. Photos 1960.

unable to escape, were put to death without mercy or thrown into the flames.

We now came to a third town in a situation capable of being defended against assailants ten times as numerous as the besiegers: this town was called Masfel.[3] It was built on rising ground, between two low hills, at the base of others forming part of the mass of the Mandara mountains. A dry watercourse extended along the front; beyond the watercourse a swamp; between this and the wood the road was crossed by a deep ravine, which was not passable for more than two or three horses at a time. The Fulani had carried a very strong fence of six feet in height, from one hill to the other and had placed their bowmen behind the palisades and on the rising ground with the watercourse before them. Their horse were all under cover of the hills and the town.

This was a strong position. The Arabs, however, moved on with great gallantry, without any support or co-operation from the

---

3. "Musfeia" in Denham's text.

Bornu or Mandara troops, and notwithstanding the showers of arrows, some poisoned, which were poured on them from behind the palisades, Bu-Khalum with his handful of Arabs carried them in about half an hour and dashed on, driving the Fulani up the sides of the hills. The women were every where seen supplying their protectors with fresh arrows during this struggle and, when they retreated to the hills, still shooting on their pursuers, the women assisted by rolling down huge masses of the rock, previously undermined for this purpose, which killed several of the Arabs and wounded others.

Barka Gana and about one hundred of the Bornu spearmen now supported Bu-Khalum and pierced through and through some fifty unfortunates who were left wounded near the stakes. I rode by his side as he pushed on quite into the town and a very desperate skirmish took place between Barka Gana's people and a small body of the Fulani. These warriors throw the spear with great dexterity, and three times I saw a man transfixed to the earth who was dismounted for the purpose of firing the town, and as often were those who rushed forward for that purpose sacrificed for their temerity by the Fulani. Barka Gana, whose muscular arm was

Bornu Horsemen. The quilting in which the horses are clad beneath their trappings was common to all heavy cavalry in the central Sudan. It served as armour by absorbing arrowheads and sword-cuts.
Photo 1960

almost gigantic, threw eight spears which all told—some of them at a distance of thirty-five yards and one particularly on a Fulani chief, who with his own hand had brought four to the ground.

'*Incidet ictus,*
Ingens ad terram duplicato poplite Turnus.'

Had either the Mandara or the Sheikh's troops now moved up boldly, notwithstanding the defence these people made and the reinforcements which showed themselves to the south-west, they must have carried the town with the heights overlooking it, along which the Arabs were driving the Fulani by the terror their miserable guns excited. But, instead of this, they still kept on the other side of the watercourse, out of reach of the arrows.

The Fulani, seeing their backwardness, now made an attack in their turn. The arrows fell so thick that there was no standing against them and the Arabs gave way. The Fulani horse now came on and, had not the little band round Barka Gana and Bu-Khalum with a few of his mounted Arabs given them a very spirited check, not one of us would probably have lived to see the following day. As it was, Barka Gana had three horses hit under him, two of which died almost immediately, the arrows being poisoned, and poor Bu-Khalum's horse and himself received their death-wounds by arrows of the same description. My horse was badly wounded in the neck, just above the shoulder, and in the near hind leg. An arrow had struck me in the face as it passed, merely drawing blood, and I had two sticking in my burnous. The Arabs had suffered terribly: most of them had two or three wounds and one dropped near me with five sticking in his head alone. Two of Bu-Khalum's slaves were killed also, near his person.[4]

At a later period the Fulani came to rely mainly on cavalry but at this time, as in the *jihad* and the wars with Bornu, their real strength still lay in footmen armed with the bow. As their arrows were light and had little penetrating power, they relied mainly on speed and steadfastness and sometimes, though not always, on the poison which played such an important part in this battle. In these qualities they were supreme however, so that, in the late eighteenth and early nineteenth centuries, Fulani bowmen dominated the battlefields of the Sudan as English bowmen had once dominated those of Mediaeval Europe.[5]

Denham's description shows how intense the arrow-storm of the Fulani was and how rapidly it could swing a battle in their favour.

4. Ibid, pp. 313-6.
5. Johnston, op. cit. *passim*.

No sooner did the Mandara and Bornu troops see the defeat of the Arabs than they, one and all, took to flight in the most dastardly manner, without having once been exposed to the arrows of the enemy, and in the utmost confusion. The Sultan of Mandara led the way, who was prepared to take advantage of whatever plunder the success of the Arabs might throw in his way, but no less determined to leave the field the moment the fortune of the day appeared to be against them.

I now for the first time, as I saw Barka Gana on a fresh horse, lamented my own folly in so exposing myself, badly prepared as I was for accidents. If either of my horse's wounds were from poisoned arrows, I felt that nothing could save me. However, there was not much time for reflection: we instantly became a flying mass and plunged, in the greatest disorder, into that wood we had but a few hours before moved through with order and very different feelings.

I had got a little to the westward of Barka Gana in the confusion which took place on our passing the ravine, which had been left just in our rear and where upwards of one hundred of the Bornowy were speared by the Fulani, and was following at a round gallop the steps of one of the Mandara eunuchs—who, I observed, kept a good look out, his head being constantly turned over his left shoulder with a face expressive of the greatest dismay—when the cries behind of the Fulani horse pursuing made us both quicken our paces. The spur, however, had the effect of incapacitating my beast altogether, as the arrow, I found afterwards, had reached the shoulder-bone, and in passing over some rough ground he stumbled and fell.

Almost before I was on my legs, the Fulani were upon me; I had however, kept hold of the bridle and, seizing a pistol from the holster, I presented it at two of these ferocious savages who were pressing me with their spears. They instantly went off but another, who came on me more boldly just as I was endeavouring to mount, received the contents somewhere in the left shoulder, and again I was enabled to place my foot in the stirrup. Remounted, I again pushed my retreat. I had not, however, proceeded many hundred yards when my horse again came down with such violence as to throw me against a tree at a considerable distance and, alarmed at the horses behind him, he quickly got up and escaped, leaving me on foot and unarmed.

The eunuch and his four followers were here butchered, after a very slight resistance, and stripped within a few yards of me. Their cries were dreadful and, even now, the feelings of that moment are

A DISASTROUS RAID

fresh in my memory. My hopes of life were too faint to deserve the name. I was almost instantly surrounded and, incapable of making the least resistance as I was unarmed, was as speedily stripped and, whilst attempting first to save my shirt and then my trousers, I was thrown on the ground. My pursuers made several thrusts at me with their spears that badly wounded my hands, in two places, and slightly my body, just under my ribs on the right side. Indeed I saw nothing before me but the same cruel death I had seen unmercifully inflicted on the few who had fallen into the power of those who now had possession of me. And they were alone prevented from murdering me in the first instance, I am persuaded, by the fear of injuring the value of my clothes, which appeared to them a rich booty. But it was otherwise ordained.

My shirt was now absolutely torn off my back and I was left perfectly naked. When my plunderers began to quarrel for the spoil, the idea of escape came like lightning across my mind and, without a moment's hesitation or reflection, I crept under the belly of the horse nearest me and started as fast as my legs would carry me for the thickest part of the wood. Two of the Fulani followed and I ran on to the eastward, knowing that our stragglers would be in that direction, but still almost as much afraid of friends as foes. My pursuers gained on me, for the prickly underwood not only obstructed my passage but tore my flesh miserably, and the delight with which I saw a mountain-stream gliding along the bottom of a deep ravine cannot be imagined. My strength had almost left me and I seized the young branches issuing from the stump of a large tree, which overhung the ravine, for the purpose of letting myself down into the water, as the sides were precipitous, when under my hand, as the branch yielded to the weight of my body, a large *liffa,* the worst kind of serpent this country produces, rose from its coil, as if in the very act of striking. I was horror-struck and deprived for the moment of all recollection. The branch slipped from my hand and I tumbled headlong into the water beneath; this shock, however, revived me and with three strokes of my arms I reached the opposite bank which, with difficulty, I crawled up and then, for the first time, felt myself safe from my pursuers.

Scarcely had I audibly congratulated myself on my escape when the forlorn and wretched situation in which I was, without even a rag to cover me, flashed with all its force upon my imagination. I was perfectly collected, though fully alive to all the danger to which my state exposed me, and had already begun to plan my night's rest in the top of one of the tamarind trees in order to escape the panthers which, as I had seen, abounded in these woods, when the idea of the *liffas,* almost as numerous and equally to be dreaded, excited a shudder of despair.

I now saw horsemen through the trees still farther to the east and determined on reaching them, if possible, whether friends or enemies. And the feelings of gratitude and joy with which I recognised Barka Gana and Bu-Khalum with about six Arabs, although they also were pressed closely by a party of the Fulani, was beyond description. The guns and pistols of the Arab sheikhs kept the Fulani in check and assisted in some measure the retreat of the footmen. I hailed them with all my might but the noise and confusion which prevailed, from the cries of those who were falling under the Fulani spears, the cheers of the Arabs rallying and their enemies pursuing, would have drowned all attempts to make myself heard had not Marami, the Sheikh's negro, seen and known me at a distance.

To this man I was indebted for my second escape. Riding up to me, he assisted me to mount behind him, while the arrows whistled over our heads, and we then galloped off to the rear as fast as his wounded horse could carry us. After we had gone a mile or two, and the pursuit had something cooled in consequence of all the baggage having been abandoned to the enemy, Bu-Khalum rode up to me and desired one of the Arabs to cover me with a burnous. This was a most welcome relief, for the burning sun had already begun to blister my neck and back and gave me the greatest pain.

Shortly after, the effects of the poisoned wound in his foot caused our excellent friend to breath his last. Marami exclaimed 'Look, look! Bu-Khalum is dead!' I turned my head, almost as great an exertion as I was capable of, and saw him drop from the horse into the arms of his favourite Arab. He never spoke after. They said he had only swooned; there was no water, however, to revive him and, about an hour after, when we came to Makeri, he was past the reach of restoration.

About the time Bu-Khalum dropped, Barka Gana ordered a slave to bring me a horse, from which he had just dismounted, being the third that had been wounded under him in the course of the day; his wound was in the chest. Marami cried *'Sidi Rais!* Do not mount him—he will die!'. In a moment, for only a moment was given me, I decided on remaining with Marami. Two Arabs, panting with fatigue, then seized the bridle, mounted and pressed their retreat: in less than half an hour he fell to rise no more and both the Arabs were butchered before they could recover themselves.

Had we not now arrived at the water, as we did, I do not think it

A DISASTROUS RAID

possible that I could have supported the thirst by which I was consumed. I tried several times to speak in reply to Marami's directions to hold tight when we came to breaks or inequalities in the ground but it was impossible and a painful straining at the stomach and throat was the only effect produced by the effort.

On coming to the stream the horses, with blood gushing from their nostrils, rushed into the shallow water and, letting myself down from behind Marami, I knelt down amongst them and seemed to imbibe new life by the copious draughts of the muddy beverage which I swallowed. . . . Of what followed I have no recollection: Marami told me afterwards that I staggered across the stream, which was not above my hips, and fell down at the foot of a tree on the other side. About a quarter of an hour's halt took place here for the benefit of stragglers and to tie poor Bu-Khalum's body on a horse's back, at the end of which Marami awoke me from a deep sleep and I found my strength wonderfully increased. Not so, however, our horse, for he had become stiff and could scarcely move.

As I learnt afterwards, a conversation had taken place about me while I slept which rendered my obligations to Marami still greater. He had reported to Barka Gana the state of his horse, and the impossibility of carrying me on, when the chief, irritated by his losses and defeat, as well as at my having refused his horse, by which means he said it had come by its death, replied 'Then leave him behind. By the head of the Prophet! Believers enough have breathed their last today. What is there extraordinary in a Christian's death?' My old antagonist, Mallam Chadili replied, 'No, God has preserved him; let us not forsake him!'

Marami returned to the tree and said 'his heart told him what to do.' He awoke me, assisted me to mount, and we moved on as before but with tottering steps and less speed. The effect produced on the horses that were wounded by poisoned arrows was extraordinary: immediately after drinking they dropped and instantly died, the blood gushing from their nose, mouth, and ears. More than thirty horses were lost at this spot from the effects of the poison.

In this way we continued our retreat and it was after midnight when we halted in the Sultan of Mandara's territory. Riding more than forty-five miles in such an unprovided state on the bare back of a lean horse, the powerful consequences may be imagined. I was in a deplorable state the whole night . . . the irritation of the flesh wounds was augmented by the woollen covering the Arab had thrown over me, teeming as it was with vermin. Barka Gana, who had no tent but the one he had left behind him with his women at Mora on our advance, could offer me no shelter and he was besides so ill, or chagrined, as to remain invisible the whole day. I could scarcely turn from one side to the other but still, except at intervals when my friend Marami supplied me with a drink made from parched corn, ... I slept under a tree nearly the whole night and day of the 29th. Towards the evening I was exceedingly disordered and ill.

Mai Migami, the dethroned Sultan of the country to the south-west of Ngornu and now subject to the Sheikh, took me by the hand as I crawled out of my nest for a few minutes and, with many exclamations of sorrow and a countenance full of commiseration, led me to his leather tent and, sitting down quickly, disrobed himself of his trousers, insisting that I should put them on. Really, no act of charity could exceed this! I was exceedingly affected at so unexpected a friend, for I had scarcely seen or spoken three words to him, but not so much so as himself when I refused to accept them. He shed tears in abundance and thinking, which was the fact, that I conceived he had offered the only ones he had, immediately called a slave, whom he stripped of those necessary appendages to a man's dress, according to our ideas, and putting them on himself, insisted again in my taking those he had first offered me. I accepted this offer and thanked him with a full heart. Migami was my great friend from that moment until I quitted the Sheikh's dominions.

We found that forty-five of the Arabs were killed and nearly all wounded; their camels, and everything they possessed, lost. Some of them had been unable to keep up on the retreat but had huddled together in threes and fours during the night and, by showing resistance and pointing their guns, had driven the Fulani off. Their wounds were some of them exceedingly severe and several died during the day and night of the 29th, their bodies, as well as poor Bu-Khalum's, becoming instantly swollen and black and sometimes, immediately after death, blood issuing from the nose and mouth, which the Bornu people declared to be in consequence of the arrows having been poisoned.

The surviving Arabs, who had now lost all their former arrogance and boasting, humbly entreated Barka Gana to supply them with a little corn to save them from starving. The Sultan of Mandara behaved to them unkindly, though not worse than they deserved, refused all manner of supplies, and kept Bu-Khalum's saddle, horse-trappings, and the clothes in which he died. He also began making preparations for defending himself against the Fulani who, he feared, might pay him a visit. On the morning of the 30 April we left Mora, heartily wishing them success should they make the attempt.

Bu-Khalum's imprudence in having suffered himself to be persuaded to attack the Fulani became now apparent, as although in case of his overcoming them he might have appropriated to himself all the slaves, both male and female, that he found amongst them, yet the Fulani themselves were Moslem and he could not have made them slaves. He was, however, most likely deceived by promises of a pagan country to plunder in the event of his success against these powerful people, alike the dreaded enemies of the Sheikh and the Sultan of Mandara[6]

My wounded horse, which had been caught towards the evening of the fight by the Shuwas and brought to me, was in too bad a state for me to mount and Barka Gana procured me another. My pistols had been stolen from the holsters but fortunately my saddle and bridle, though broken, remained.

Thus ended our most unsuccessful expedition. It had, however, injustice and oppression for its basis, and who can regret its failure?[7]

Seen in its historical perspective, the raid on Masfel was only an isolated episode in the long struggle between Mandara, supported by Bornu, and Adamawa. The next important success was gained by the Sultan of Mandara when he succeeded in almost completely wiping out a Fulani clan. But this disaster prompted Adama, the formidable Fulani Emir after whom the Emirate was called, to concern himself personally with the war. Soon afterwards he routed the Mandara army at Gider and occupied Mora. Although he was not strong enough to hold the place, his victory enabled him to annex the principality's western districts of Mubi, Michika, and Uba and incorporate them in his own domains.[8]

* * *

Meanwhile Denham had lost almost all his possessions—his trunk with most of his linen, his canteens, his azimuth-compass, and his sketching case. Moreover his servant, who had followed him into the action and had

---

6. Actually, as has already been mentioned, the rule that one Moslem could not enslave another was constantly evaded in the warfare of the Sudan, often under the pretext that the captive was a backslider or a heretic. Nevertheless, therefore the fact that the women and children at Dirkulla were killed and not rounded up confirms the view that the object of the raid was simply to annihilate a troublesome Fulani outpost. If this was in fact the case, the rumour recorded by Denham, that success was to have been rewarded by the provision of an easy target elsewhere, seems inherently probable.
7. Denham, 1, pp. 316-327.
8. Johnston, pp. 86-87.

also had a narrow escape from death after the loss of his mule, was too lame and bruised to keep up with the column which covered between 25 and 30 miles a day on the long march back to Kuka. For the most part, therefore, Denham was left to fend for himself. He had a most painful journey but, seeing others in worse state than himself, he bore the hardship stoically.

> In the mid-day halts I usually crept under Mai Migami's tent but at night I laid me down on the ground, close to that of Barka Gana, in order that my horse might get a feed of corn. I always fell into a sound sleep at night as soon as I lay down after drinking Marami's beverage, who had supplied me with a little bag of parched corn which he had procured at Mora. And about mid-night a slave of the chief, whose name was most singularly like my own, Dunama, always awoke me to eat some millet-paste and fat mixed with a green herb called *maloheia* in Arabic. This was thrust out from under Barka Gana's tent and consisted generally of his leavings. Pride was sometimes nearly choking me but hunger was the paramount feeling: I smothered the former, ate, and was thankful. It was in reality a great kindness for, besides myself and the chief, not one, I believe, in the remnant of our army tasted anything but parched corn and cold water during the whole six days of our march. On the night of the 4 May we arrived at Ngornu.
>
> The extreme kindness of the Sheikh, however, was some consolation to me after all my sufferings. He said, in a letter to Barka Gana, 'that he should have grieved had anything serious happened to me, that my escape was providential and a proof of God's protection, and that my head was saved for good purposes'. He also sent me some linen he had procured from our huts at Kuka and a dress of the country. The interest taken by the Governor in the fate of such an unbeliever, as they thought me, increased exceedingly the respect of his servants.[9]

Next morning, having covered 160 miles in six days[10] they reached Kuka.

Barka Gana was presented by Denham with a brace of French ornamented pistols and enough pink taffeta to make a gown. With these gifts, which to him seemed in no way incongruous, he was highly delighted.

---

9. Denham, I, pp. 328-9.

10. As the crow flies, the distance is about 145 miles. Over the ground it must have been at least 160, perhaps a little more. Given his painful condition, it is easy to understand than Denham's estimate of 180 miles should have been a little high.

Denham himself received another horse from the Sheikh in place of the one which he had had to leave behind. At the same time El-Kanemi, laying all the blame for the defeat on the Mandara troops, assured Denham that, if he was ready to accompany another expedition which was being planned, he would show him how the Kanuri and Kanembu could fight when he was leading them.[11]

11. Denham, 1, pp. 329-30.

XI
The Manga Rebellion

Back in Kuka, Denham found that the townspeople were completely preoccupied with their preparations for the expedition of which the Sheikh had spoken. To understand exactly what was afoot, we must make a brief digression into history.

The Mangawa were one of the clans which made up the Kanuri people. They claimed indeed to be the descendants and followers of a member of the ruling family who, early in the eighteenth century, had been forced to flee after incurring the displeasure of his brother the Sultan. Since that time they had lived partly in Damagaram, an Emirate to the northwest which was tributary to Bornu, and partly in the western marches of Bornu itself. One branch, which occupied the debateable lands between Bornu and Damagaram, succeeded gradually in asserting its independence of both and later established the semi-independent Emirate of Gumel.[1]

The old quarrel with the Sultan of Bornu and their remoteness from the capital seem to have given the Mangawa an independent outlook and to have weakened the links that bound them to Bornu. The Gumel branch even abandoned their mother tongue, Kanuri, for Hausa and might well have been drawn right into the Hausa orbit if it had not been for the *jihad* and the war between the Fulani and the Kanuri that grew out of it. This caused them and the rest of the Mangawa to rally to Bornu and, so long as the danger of a Fulani conquest lasted, they remained staunch and loyal. With the peace, however, the Manga independence of

1. Johnston, p. 223.

149 | THE MANGA REBELLION

spirit began to reassert itself. At the same time, the Kanuri withdrawal towards Chad increased the distance between them and the capital, making the task of controlling them more difficult than ever. Finally their connection with the ruling family enabled them to question the propriety of El-Kanemi's seizure of power from the Sultans and his right to rule Bornu.

For El-Kanemi, the disaffection of the Mangawa was all the more dangerous for being aimed at his personal authority, rather than at the government of the realm generally, and this doubtless accounts for the vigour of his response.

> These people had never thoroughly acknowledged the Sheikh's supremacy and the collecting of their tribute had always been attended with difficulty and bloodshed. They had, however, now thrown off all restraint and put to death about one hundred and twenty of the Sheikh's Shuwas and declared they would no longer be under his control as the Sultan of Bornu was their king, and headed by a Mallam of great power had begun to plunder and burn all the Sheikh's towns near them. It was reported, and with some truth, that they could bring 12,000 bowmen into the field, by far the most efficient force to be found in the black country.
>
> To oppose these, the Sheikh assembled his Kanembu spearmen (who had accompanied him from their own country and assisted him in wresting Bornu from the hand of the Fulani) to the amount of between eight and nine thousand. These, with about five thousand Shuwas and Bornu men, composed the force with which he meant to subdue these rebels.
>
> Another complaint against the Mangawa was 'That they were backsliding and not saying their prayers, the dogs!' This is, however, a fault which is generally laid to the charge of any nation against whom a true Moslem wages war, as it gives him the power of making them slaves. By the laws of Muhammad, one believer must not bind another.[2]

El-Kanemi left Kuka on May 8, only three days after Denham's return from Mora, in order to drum up reinforcements and muster his forces before marching against the Mangawa. But before his departure, it was arranged that Oudney and Denham should be escorted to Ngazargamu, the old capital of Bornu, which they wanted to see and that they should then make a rendezvous with the Sheikh at Kabshari so that they could

2. Denham, 1, pp. 340-1.

witness the campaign as well. Their guide on this expedition was to be Umar Gana, one of the El-Kanemi's most trusted slaves.

The fast of Ramadan began on May 13 and it was not until the 22nd that Oudney and Denham set out. They took four servants with them and five camels carried their tents and luggage. With marches of ten to fourteen miles, morning and evening, they covered the seventy miles to the River Yobe in three days.

Taking out his gun in the evening in search of wild fowl, Denham had an experience which brought home to him the fear and uncertainty in which the people of this valley now lived.

> I walked out following the easterly course of the stream in search of game but, within four hundred yards of the banks, the ground was so choked with high grass and prickly underwood that I was obliged to take a path more inland where a partial clearance had been made for the sake of some scanty cotton plantations. Pursuing some guineafowl across one of these, I was assailed by the cries of several women and children who, having thrown down their water jugs, were flying from me in the greatest alarm. I however went on but had not proceeded above a quarter of a mile when my negro pointed out several men peeping from behind some thick bushes and evidently watching our motions. I desired him to be on his guard, as he carried a carbine loaded with slugs, and we called repeatedly to them without any effect. They had been alarmed by the women who had represented us to be Tuaregs, of whom they are constantly in dread as their country is not more than seven days distant from where these marauders are often seen...
>
> The inhabitants of these wilds cannot be induced to quit their present homes and they patiently submit to have their flocks and children taken from them, and their huts burnt, rather than seek a more secure residence in the larger towns. They have, however, a manner of defending themselves against these cruel invaders which often enables them to gratify their revenge: the ground is covered often by the high grass and jungle close to the banks of the rivers and they dig very deep circular holes, at the bottom of which are placed six or eight sharp stakes, hardened by the fire, over the top of which they most artfully lay the grass, so as to render it impossible to discover the deception. An animal with its rider stepping on one of these traps is quickly precipitated to the bottom, and not infrequently both are killed on the spot.
>
> In returning to the tents with the people whom I had alarmed, and who cautioned me not to proceed farther in that direction, I trembled at the recollection of the various escapes I had had, as

some of these *blaka,* as they are called, were not a yard distant from the marks of my former footsteps.³

The explorers were now nearing the old capital and had reached that part of the Yobe valley which had once been the heart of Bornu. But it had all been devastated in the war with the Fulani and there was little to be seen except for the ruins of former towns of which they counted thirty or more. Since then fifteen years had passed, the population had been reduced to a mere sprinkling and the land had gone out of cultivation. Now the paths were over-hung by thorn-bushes, game had again become plentiful and the woods were infested by outlaws who attacked passing caravans.⁴

We had this morning met a caravan from Hausaland, consisting of about twenty persons and bringing one hundred and twenty slaves, and some hours afterwards we came to the place where they had passed the preceding night. They had lit their fires in the very centre of the path and made a good fence all round them of large branches of trees and dry wood. This fence is sometimes set fire to when their four-footed visitors are numerous and approach too near. Camels and animals of every description are placed in the centre and, should one stray in the night, he is seldom again recovered. Caravans seldom travel after dusk, particularly those on foot, and our negroes had such a fright during the latter part of this day's march that they declared on coming up with the camels that their lives were in danger from such late marches, an immense lion having crossed the road before them only a few miles from where we halted.... They said that he had stopped and looked back at them and, if they had not had presence of mind sufficient to pass on without at all noticing him or appearing alarmed, some of the party would have suffered.

In these woods caravans from Hausaland are often robbed and the runaway negroes, who are good bowmen, pick off the leaders from behind the trees and then plunder the baggage. Ten men from one caravan had, we were informed, been so murdered during the last year.⁵

On May 26 the travellers reached the neighbourhood of Ngazargamu which, as the capital of Bornu, had once ranked with Kano and Timbuktu as one of the great centres of the Sudan. The city had been founded in

3. Ibid, pp. 342-4.
4. Ibid, pp. 346-7 and 352.
5. Ibid, pp. 345-7.

the second half of the fifteenth century at the time when the Sefawa dynasty, having been expelled from Kanem, was re-establishing itself in Bornu. For well over three hundred years it had been the capital of Bornu and during the whole of that period it had remained inviolate. In the early nineteenth century however, with the outbreak of the *jihad,* its immunity had come to an abrupt end. Then, in the space of four years between 1808 and 1812, it had been stormed by the Fulani under Gwani Muktar, recaptured by the Kanuri under El-Kanemi, retaken by the Fulani under Ibrahim Zaki and finally abandoned by both sides.[6] Now it was no more than a ruin.

> After our tents were pitched, and we had refreshed ourselves by a mess of ducks and rice, we determined on riding to visit the remains of Old Birni.... We proceeded by the high road to Hausaland and, after about two miles, came to the spot on which once stood the capital of Bornu; and the ruins of the city certainly tended more strongly to convince us of the power of its former Sultans than any of the tales we had heard of their magnificence. Old Birni covered a space of five or six miles and is said to have had a population of two hundred thousand souls. The remains of the walls were in many places still standing, in large masses of hard red brick-work, and were from three to four feet in thickness and sixteen to eighteen feet in height.[7]

Nearly thirty years later, Barth also visited the ruins and estimated the circumference of the walls as only five or six miles. As this would have given an area of less than two square miles, the population of the city can never have approached the figure of 200,000 quoted by Denham. In fact it is more likely to have been between 50,000 and 75,000.

On the following day the party moved on to Gambaru so that they could see the ruins of the riverside palace which the Sultan once had there.

> The ruins now standing give a proof of the buildings having been, for this country, of a princely kind: the walls of a mosque, which were more than 20 yards square, are still visible and those of the Sultan's house, with gates opening to the river, still remain. A private mosque appears also to have been attached to the Sultan's residence. The buildings were all of brick and must have had had a superior appearance to any town we had seen in Africa. The

---

6. S.J. Hogben and A.H.M. Kirk-Greene, *The Emirates of Northern Nigeria,* London, 1966, p. 124.
7. Denham, 1, p. 348.

situation was beautiful and, although labyrinths of thickets and brambles now overspread the banks of the river, while wild plants and useless grass were in the meadows, yet I was assured that the whole neighbourhood of Gambaru was once in a superior state of cultivation and that, in the old Sultan's time, boats were constantly moving to and from Kabshari and other towns to the west.[8]

* * *

That evening Denham and Oudney found that they were in a position of some danger. When they had arranged with El-Kanemi to meet him at Kabshari, they had naturally assumed that he would arrive there first. Now they discovered, with some alarm, that he had not yet come up and that there were no friendly forces between them and the insurgents.

> Kabshari, to which place we intended proceeding and there awaiting the arrival of the Sheikh, had been attacked and partly burnt by the Manga people since our leaving Kuka and deserted by the inhabitants. While we were debating on what steps we should take in consequence of this intelligence, two Kanembu spearmen came to us, in great consternation, with news that the Manga horse had been reconnoitring all around us, had even visited the part of the river we had been exploring in the morning, and after murdering several Kanembu who were proceeding to join the Sheikh, had carried off the bullocks and whatever they had with them. The Sheikh's delay in coming up had made them bold and their approach had caused all the Shuwas we had left at Muggabi to beat a retreat. We were therefore left quite alone and, as it seemed, might expect every minute to be surrounded, taken prisoner, and with an iron round our necks, with which slaves are coupled like greyhounds in slips, marched off to Manga.
>
> Umar Gana was greatly alarmed and, dressing himself in his steel jacket, with red waistcoat over it and black turban, calmed our fears but little by leaving us for a full hour to see if the Shuwas had really left Muggabi, notwithstanding he at the same time assured us that the sight of his red jacket would frighten a hundred Mangawa. On his return, which we looked for with much anxiety, we found the alarming reports in part confirmed. No Shuwas were near the lake and he was quite sure the enemy had been there. He proposed going to Kabshari along the banks of the river to the west but acknowledged that the Sheikh was not there and that the people had moved off towards Ngornu. We considered this bad advice and determined

8. Ibid, pp. 350-1.

on returning at least to the Kuka road. That was, however, no easy task and after some consideration it was determined that we were to keep close to the bank of the river and creep through the woods as well as we could, avoiding all beaten paths. We moved at three in the afternoon and crossed about two miles distant to the north bank of the river, our road being extremely intricate and overgrown with trees and underwood.

Just before sunset we came upon a herd of elephants, fourteen or fifteen in number; these the negroes made to dance and frisk like so many goats by beating violently a brass basin with a stick. As night now began to cast over us its gloomy veil, we determined on fixing ourselves until morning in a small open space where a large tree, destroyed by the attacks of the white ant, had fallen and afforded us firewood to prepare our supper: to seek it any distance would have been dangerous at that time in the evening on account of the lions. The little grass which was gathered for our horses was furnished by the space within sight of our tents. Our animals were brought as close to us as possible and we kept up fires the greater part of the night. A few roaring salutations, and those principally from the elephant and jackal, were the only disturbance that we met with.

We proceeded on our course on the following day, winding with the river.... Towards noon the wood became much thicker, no pathway was to be discovered, and our guide declared that where we were he had not the least idea. A little further on we came to a complete stoppage: brambles were wound round the before thickly-clustered branches of mimosa and prickly acacias and, on removing with great difficulty some of those, we found the treacherous grass underneath merely covering *blakas,* large, deep, and well staked, capable of receiving and destroying a Tuareg and his camel. In endeavouring to find a passage at a short distance, Dr. Oudney was very nearly precipitated, horse and all, into one of these graves for the quick. We were absolutely afraid to move and Umar Gana, who declared these fortifications indicated our being near some town which was thus prepared against the Mangawa, desired me to fire a gun in order to bring some of the inhabitants to serve as our guide. Accordingly two sturdy negroes came to our assistance who, after eyeing us through the trees and ascertaining who we were, conducted us to the village which, although at no great distance, would have foiled all our efforts to discover: the avenues were completely barricaded on every side, the paths cut up, and these *blakas* so scattered in all directions that, even with a guide and going one by one, it was with the greatest difficulty we avoid them.

Arrived at the village, which was called Wallad, of so miserable a description that it could not even furnish a jar of milk, notwithstanding we produced both needles and beads, a new difficulty arose for, although the camels were sought after and brought in safe by the people, yet my servant Columbus, who was behind on a mule, did not make his appearance. We were in considerable anxiety, both on account of the wild beasts and these pits which were almost equally frightful. Our alarm was a good deal increased when, after having sent people in every direction, giving them pistols, and desiring them to fire signals and not return without him, the people of the village came running to the jujube tree under which we were resting to tell us that Columbus and the mule had fallen into one of these *blakas* and that they believed the mule was dead.

We hastened to the spot and found the poor mule indeed very near it: she was sticking on four stakes, one in her flank and two in her hind quarter, with her knees dreadfully torn by struggling. Had she been a larger and heavier animal, nothing could have saved her. The man had, by a violent exertion, thrown himself out, how he knew not, almost as soon as he fell in and escaped with his leg only bruised. He said he had lost his way hours before and had climbed to the top of several tamarind trees in order to discover traces of our route, without success; once he thought he heard a gun but, having only two charges of powder with him, he kept them as a defence against the wild animals at night and was afraid to answer the signal.

After all our difficulties, it was some comfort at length to find that the Sheikh was within only a few hours' march of us, on the south side of the river, and in the evening we determined on joining him. Again therefore crossing the Yobe at a dry spot, we came to the outskirts of the Bornu camp on the banks of a large water called Damasak, about five miles distant from the ford. At the river we again saw the footmarks of a very large lion and also those of a hippopotamus. It was after sunset when we arrived and, passing through numerous groups of the Kanembu spearmen, who were lying about without any covering, we came to the open space where the Sheikh's tent and the huts of his principal people were fixed.[9]

* * *

The Sheikh, when he went to war, always insisted on being accompanied by the Sultan. This was a prudent precaution because in the Sudan

---

9. Ibid, pp. 352-7.

a recognized method of bringing about the death of an unwanted ruler or a dangerous rival was to arrange matters in such a way that he was left in the lurch in battle. Six years earlier, for example, El-Kanemi had nearly been surrounded and killed by the Baghirmis at the battle of Ngala. The common people afterwards believed that the danger had arisen simply through an unexpectedly fierce charge of the enemy and that the Sheikh had saved himself by possessing the charm of invisibility.[10] Among the more sophisticated however, it was said that the Sultan, Mai Dunama Lefiami had been in secret league with the Baghirmis and had engineered the whole incident to rid himself of the Sheikh.[11] In the end, ironically enough, it had been the Sultan and not the Sheikh who had been killed at Ngala. This reversal of fortune had of course enhanced the prestige of the Sheikh who was afterwards regarded as so powerful and astute that he could not only defeat intrigues against him but actually turn them against their authors.

On the Manga expedition, therefore, El-Kanemi was, as usual, accompanied by the Sultan.

> The Sheikh is preceded by five flags—two green, two striped, and one red, with extracts from the Koran written on them in letters of gold—and attended by about a hundred of his chiefs and favourite slaves. A negro high in confidence rides close behind him, bearing his shield, jacket of mail, and wearing his skull-cap of steel; he also bears his arms. Another, mounted on a swift camel and fantastically dressed with a straw hat and ostrich feathers, carries his timbrel or drum which it is the greatest misfortune and disgrace to lose in action . . .
>
> Close in the rear of the camels follow eunuchs and the harem. The Sheikh takes but three wives who are mounted astride on small trained horses, each led by a boy-slave or eunuch, their heads and figures completely enveloped in brown silk burnouses and a eunuch riding by the side of each.
>
> The Sultan of Bornu has five times as many attendants and his harem is three times as numerous. He is attended also by men bearing trumpets of hollow wood, ten and twelve feet long. With these a kind of music is constantly kept up. (As this instrument is considered an appendage of royalty alone, the Sheikh has none.) The *Kaugama* or standard bearer rides in front of him, carrying a

---

10. Ibid, p. 361. Belief in this charm, which in Hausa is called *layyar zana*, is general throughout the central Sudan.
11. *Gazetteer of Bornu Province*, Lagos, 1929, p. 21.

very long pole hung round at the top with strips of leather and silk of various colours in imitation probably of the Pasha's tigue or tails, and two ride on each side of him called *Mistruma Dandelma,* carrying immense spears with which they are supposed to defend their Sultan in action, whose dignity would be infringed upon by defending himself. But the spears are so hung around with charms, and the bearers so abominably unwieldy, that the idea of such weapons being of any use in the hands of such warriors is absurd. Indeed the grotesque appearance of the whole of this prince's train, with heads hung round with charms and resembing the size and shape of a hogshead, their protruding stomachs and wadded doublets, are ridiculous in the extreme.

The town of Kabshari, where we halted, had been nearly destroyed by the Mangawa. On attacking a place, it is the custom of the country instantly to fire it and, as they are all composed of straw huts only, the whole is shortly devoured by the flames. The unfortunate inhabitants fly quickly from the destructive element and fall immediately into the hands of their no less merciless enemies who surround the place. The men are quickly massacred and the women and chiefs, lashed together and made slaves. Ramadan, one of the Sheikh's chiefs, a slave from Hausaland, had been stationed here for the last fifteen days and, under his protection, the survivors of the attack had returned and were already rebuilding their dwellings. . . .

These unfortunate people seldom think of defending their habitations but rather give them up and by that means gain time to escape themselves. . . . The Kabsharians had long been in dread of a visit from the people of Manga and, on their approach, the greater part of them had retreated to the banks of the river, to the north-west of the town, which are there extremely high, and they had made a strong post by digging *blakas* and placing pointed crossed stakes in trenches which rendered their retreat nearly inaccessible.[12]

Just as in the recent wars the Fulani had relied principally upon their bowmen, so had the Bornu armies depended mainly on the stiffening provided by the Kanembu pikemen. 'The infantry here' wrote Denham 'as in our own quarter of the globe, most commonly decide the fortune of war. The Sheikh's former successes may be greatly, if not entirely, attributed to the courageous efforts of the Kanem spearmen in leading the Bornu horse into battle who, without such a covering attack, would

---

12. Denham, I, pp. 361-4. Ramadan is a nickname sometimes given to boys born in the month of the fast. In Hausa it is usually corrupted to Ladan.

never be brought to face the arrows of their enemies.'[13] Because of the important part that these troops played in the wars of the day, Denham's description of them is particularly interesting.

> June 1—The sun had scarcely risen this morning when the Sheikh was on horseback, inspecting his favourite troops, the Kanembu infantry. A hollow space under some sandhills was chosen, about a quarter of a mile from the camp, and the whole was conducted with a good deal of order and system. He was attended to the ground by the four chiefs who accompanied the expedition under his orders and a circle was formed by the Arabs and the Bornu horse. The Sheikh's principal slaves and commanders were dispersed in different parts, habited in their scarlet burnouses with gold lace, and surrounded also by their followers. His own dress was, as usual, neat and simple: two white figured muslin gowns, very large, with a burnous of the same colour and a Cashmere shawl for a turban, composed his dress. Over the whole, across his shoulders, hung the sword which, as he repeatedly said 'the Sultan Inglese had sent him'. He was mounted on a very beautiful bright bay horse from Mandara and took his station on the north side of the circle, while the Kanembu were drawn up on the opposite extremity in close column to the number of nine thousand.
>
> On the signal being made for them to advance, they uttered a yell or shriek, exceeding anything in shrillness I ever heard, then advanced by tribes of from eight hundred to one thousand each. They were perfectly naked with the exception of a rather fantastic belt of goat or sheep's skin, with the hair outwards, round their middles and a few narrow strips of cloth round their heads and brought under the nose. Their arms are a spear and shield, with a dagger on the left arm reversed, secured by a ring which goes on the wrist, the point running up the arm and the handle downwards. The shields are made of the wood of the *fogo*, a tree which grows in the shallow waters of the great lake, and are so extremely light as to weigh only a few pounds; the pieces of wood of which it is formed are bound together by thongs of the hide of bullocks, with the hair on, which is also carried along the edge of the outside of the shield in vandykes and forms an ornament. They are something the shape of a gothic window and most of them slightly convex. Under cover of these the Kanembu attack the bowmen with great order and at a slow pace. Their leaders are mounted and are distinguished merely by a gown of dark blue and a turban of the same colour.
>
> On nearing the spot where the Sheikh had placed himself they

---

13. Ibid, p. 378.

THE MANGA REBELLION

> quickened their pace and, after striking their spears against their shields for some seconds, which had an extremely grand and stunning effect, they filed off to the outside of the circle where they again formed and awaited their companions who succeeded them in the same order. There appeared to be a great deal of affection between these troops and the Sheikh. He spurred his horse onwards into the midst of some of the tribes as they came up and spoke to them, while the men crowded round him, kissing his feet and the stirrups of his saddle. It was a most pleasing sight. He seemed to feel how much his present elevation was owing to their exertions, while they displayed a devotion and attachment deserving and denoting the greatest confidence. . . .
>
> On seeing the Sheikh after this inspection, he asked me what I thought of his Kanembu; I could not help expressing my pleasure at their orderly and regular appearance and he smiled when I assured him that I thought with such troops as these he need fear but little the attempts of the Arabs and Fezzaneers.[14]

In the field, the post of honour, nearest to the enemy, was always accorded to the Kanembu and Denham described their system of mounting guard and keeping watch.

> They have a regular chain of posts or pickets, consisting of five or six men each, extending from the main body to one of the tribes who always act as an advance guard about two miles in front and cover the whole front of the army. They lie very snugly in the shelter of their shield which protect them both from wind and rain as well as the arrows of their foes. One or two of each party are always on the look out and their peculiar watch-cry is passed from one sentry to the other at every half hour or oftener the whole night through. On the least disturbance taking place in the camp, or horses breaking loose after a sudden storm, the whole body strike their shields and set up a yell to show that they are awake to the circumstance. This also is their tattoo, may be heard for miles, and answers the blowing of the Sheikh's horn for the last prayers at Lisha.[15]

The leader of the rebellion was a well-known divine called Mallam Fanami who had captured the hearts and minds of the Mangawa in much the same way that El-Kanemi had previously won the hearts and minds of the Kanuri and Kanembu. When Denham and Oudney reached the scene

---

14. Ibid, p. 364-6.
15. Ibid, pp. 368-9. *Lisha* is the last of the Moslem's five obligatory prayers and is said after nightfall.

of operations there had been no major battle but skirmishing had taken place and blood had already been shed.

> Ramadan, who had been stationed in Kabshari since the burning of the town, gave me an account of a second attack made by the Mangawa since his arrival. He had about two hundred and fifty people with him, amongst whom were about a dozen Arabs in the Sheikh's service who had guns. Eight or nine hundred Manga people made their appearance by daylight one morning, principally to try the strength of their enemies, which it was of course Ramadan's business to prevent their ascertaining. He succeeded in driving them back, although not without some loss, quite to the enclosed country where they had greatly the advantage of him and killed nearly thirty of his men with their arrows. Ramadan now practised a *ruse de guerre* by which means he destroyed nearly half the force of his enemies: he appeared to give up the chase and retired with his party; towards evening, however, he moved round by the river to a watering place where he expected the Mangawa would go to drink and refresh themselves and, rushing upon them unperceived, slaughtered upwards of four hundred.[16]

For the Sheikh the problem was much more than just military. The Mangawa were excellent fighting men who could put 12,000 bowmen into the field. If the kingdom was not to be very seriously weakened, therefore, it was not enough just to suppress the revolt, not even to avoid civil war: more important, the insurgents had to be weaned away from Mallam Fanami and brought back to their allegiance. El-Kanemi was statesman enough to see that this could only be done by magnanimity.

> June 3—A reconnoitring party of cavalry went out soon after daylight with Ramadan and Da'ud at their head. About three in the afternoon they began to return, bringing with them women and children of both sexes to the amount of eight hundred. One Shuwa, a friend of mine, brought a poor woman with four children, two in her arms and two on the father's horse, who had been stabbed for defending those he held most dear upon earth. They also brought a number of very fine horses and several hundred bullocks and sheep. The poor wretches, on being brought to the Sheikh's tent, uttered the most piteous cries and, after looking at them, he desired that they might all be released, saying 'God forbid that I should make slaves of the wives and children of any Moslem! Go back; tell the wicked and powerful chiefs who urge your husbands to rebellion

16. Ibid, pp. 366-7.

THE MANGA REBELLION

> and backsliding that I shall quickly be with them. And it is them I will punish, not the innocent and the helpless.'[17]

Whether El-Kanemi acted as he did on strict principle or from shrewd calculation, his policy proved eminently successful and, after very little fighting, the revolt began to collapse.

> June 5—Many hundreds of the Manga people now came in, bowing to the ground and throwing sand upon their heads in token of submission. At night everything was prepared for our marching to the capital, leaving the women, camels, and baggage, at this place, but the people sent word that, if the Sheikh remained where he was, they would come to him and surrender themselves.
>
> June 6—Several towns sent their chiefs and submitted in this manner—bringing peace-offerings on the Sheikh's swearing solemnly not to molest them further. But Mallam Fanami, a divine of great talent, the mover of the rebellion, refused to come because he feared to lose his head, although offering two thousand slaves, one thousand bullocks, and three hundred horses to the Sheikh as the price for peace. The offer was refused, the Sheikh's object being the subjection of this rebellious chief and not his death or plunder.[18]

With the rebels wavering, and some of their emissaries already suing for peace, El-Kanemi brought off an imaginative stroke.

> We had the night before attempted to send off two rockets which to my great disappointment, as well as the Sheikh's, had failed: they had been carelessly carried and the composition had fallen out of them. This evening he sent 'to beg that I would try two more and, please God, make them go better.' I replied 'that I would do my best' and, most fortunately, they succeeded to my wish. They were, indeed, a beautiful sight, as the night was extremely dark, and created exceeding wonder. Some of the messengers who had come from the towns to the west fell on their faces and began to pray most fearfully when the rockets burst in their descent.[19]

The Sheikh was well pleased with the result and later said to Denham: "Why did you not bring plenty of rockets? They are the most wonderful things I ever saw".

Among those who witnessed this demonstration was Fanami's son and

17. Ibid. pp. 367-8.
18. Ibid. pp. 369-70.
19. Ibid. pp. 370-1.

it was probably no coincidence that, very soon afterwards, the father decided to make his submission.

> The following day, Mallam Fanami himself made his appearance. His people had become clamorous and, having no alternative, he came superbly mounted on a white horse with full one thousand followers and, dismounting at the door of the Sheikh's tent, humbled himself to the dust and would have poured sand on his head but this was by the Sheikh's order prevented and the Mallam brought into his presence. As is the custom on these occasions, he came in poor habiliments with an uncovered head. The Sheikh received his submission and, when he really expected to hear the order for his throat to be cut, he was clothed in eight handsome gowns and his head made as big as six with turbans from Egypt.[20]

Mallam Fanami proved to be a man of strange appearance, almost a freak of nature, with a face that was hairless on one side and heavily bearded on the other. This had apparently helped him to win adherents among the unsophisticated Mangawa but as a man of learning he had only moderate attainments and was certainly no match for the Sheikh. After his submission Denham was told that El-Kanemi had spent three successive nights writing charms which had had the effect of causing his enemies to fall ill, of blunting their swords, and of snapping their arrows; when, on top of all that, he had conjured up the rockets, Mallam Fanami had conceded victory and declared that "to withstand a Sheikh of the Koran who performed such miracles was useless and, at the same time, a sin."[21]

El-Kanemi's handling of the revolt had been masterly. By displaying just the right mixture of firmness and clemency and above all by convincing the Mangawa that his spiritual and supernatural powers were superior to those of Mallam Fanami, he had recalled them to their loyalty with very little bloodshed and no aftermath of bitterness.

* * *

On June 11 the *Id el-Fitr,* the Moslem festival that marks the end of the fast of Ramadan, was celebrated in the field. Then, when the army was preparing to return to the capital, a clash of personalities occurred which threw an interesting light on El-Kanemi's character and showed how he maintained his ascendancy.

20. Ibid. p. 371.
21. Ibid. pp. 378-9.

THE MANGA REBELLION

A circumstance happened during the last two days which created a great sensation amongst the chiefs and, while it proved that absolute power in the person of the Sheikh was not unaccompanied by a heart overflowing with feelings of mercy and moderation, it also displayed many amiable qualities in his untutored and unenlightened subjects.

Barka Gana, his General and his favourite, a governor of six large districts, the man whom he delighted to honour, who had more than fifty female slaves and twice the number of male, was taught a lesson of humility that made me feel exceedingly for him. In giving presents to the chiefs, the Sheikh had inadvertently sent him a horse which he had previously promised to someone else. On Barka Gana being requested to give it up, he took such great offence that he sent back all the horses which the Sheikh had previously given him, saying that he would in future walk or ride his own. On this the Sheikh immediately sent for him, had him stripped in his presence and a leather girdle put round his loins; and, after reproaching him with his ingratitude, ordered that he should forthwith be sold to the Tubu merchants, for he was still a slave.

The favourite, thus humbled and disgraced, fell on his knees and acknowledged the justness of his punishment. He begged for no forgiveness for himself but entreated that his wives and children might be provided for out of the riches of his master's bounty. But on the following day, when preparations were made for carrying this sentence into effect, the *Kaganawa* (black Mamelukes) and Shuwa chiefs about the Sheikh's person fell at his feet and, notwithstanding the haughtiness of Barka Gana's carriage to them since his advancement, entreated to a man pardon for his offences and that he might be restored to favour. The culprit appearing at this moment to take leave, the Sheikh threw himself back on his carpet, wept like a child, and suffered Barka Gana, who had crept close to him, to embrace his knees, and calling them all his sons, pardoned his repentant slave. No prince of the most civilized nation can be better loved by his subjects than this chief. And he is a most extraordinary instance, in the eastern world, of fearless bravery, virtue, and simplicity. In the evening, there was great and general rejoicing. The timbrels beat; the Kanembu yelled and struck their shields; everything bespoke joy; and Barka Gana, in new gowns and a rich burnous, rode round the camp followed by all the chiefs of the army.[22]

22. Ibid. pp. 375-7.

On June 18, with its mission accomplished, the army began its return march. At Kabshari, Denham observed that good progress was being made in rebuilding the quarter of the town that had been destroyed in the fighting. The Sheikh encouraged the inhabitants by exempting them from paying tribute for a season and by himself making them a present of money.

At Demasak the army was disbanded, the Kanembu and Shuwa contingents being given leave to return direct to their homes. A few days later, as the Bornu contingent was approaching Kuka, the Sheikh sent for Oudney and Denham to come and ride in his train. The whole population turned out to meet them and thus, amid the shouts of the men and the joyful ululations of the women, they made a triumphal entry into the capital.

XII

The Onset Of The Dry Season

When the explorers had set out from North Africa they had entrusted the whole of their cash reserve, 2,000 silver dollars, to the safekeeping of Bu-Khalum. The only evidence of this transaction, however was the receipt, written in Italian, which had been prepared in the Consul's office in Tripoli. On Bu-Khalum's death, all his possessions in the Sudan had passed to his brother, Haj Ali and the solvency of the explorers had therefore depended on his acknowledging and repaying the debt.

When the majority of the Arabs had set off on the Mandara expedition, Haj Ali had not accompanied them. Instead he had gone to Hausaland with the minority in order to dispose of the merchandise which he and his brother had brought from North Africa. Until he returned therefore, there was nothing that the Europeans could do but be patient. But to Denham, an active man who evidently believed that they should never have allowed themselves to be put in so insecure a position, patience did not come easily. When he subsequently wrote his narrative, Oudney was already dead and so he refrained from criticizing him openly, but some of his comments are clearly critical by implication. 'We had left Murzuk' he wrote 'with thirty-three of our own and four hired camels and yet the store (of cash), of all others the most needful, we had not taken into our own keeping.'[1]

In late June, when Denham and Oudney came back from the Manga expedition, there was still no news of Haj Ali's return. By this time,

1. Denham, I, p. 399.

though not yet completely impoverished, the explorers were already seriously short of funds. In this predicament, they were doubly grateful for the supplies with which the Sheikh continued to furnish them.

> The embarrassed state of our finances had been known to him ever since the exposure which took place on Bu-Khalum's death and, since that period, scarcely a week had passed without a supply of wheat, sheep, honey, and fat being sent to us, unsolicited. Without such assistance, the small stock of money which remained after the death of our friend would have been insufficient to have supported us beyond a few weeks, notwithstanding it was increased by the sale of all our red and yellow cloth, the most valuable part of our stores. The necessaries of life sufficient to support nature we never could have been said to want: one hot meal every evening had never failed us and boiled rice, or rice and milk, was the usual breakfast, but the luxuries of tea, coffee, and sugar, had been long dispensed with. We had, however, by not having been sufficiently on our guard . . . exposed our poverty to the whole town and the falling off in the number of our visitors proved that the feelings of the people were not exactly in unison with those of their leader.[2]

The worries of the Europeans were greatly aggravated by sickness. Clapperton had been intermittently ill ever since his arrival in Bornu four and a half months earlier and Hillman was similarly suffering frequent attacks of fever and delirium. Oudney too, since his return from Manga, had been virtually confined to his hut and now Denham, though still much the fittest of the four, was being troubled by his eyes. With nearly all their horses and most of their camels already dead, they began to brood whether they would ever be able to extricate themselves from the Sudan. 'The regrets which accompanied the contemplation of our unprovided state' wrote Denham 'and the perilous uncertainty as to what would be our situation on the least falling off on the part of the Sheikh, occasionally filled us with indescribable alarm'. So oppressed were they by these gloomy reflections that they no longer found pleasure in each other's company or conversation and normally dispersed to their own huts as soon as they had finished their evening meal. Indeed in one passage Denham speaks of their disagreements being aggravated by the peevishness and discontent brought on by sickness, by having to live in huts that did not protect them from the rain and by worrying about money and supplies.[3] Though this friction never developed into a serious

2. Ibid, pp. 399-400.
3. Ibid, p. 409.

THE ONSET OF THE DRY SEASON

rift or approached, even remotely, the bitter quarrels and rivalries that marred the history of some other African expeditions, it should not be glossed over altogether.

It was not until the third week in August that Haj Ali and the other merchants returned from their trading expedition to Hausaland. By that time the explorers were living entirely on provisions furnished by the Sheikh, except for a little milk and a few fowls which they bought for themselves and their funds were all but exhausted. They learnt that more of the Arabs and Fezzaneers had died in Hausaland than in any previous year and found that Haj Ali, who had also suffered ill health was greatly altered in appearance. Nevertheless, with his safe return, they imagined that their financial difficulties were over. The shock was all the greater therefore, when he denied knowledge of any deposit and refused to recognise the validity of the receipt made out in Tripoli.

> Haj Ali Bu-Khalum had been now returned more than a week and nothing satisfactory had ever been extracted from him as to the money left in his brother's hands. I had great fears of his honesty from the first and urged the necessity of our taking some decided measures with him. We accordingly summoned him to appear before the Sheikh, the result of which was our failure for want of sufficient documents and the tergiversation of the Arabs. . .
>
> We received visits of condolence from several of our Bornu friends who were all extravagant in their abuse of Haj Ali. 'Are these your Murzuk friends,' said they 'who were to assist you with everything? Why, this is robbing you! However, they called God to witness to a lie and they will die soon: only wait a day or two.'[4]

This description suggests that the case was heard by the Sheikh himself but it is clear from the more detailed court record, which Denham included as an appendix to his narrative, that it was tried by a *Kadi*, or Judge, in an ordinary court. Now in the absence of documentary evidence, Moslem law requires the testimony of two witnesses. Here the receipt, being written in Italian, was unintelligible to the court and was consequently not accepted as written evidence. As for witnesses, since the explorers were able to produce only one, the court decided, perfectly correctly, that the defendant had the right to exculpate himself by taking a formal oath on the point at issue. This he evidently did and so judgement was given in his favour.[5]

4. Ibid, p. 414.
5. Ibid, I, p. 414 and II, pp. 431-3.

Considering that the Europeans had been entrusted by the Pasha to the personal protection and care of his brother, the late Bu-Khalum, Haj Ali's action was indefensible. He was admittedly beset by difficulties of his own and, at the time, these may have seemed more pressing than the troubles of the explorers or the future displeasure of his sovereign. But soon afterwards, as we shall see, rumours began to circulate in Kuka that the Pasha was preparing an expedition to conquer Bornu and annex it to Tripolitania. If these stories were true, Haj Ali must have reflected, he was liable to be called to account much sooner than he had reckoned. This calculation, coupled with a sense of guilt for having sworn a false oath, seems to have brought him round to a more accommodating mood.

> Feeling that our situation required an appearance of spirit and determination, I sent for Abdul Wahad, an Arab of Zehren distantly related to Bu-Khalum to whom on two occasions of distress I had been kind, and upbraided him with his falsehood and ingratitude. Nor was my remonstrance altogether without effect. He acknowledged that 'His heart had been too big for his stomach ever since he left the palace; that his eyes had been dim and he had enjoyed no rest; for' said he 'I swore to myself to be as faithful to you as a brother.'
>
> 'All this is very fine' said I 'but what proof will you give of this remorse?'
>
> 'Every proof' he replied. 'Haj Ali will come this very day and acknowledge the debt—that must be the consequence. I have been to the Sheikh and said how you had assisted me and that I had sworn and could not see you wronged.'
>
> Even as Abdul Wahad predicted, so it happened. Karouash came in the course of the day to say that Abdul Wahad had been to his house and told him the debt was just, and that he had reported the conversation to the Sheikh. The Sheikh's answer was 'He is quite right. After what the Rais Khalil (Denham) said, everyone would have known where justice lay, for the English have not many words, but they are true, and the Arabs, you know, will lie a little.'
>
> In the evening Haj Ali came himself. He made, however, but a blundering excuse, saying he had never inquired into it, did not even know whether we gave any money or not to Bu-Khalum, but now that he knew, and God forbid he should ever be otherwise than friendly with the English, and that not only two but five thousand dollars were at our service. All this, however, ended in his begging us to wait until he had sent off his caravan to Murzuk and that then he would try to give us eight hundred or one thousand dollars in gowns and strips of cloth for not ten dollars in money had he, and the rest

he hoped we would wait for until he sent to Hausaland. Unsatisfactory as this was, we thought it better not to make objections, merely saying that we were without money and begging that he would settle it as soon as he possibly could.[6]

But even this compromise proved to be unsatisfactory. As the gowns and cloth that Haj Ali made over to them were worth only 600 dollars and as they still had no firm acknowledgement of the balance of the debt, they decided to go back to the *Kadi*. The following extract from the court record is interesting because it shows that the proceedings were well regulated and far from unsophisticated.

> They (the Europeans) appeared a second time at the said court of justice and alleged that Haj Ali, after their first appearance, acknowledged and pledged himself to pay them the two thousand dollars which they claimed from his late brother, that he paid them a part of the said sum in cotton cloth to the value of six hundred dollars in Bornu money, and that the remaining fourteen hundred were to be repaid to them by him at the city of Kano in Hausaland. They therefore wished to legalize this before the judge.
>
> Haj Ali, however, said, that he gave them the six hundred dollars merely as an act of kindness on his part and as a loan from him to them, which they were to return to him at Kano, that he never acknowledged or promised to pay his brother's debt, but that he told them, if they should be in want of more money at Kano, he would advance them as much as he could afford.
>
> They then requested the judge to restrict him from selling or sending his brother's property to Kano (lest it should be lost on the road) until they had proved their claim by better evidence. Haj Ali agreed, either himself or through his agent, to pay them five hundred dollars more, in addition to the six hundred, two months after their arrival at Kano and fixed a period of one year from the date of this document between them and him for the proof of the justice of their claim. If they failed to prove their demand upon his deceased brother before the lapse of the said period, they were to repay him the eleven hundred dollars and forego all their claims. But if, on the contrary, they should be able to substantiate their demand within the stipulated period, he would then repay to them the nine hundred dollars, balance of the two thousand.
>
> Upon these conditions both parties agreed and declared themselves content and satisfied, while they were in a perfect state of health and mind as to deserve reliance and dependence upon.

6. Ibid, I, pp. 415-6.

Issued from the Court of Justice of the honoured and learned Sheikh Mohammad El-Amin ben Mohammad El-Kanemi at Bornu on the 27th day of Rabi'ul Awal, one thousand two hundred and thirty-nine of the Prophet's Hijra.

With this partial settlement, which was not reached until December 1823, the plaintiffs had to be content.

* * *

The explorers were always on the alert to pick up geographical information and lost no opportunity of questioning the Africans and Arabs whom they met in the course of their travels. As anyone who has ever attempted it will know, however, this is an exercise fraught with many difficulties and hazards. First, there are the ordinary barriers of language. Next, and much more formidable, there are the vagaries of African nomenclature. The River Niger, for example, is known in the Western Sudan as the *Joliba* but to the Hausas it is the *Kwara*. Bauchi, the land of the slaves, is not only the Emirate of that name but may equally well be any pagan district adjoining Moslem Hausaland.[8] The Bahr el-Ghazal is an underground river running into Lake Chad as well as a tributary of the Nile.[9] Finally there is the perennial problem of judging how far an informant is speaking from firsthand knowledge, how far he is repeating hearsay and how far, in his effort to please and earn a reward, he is simply drawing on a lively imagination.

Though Denham and his friends were fully alive to these dangers, they were sometimes deceived, particularly when a plausible informant mixed fiction with a leavening of fact. On the Mandara expedition, for example, Denham met a man who said that he had travelled between Nupe in the west and Darfur in the east. Despite his claim to be Hornemann's son, which was palpably a fabrication, Denham was sufficiently impressed by his information to record and later publish it.

> I met with a man who wanted to persuade me that he was a son of Hornemann by his slave, although from his appearance he must have been born ten years before that unfortunate traveller entered this country. He said he had been twenty days south of Mandara, to a country called Adamawa which he described as being situated in

---

7. Ibid, II, pp. 432-3.
8. In Sokoto, for example, the pagan districts of Zuru are often referred to as Bauchi.
9. H.R. Palmer, *Sudanese Memoirs*, I, map.

the centre of a plain surrounded by mountains ten times higher than any we could see ... and here, for one Hausa gown, the Sultan gave him four slaves. ... These people, he says (that is, the pagans on the hills, for Adamawa itself is occupied by the Fulani) eat the flesh of horses, mules, and asses, or of any wild animal they kill. Nobody but the chiefs and their children are clothed; all the rest of the nation go naked; the men sometimes wear a skin round the loins but the women nothing.

This man, who was called Kaid Musa ben-Yusuf (Hornemann's name), spoke to me of several extensive lakes which he had seen in this journey and also described with great clearness a river running between two very high ridges of the mountains which he crossed previous to arriving at Adamawa. This river he declared to run from the west and to be the same as the Quolla or Quarra at Nupe but not the same as the river at Kano which had nothing to do with the Shari and which ran into the Chad; but the main body of the water ran on to the south of Baghirmi, was then called the Dago, and went eastward to the Nile. Kaid Musa was a very intelligent fellow, had visited Nupe, Raka, Wadai and Darfur, by which latter place also, he said, the river passed. He was most particularly clear in all his account and his statement agreed in some points with the information a Shuwa named Dris Bu-Ras-ben-Abu-Delil had given me; therefore I was the more inclined to pay attention to it.

To the south of this river, the population is entirely pagan, until the Great Desert. This desert is passed several times in the year by caravans with white people, not Christians, who bring goods from the great sea. Some of these reach Adamawa. He himself saw white loaf sugar, such as the merchants brought here from Tripoli to the Sheikh, and a gun or two, with metal pots and pans, and arrack (gin or rum).[10]

We now know that this statement, though it contained a modicum of truth, was riddled with inaccuracies. The mountains of Adamawa are not much higher than those of Mandara. The river, the Benue, flows westward, not eastward. There is no link between it and the Nile and the two systems are in fact separated by the Cameroon highlands which drain into the Chad basin. But these things were still hidden from the geographers of the day and Denham had no means of separating the truth from the falsehood. He therefore set it all down, for what it was worth, and the map which was published with his narrative illustrated Kaid Musa's

10. Denham, I, pp. 333-5. But see later for what may be further elucidation of this point.

assertions by showing the Niger, when it reached Nupe, turning eastward, making a pass towards Lake Chad from the south, and then, veering east again heading away for Darfur and the Nile.

Denham was assured by all his informants that the mountains stretched southward from Mandara for two months' journey, say for 900 miles, and he was later to see for himself the Shari and the Logone, two major rivers flowing northward into Lake Chad. Perhaps, therefore, he should have been more sceptical about the story that somehow an eastward flowing Niger managed to cut through the mountain barrier and cross the line of the other two rivers. Though this theory was put forward as only one of four which had at one time or another been propounded to the explorers, it contributed to the confusion about the Niger's course that was to persist until, eight years later, the mystery was finally cleared up by the Lander brothers.

On another occasion, after his return from the Manga expedition, Denham met a young man, a Fulani from the western Sudan, who gave him some interesting information about Mungo Park's second expedition.

> Many years ago (he said) white men, Christians, came from Segu to Jenne in a large boat, as big as two of our boats. The natives went out to them in their canoes; they would not have done them any harm but the Christians were afraid and fired at them with guns and killed several in the canoes that went near their boat. They proceeded to Timbuktu and there the Sultan sent to them one of his chiefs and they held a parley. The Christians complained that the people wanted to rob them. The Sultan was kind to them and gave them supplies. Notwithstanding this, they went off suddenly in the night, which vexed the Sultan, as he would have sent people with them, if they had not been afraid of them a little, and he now sent boats after them to warn them of their danger, as there were many rocks in the belly of the river, all pointed. However, the Christians went on and would not suffer the Sultan's people to come near them, and they all perished.
>
> My informant never heard that anything belonging to them was saved but remembers himself seeing a man often with his father who was in one of the canoes that followed them and who had seen them strike against the rocks—indeed he brought the news to Timbuktu. Their appearance excited a great sensation amongst the people—[he] had frequently heard people talk about the Christians and the large boat for a whole day at his father's—to this day they talk about them. They had guns fixed to the sides of the boat, a

thing never seen before at Timbuktu, and they alarmed the people greatly.[11]

This narrative agrees with accounts later given to Barth in suggesting that Mungo Park, in his unswerving determination to win through to the sea, was too ready to use force. At the same time it completely ignores the repeated attacks which, according to the only eye-witness account, were made against his party in the great bend of the Niger and the determined attempts that were made to waylay and overwhelm it.

Denham's informant, whose name was Abdul Gassam, was a young zealot reared in the Fulani tradition of ascetic piety. Though only sixteen, he had already achieved one of the ambitions of all Islamic scholars and learnt the whole of the Koran by heart.

> He was on his way to the pilgrimage and had left Timbuktu, as is the custom, without anything beyond the shirt on his back, the rags of which he exchanged on the road for a sheep's skin, subsisting entirely on charity. He was a very fine and intelligent lad of a deep copper colour but with features extremely handsome and expressive. He was five months from Jenne and greatly exhausted by fatigue and the want of nourishing food. His whole wardrobe was his sheep's skin and, although the Sheikh gave him a gown, he said he almost thought it a sin to indulge in the luxury of putting it on...
>
> About the time of our evening meal, Abdul Gassam generally made his appearance at our tents. Bad as the fare was, he found it preferable to the cold mess of flour and water he got elsewhere. He knew little or nothing of the road by which he had come to Kano, not even the names of the places he had halted at. He said he could scarcely believe that such good people as we were could be anything but Moslem...
>
> He left Kuka in the month of August, in company with an old Mallam for Wadai, with a small leather bag of parched corn and a bottle for his water. I gave him a dollar to pay for his passage across the Red Sea which he sewed up in his sheep's skin. I however heard that he had been drowned in crossing one of the branches of the Chad. My informant was a Wadai Shuwa but, if they found out that he had the dollar, he was most likely murdered for the sake of such a booty.

*   *   *

11. Ibid, pp. 385-6.
12. Ibid, pp. 384 and 387-8.

The rainy season was now well under way and thunder-storms, accompanied by torrential downpours, were frequent.

> Previous to a storm, gusts of wind would accompany the black clouds which encompassed us and blow with great force from the north-east. These winds, however, were not accompanied by such violent or lasting rains. But, when the clouds formed themselves to the south-east, they were tremendous, accumulating as it were all their force and gradually darkening into a deep and more terrific black with frequent and vivid forked lightning, accompanied by such deafening and repeated claps of thunder as shook the ground beneath our feet like an earthquake. The rain always at these times burst upon us in torrents, continuing sometimes for several hours, while blasts of wind from the same quarter drove with a violence against our unsheltered huts that made us expect every instant, low as they were, to see the roofs fly from over our heads and deprive us of the trifling protection they afforded. After these storms, the enclosures round our huts were often knee deep in water and channels were formed with all possible speed or our habitations would have been inundated. At the full and change of the moon these storms were always most violent.[13]

Denham noted that the seed was sown with the first heavy rains and that throughout July, the slaves were busily employed on the farms. By mid-August, as the millet shot up, the arid plains round Kuka underwent an extraordinary transformation and an annual hazard, peculiar to the Chad region, appeared again.

> At this season of the year there are other reasons besides the falls of rain which induce people to remain in their habitations—when the great lake overflows the immense district which in the dry season affords cover and food by its coarse grass and jungle to the numerous savage animals with which Bornu abounds, they are driven from these wilds and take refuge in the standing corn, sometimes in the immediate neighbourhood of the towns. Elephants had already been seen at Duwergu, scarcely six miles from Kuka, and a female slave, while she was returning home from weeding the corn to Kauwa, not more than ten miles distant, had been carried off by a lioness.
> The hyenas, which are everywhere in legions, grew now so extremely ravenous that a good large village, where I sometimes procured a draught of sour milk on my duck-shooting excursions,

175 | THE ONSET OF THE DRY SEASON

had been attacked the night before my last visit, the town absolutely carried by storm, notwithstanding defences nearly six feet high of branches of the prickly mimosa, and two donkies, whose flesh these animals are particularly fond of, carried off in spite of the efforts of the people. We constantly heard them close to the walls of our own town at nights and, on a gate being left partly open, they would enter and carry off any unfortunate animal that they could find in the streets.

There are a particular class of female slaves here to whom the duty of watching and labouring in the fields of grain is always allotted. I have before said that all laborious work is performed by that sex we consider as the weakest, and whom we employ in the more domestic duties only, and it is to them this perilous work is assigned. The female slaves from Musgau are never bought by the Tripoli or Fezzan traders: their features, naturally large and ugly, are so much disfigured by the silver stud which they wear in the under lip that no purchaser would be found for them. Besides the loss of the two front teeth, which are punched out to make way for the silver which goes quite through into their mouths, the weight of the metal after a year or two drags the lip down so as to make it quite lie on the chin and gives a really frightful appearance to the face. These poor creatures, therefore, who are generally of a strong make and patient under their sufferings, guard the crops and collect the harvest, and a year seldom passes without several of them being snatched away by the lions who, crouching under cover of the ripening corn, spring on their prey and bear it off.[14]

In the Sudan, July and August are the months of heaviest rainfall. During this period the rivers are so swollen and low-lying ground becomes so water-logged, that travelling on foot or on horseback becomes excessively difficult, indeed in some places almost impossible. Even if they had had plenty of money, therefore, the explorers would have been unable to venture far afield. As it was, they had no choice in the matter and were confined to Kuka by their penury as well as by the climate.

XIII
Life In Kuka

The explorers' long sojourn in Kuka, though it was marred by constant illness and rendered highly uncomfortable by the inadequacies of their lodgings and their own shortage of ready money, nevertheless afforded an excellent opportunity of studying at close quarters the society of the capital. Denham had the nose of a journalist and the incidents that he observed and recorded some unusual, some humdrum, give us a vivid picture of the life and times.

> Soon after our return from Manga, in consequence I imagine of representations rather to the prejudice of the ladies generally during the absence of their lords, the matrons were ordered to assemble at the palace of the Sheikh. It must be understood that he was most rigorous with the gentler sex, visited any little aberrations with severe punishments, in some cases even unto death, and justly piqued himself on the beneficial change he had effected in their lives and manners since his residence amongst them. The women of Kuka were always held up as patterns to those of Ngornu and Birni. The sum of their offending appeared to be having been too often seen in the streets during the absence of the lords of creation and with their faces uncovered. Their husbands also generally complained of their having acquired a habit of loud talking, from thence arguing that they must have talked a great deal.
> They were severely lectured and dismissed, and an order was issued that no married woman who had slaves should ever be out of her house or receive visitors at home. The single, who from the frequency of divorces are numerous, were most strictly admonished

and when they pleaded as an excuse for receiving visitors their wish to be married, the *Kadi* exclaimed most sagely: 'But as only one man can marry one woman, is it necessary several should come to the house? Surely only one should be allowed to pay his visits.' The *Kadi* was however silenced by the still more sagacious Sheikh who saw greater danger likely to occur from these tete-a-tetes without chance of interruption. 'No' said he 'to debar any woman from receiving her suitors would be to discourage marriage, which is contrary to the law of the Prophet. But these visits must not be made at unreasonable hours in the night, and let her take care there is no preference and that no one person is admitted to the prejudice of another. Should her door be once found barred on the inside, *Shaitan* (the devil) will have got hold of her and she shall have her head shaved.'[1]

Soon afterwards El-Kanemi showed how severe he could be in enforcing moral laws.

Two decisions of the Sheikh lately had created a considerable emotion amongst the people. The slave of one had been caught with the wife of another, a free man, and the injured husband demanded justice. The Sheikh condemned both the man and the woman to be hanged side by side. The owner of the slave, however, remonstrated and said that the decision, as far as respected the woman, was just, for she was always endeavouring to seduce his slave from his work and that if he, the Sheikh, condemned his slave to death, the man whose wife was the cause of it ought to give him the value of his slave as he was poor. This the husband objected to. 'Ah' exclaimed the Sheikh 'how often is a man driven to his destruction by woman! Yet of all his happiness she is the root or the branch'. He himself paid the value of the slave to the owner and, the next morning, the guilty pair were suspended outside the walls.[2]

Towards the end of the rainy season there was another instance of the diligence with which the Sheikh sought out immorality and the rigour with which he prosecuted it. This time the offenders were two young girls of easy virtue.

Two of these unfortunates fell into his hands, whose sinnings were placed beyond all doubt by the activity of the spies he employed to watch over this department. And, although his decisions on ordinary occasions were ever on the side of mercy, these

1. Denham, I, pp. 389-90.
2. Ibid, pp. 395-6.

poor girls were sentenced to be hanged by the neck until they were dead. The agitation and sorrow which the threatened execution of these two girls, who were both of them under seventeen excited in the minds of all the people were most creditable to their feelings and, although on other occasions their submission to the decrees of their chief was abject in the extreme, yet on this (to say the least of it) rigorous sentence being made public, loud murmurs were uttered by the men and railings by the women. The lover of one of the girls swore that he would stab any man who attempted to place the rope. He had offered to marry, which offer had been refused. The general feeling was pity and the severity of the punishment caused the sin to be almost forgotten, which would not have been the case had the penalty been of a more lenient nature. Indeed it was natural that pity should be felt—notwithstanding all one's morality, it was impossible to feel otherwise.... The Sheikh's unmerciful edict in this case excited an abhorrence and rendered him more unpopular than any act of his since I had been in the country.

The day after (for punishments are summary in eastern countries) was fixed for the expiation of their crime, but a divine, nearly equal to the Sheikh in skill, took upon himself to remonstrate and declared such punishments were themselves *haram,* impermissable, for in no part of the Koran could an authority be found for such a sentence. To disgrace or set a mark on such culprits was the law of the Prophet—not death—and that, should these poor offenders suffer, God would avenge their death on the country and sickness, with bad crops, would come upon them. The Sheikh for a long time continued inexorable and observed that riches, plenty and prosperity, without virtue, were not worth possessing—the punishment of the two girls, however was eventually commuted to that of head-shaving, a heavy disgrace which was performed in the public street.[3]

During the *jihad* there had been a long controversy between the Fulani leaders on the one hand and El-Kanemi on the other on various theological and moral questions,[4] and at that time El-Kanemi gave the appearance of being more tolerant and flexible than the Fulani reformers. It is therefore all the more surprising to find that, in this matter of sexual morality, his regime in Kuka was harsher than those of Sultan Bello and the Emir Abdullahi, the Fulani rulers in Sokoto and Gwandu.

Not long afterwards, in another case, Denham had an opportunity of witnessing the operation of the Moslem law of retaliation.

3. Ibid, pp. 443-4.
4. For details, see Johnston, pp. 105-40.

We had a curious trial this morning before the Sheikh, the result of which furnishes a singular proof of his simplicity and submission to the word of the Prophet. The circumstances were these: a Shuwa had stabbed a man the night before, upon some disagreement, and death was the consequence. The brother of the defunct demanded blood and, on application to the *Kadi,* it came out in evidence that the Shuwa had desired the deceased to quit his door three times, if he had any faith in the Prophet, but he still continued to resist and aggravate him till at last he stabbed him in six places. The *Kadi*'s decision was that, upon so solemn a caution, the unfortunate man should have retired; that his not doing so was a proof he had no faith in the Prophet, was an unbeliever, and was the cause of his own death; and therefore that the murderer should not suffer punishment.

The accuser, however, appealed to the Sheikh who told him that certainly by God's law, communicated to the Prophet and written in the Koran, an eye for an eye, a tooth for a tooth, and life for life, should be given, but recommended his taking a fine instead of blood. The sturdy Arab, however, was unmoved, and called loudly for justice. The Sheikh then said he had the law in his own hands and he might do as he pleased. The prisoner was then taken outside of the walls and the brother of the deceased beat his brains out with an iron-headed club which the Shuwas sometimes carry. This was considered a very extraordinary occurrence in Bornu.[5]

For El-Kanemi, the rainy season of 1823 was a time of great anxiety because, soon after his return from the Manga expedition, reports began to circulate in Kuka that the Pasha of Tripoli had designs on Bornu. In the past, relations between the two powers had always been friendly. Separated as they were by the Sahara, they were far enough apart to avoid military and political rivalries and yet near enough to have close commercial ties which were very profitable to them both. Though not formally bound by a treaty, they were allies in fact and, if Tripoli was recognized to be the senior partner, there was no question of Bornu's being in any way subordinate or tributary. Seven years earlier moreover, the alliance had been sealed in the joint enterprise against Baghirmi. This had been an unqualified success from the point of view of both participants. The Sheikh, reinforced by the Sultan of Murzuk, had inflicted very severe damage on his enemies, while the Sultan had taken back to his

5. Denham, I, pp. 393-4.

overlord the Pasha an immense haul of booty, mainly in the form of slaves.

But now, it was freely rumoured, the Pasha was considering a move against his ally. As the explorers had arrived in Bornu accompanied by an escort furnished by the Pasha and as they were consequently regarded as enjoying his confidence and friendship, it was clear that if any such move was made they could hardly escape involvement.

> Private information, it was said, had by several channels reached the Sheikh that the Pasha had it in contemplation to send an expedition, for the purpose of taking possession of Bornu, under the joint command of Mukni, the late, and Mustafa, the present Sultan of Fezzan. . . . The report, credited as it was by the majority of Bornu people, was of itself sufficient to excite in us excessive alarm, both for our own safety as well as for the success of our mission. The Sheikh caused it to be understood, both here and at Ngornu, that the caravan about to leave Kuka for Fezzan would be the last. . .[6]

For El-Kanemi this delicate political problem was complicated by a personal factor: some of his children were in the Fezzan and were being detained there by the intrigues of the same Mustafa who was now mentioned as a possible leader of the intended expedition. As for the explorers, they found what comfort they could in the report that the Pasha would not move against Bornu while they were still there and in the fact that El-Kanemi's kindness and attention to them remained undiminished.

By September, with the end of the rains in sight, there had still been no definite news from the north. The tension in Bornu therefore rose.

> The caravan for Murzuk left Kuka on the 13th. Several Arabs who had determined on remaining here some time, took their departure in consequence of their fears of the Pasha's visit. Nothing had arrived and, in the absence of authentic intelligence, all was alarm and confusion and reports of every kind arose. They said the caravan, which had been expected more than two months, could not be delayed from any other cause than the hostile intentions of the Sultan. Trusty persons were accordingly stationed at the commencement of the desert to give the earliest information of anything approaching. . .[7]

El-Kanemi evidently took the rumours seriously because, in addition

6. Ibid, pp. 405-7.
7. Ibid, pp. 423-4.

to posting these pickets, he had various defensive measures put in hand. To supervise one of them, the help of Hillman, the shipwright, was enlisted.

> Hillman had been for a long time employed in making a guncarriage for a four-pounder which the Sultan of Fezzan had formerly brought as a present to the Sheikh. The scarcity of iron, the awkwardness of the negro blacksmiths, and the clumsiness of their work when finished were so distressing to the correct eye of an English shipwright that, even after the carriage was completed (and, considering the means he had, it was very well done), Hillman was far from being satisfied with his work. Not so, however, the Sheikh. We took it to him this afternoon and he was greatly pleased and surprised at the facility with which its elevation could be increased or decreased. Both this and the wheels were subjects of great wonder. During the work, on several occasions, the Sheikh had sent Hillman presents of honey, milk, rice, wheat, and sweet cakes...[8]

Next, early in October, the Sheikh summoned some of his feudal levies so that he could inspect them and their accoutrements. About 3,000 horsemen from the Chad and Shari districts answered the call and mustered in the capital. The examination, which El-Kanemi conducted himself, was thorough and searching. Special attention was paid to the condition of the horses: if they had grown too old to serve as chargers, they were replaced, but if they were too young and immature, the troopers were blamed and summarily punished for failing to equip themselves properly.[9]

Later in October, Denham services, as well as Hillman's, were harnessed to the military preparations.

> I had been fully employed (convinced that I was best consulting the interests of the mission by cultivating the favour and good will of the Sheikh) during the two last days in superintending the manufacture of cartridges for the two field-pieces, which were now both mounted, as we had plenty of very good paper for the purpose with us. In this I succeeded to my wishes but the providing of shot was a great difficulty. After trying a number of musket balls in a small linen bag, which would not answer, I succeeded in getting from the negro blacksmith, by means of a paper model, a small tin canister, the size of the mouth of the piece, and holding sixteen

8. Ibid, p. 428.
9. Ibid, p. 433.

musket-balls. The Sheikh's delight was extreme at this acquisition to his own implements of war and he became impatient to see the guns exercised. I offered, if he would appoint six of his best slaves, three to each gun, that I would instruct them as well as I was able—as firing them quick was a very material augmentation of their utility—and I at the same time strongly recommended his holding forth to his people the promise of reward, in the event of their being brought safe out of battle, and that the punishment would be most severe in case they were deserted and fell into the hands of an enemy.

The Sheikh's preparation for war had been carried on for the last two months with great vigour. His whole armoury had been renovated and he told me exultingly that he had two hundred guns, pistols, and carbines—although from the looks of full fifty it would have been in vain to attempt producing fire. Nearly forty men were daily employed in sharpening and new-heading the spears, weekly inspections took place of all the horses of the Shuwa and Bornu towns all round the country, and within the last month more than one thousand horses had been given in lieu of those that had been cast as unfit for service.

Whether these preparations were a prelude to a new attack on Baghirmi, or intended merely as a defence in the event of the still dreaded expedition of the Pasha being realized, the conjectures of the people were nearly balanced. It was a vain endeavour to persuade the Sheikh of the bad policy of such an attempt on the part of the Pasha of Tripoli: he knew too well the disposition and motives which governed all Turkish policy for such considerations as these to have any weight and that, whenever they thought treasure was within their reach, considerations of future policy or distant consequences would have little or no influence on their measures. By thus increasing his powers, El-Kanemi became prepared either for offensive or defensive operations and, in the particular state of his government, such a situation was peculiarly requisite. . . .

The ceremony of the trial of the brass guns for which, after consulting Mr. Clapperton who was too ill to undertake it himself, I had succeeded in making charge and wadding, took place this afternoon before the Sheikh and a thousand spectators. The distance to which they threw the balls, and the loudness of the report, created the greatest astonishment, but I could not persuade the Sheikh to suffer a second canister to be shot. 'No, no!' said he "they are too valuable; they must not be thrown away. Curses on their race! How these will make the Bagharmis jump!'

I had cut them out a harness in paper, as a pattern, which had been tolerably made in leather. This was attached to each gun, with a man mounted on the mule that drew it, and altogether the guns had a far better appearance and effect than I expected. The carriages answered extremely well—were very steady—and I much regretted that poor Hillman, to whom all the credit of mounting them belonged, was confined to his mattress and unable to see how well they answered, but the Sheikh's anxiety would not brook delay.

In addition to the Sheikh's other preparations for defensive warfare, that of repairing the walls of the town was now set about with an activity which it was exhilarating even to be spectators of. Each chief had a portion assigned him who, with his followers, carried on the work for seven or eight hours each day, superintending themselves the labourers. A covered way was run all round the town on the inside of the wall, as an additional defence which had never been before resorted to, and several feet were added to its height. I found myself as anxious about the walls as if I were to defend them from escalade. The Sheikh sent to know how I thought they went on and Barka Gana, who had the largest portion, begged me to look now and then at his people. The wall, however, was a good wall, and wanted nothing but stout hearts to man it...

* * *

Because of the constant ill-health of Oudney and Clapperton, the task of cultivating good relations with the Court at Kuka fell almost entirely to Denham.

I continued to work at the Arabic and Kanuri languages. Besides this, I usually visited Barka Gana two or three times a week and sometimes he came to see me so that my time rarely hung heavy on my hands. But he always came mounted and with so many attendants that my little hut was put in disorder for the whole day after. I believe he entered no person's habitation in the town, but my own, except the Sheikh's. No great man here ever visits his inferior, or moves from his own house to the Sheikh's, without a retinue agreeable to his rank. The Kachalla, on remonstrating with me for coming through the streets alone, was surprised when I told him that even our king did the same and, often habited like his subjects, rode attended only by a single servant. Convinced as he was before of his importance, this astonished him greatly. 'Why' said he 'were the Sheikh to do so, nobody would respect him.'

'And' replied I 'in England, the oftener the king does this, the more he is both loved and respected.'[11]

10. Ibid, pp. 439-441 and 445-6.
11. Ibid, pp. 394-5.

184 | DENHAM IN BORNU

Denham was equally assiduous in calling at the Palace to pay his respects to the Sheikh.

> I found the morning and evening visits, which I had lately made to the Sheikh in his garden when the weather would permit, a source of some little amusement. He became more free, took a lesson in making tea, of which he had become greatly enamoured, and would frequently converse on different subjects, amongst others on religion, with as much liberality as any man I ever met with. He said one day: 'Yours is the best belief of any of those unfortunates who are in the wrong path; your book is generally written by the command of The Most High, but the words are not his own words, as with the Koran. But Isa (our Saviour), the first of prophets save one, had the Divine Laws communicated also to him but they were all burnt by the Jews, confusion to their posterity!'
>
> Encouraged by his liberality and freedom I said 'that we believed our New Testmanet to be the final dispensation of the Almighty, communicated by the mouth of his Son Jesus.'
>
> This he rebutted by an exclamation of 'this proves the errors of your belief. What then do you say of the Koran?'
>
> 'We do not believe in it' said I.
>
> 'Nor its divinity?'
>
> 'No' said I 'none of these are part of our belief'.
>
> 'Lord have mercy on you and open your eyes before you die!' He replied.
>
> 'Amen!' said I. 'But remember we despise no man's religion and boldly proclaim our own.'
>
> 'There you are right' answered he. 'Any thing is better than lies'
>
> The Sheikh argues clearly and cooly, and apparently much more for the sake of gaining information than from any other motive. [12]

Whatever El-Kanemi's motive, however, he had to keep up an appearance before his courtiers of being at least as well informed as his guests. Denham clearly derived some quiet amusement from the way in which he did this.

> We had one day a renewal of a conversation which had taken place when we were all present relative to the shape of the earth and particularly whether the sun was stationary. He was incredulous and, in my best manner, I drew a diagram on the sand of his floor representing the section of a cone. He paid the greatest attention and affected perfectly to understand what I attempted to show, how a body revolves in an ellipse round the sun in one focus. He

12. Ibid, pp. 409-10.

now demanded how, supposing the earth to be globular, those on the opposite side to ourselves could walk and move as we did. This I could only explain with a reference to the load-stone, which he had been amusing himself with a few days before, and by this means gave him an idea of gravity and attraction. 'And by the force of this gravity' said I 'all bodies, on whatever side, fall in lines perpendicular to its centre.'

'I observe' said the Sheikh. 'It is wonderful!'. And, turning to his attendants, 'You' said he 'understand nothing of all this!'

They bowed their heads with a 'No, my lord.'

Then, with a look of the most perfect satisfaction, he added 'These people know everything: I have now proved it', affecting to have made these enquiries for the purpose of ascertaining our knowledge, rather than improving his own.

On one of these visits to the Palace, Denham caught a glimpse of the least attractive aspect of domestic slavery as it was practised in the Sudan.

> The Sultan of Bornu had more than two hundred youths under twenty, from Baghirmi, in his hareem as eunuchs, while the Sultan of Baghirmi (who was said to have nearly one thousand wives) had treble that number of unfortunate Kanuri and Kanembu eunuchs, chosen out of the most healthy young men who had fallen into his hands as prisoners and spared from the general masacre for the purpose of serving him in that capacity. Even the moral, and in many respects the amiable, Sheikh had more than thirty Baghirmi lads thus qualified to enter the apartments of his wives and princesses.
> As I was one day taking shelter in the portico of the Sheikh's garden from the violence of a sudden storm of rain, the chief of those privileged persons brought me to see about a dozen of this corps who were just recovering from the ordeal of initiation which they had gone through. Thin and emaciated, though fed and taken the greatest care of (for they become extremely valuable and will sell to any Turkish merchant for two hundred and fifty or three hundred dollars), these poor remnants of promising healthy young men passed before me. I could not contain my emotion or disguise the distress which was apparent in my countenance so that the old hardened chief of the seraglio, who seemed happy that so many of his fellow-creatures were reduced to the same standard as himself, exclaimed: 'Why, Christian, what signified all this? They are only Baghirmis! Dogs! Unbelievers! Enemies! They ought to have been

13. Ibid, pp. 410-11.

cut in four quarters alive, and now they will drink coffee, eat sugar, and live in a palace all their lives.'[14]

It is true that some eunuchs rose to positions of trust and privilege in the slave-hierarchies of the rulers whom they served. But to rise they first had to survive and it is equally true that many more succumbed to the rough surgery that was practiced upon them.

* * *

The explorers had first heard of the state of Wadai during their journey across the desert when they had met the survivors of a party of Mamelukes who, after Muhammad Ali's *coup d'etat* in Egypt, had retreated to the south and west, first to Kordofan, then to Darfur and finally to Wadai itself. These people had described the inhabitants as savages of the worst description and had earnestly warned Denham not to go there if he valued his life.[15]

Later, in Kuka, Denham had heard that for the past five years Bornu and Wadai had been at feud over the suzerainty of Kanem and that trade between them had come to a complete standstill. Now, from the Arab who was the sole survivor of the last trading caravan, he learned why the people of Wadai had such an unsavoury reputation throughout the Sudan.

> Since the death of the good Sultan Sabon, as he was called, no intercourse [with Wadai] had been attempted either from hence or even from Fezzan. The only man who escaped from the last caravan, five years ago, was now here and gave the following account of the treatment he received.
>
> He was named Abdu Nibbe, the confidential servant of the Pasha's palace governor, and had gone from Tripoli to Wadai by way of Murzuk, having been entrusted with a very considerable sum with which he was to trade. They arrived at Wadai in safety, and at Wara the capital, and after residing there more than twenty days, during which time he had purchased thirty-seven slaves and was apparently upon friendly terms with the natives, one morning they entered his hut, seized all his property, and stripped and bound him. . . . Naked, he was carried before the Chief who acted as regent, Sabon's son the Sultan being but an infant. Abdu Nibbe there found forty persons, consisting of his fellow-travellers and their followers, bound in the same manner as himself. After being insulted in every possible way, they were taken outside the town in order to have their throats cut.

14. Ibid, p. 455.
15. Ibid, p. 47.

Abdu Nibbe, who was a powerful fellow from Towergha, a town near Mesurata, after seeing many of his companions suffer themselves patiently to be massacred and feeling the cord with which his hands were tied but loosely fastened, determined on making an attempt, at least, to save his life. He burst the cord asunder and ran towards the hills. Twice they caught him and twice he escaped from their keeping, carrying with him three wounds from spears and one from a knife which very nearly severed his right hand from his body. Night, however, came on and, creeping into a hole which had been, and still might be, the habitation of a brood of hyenas, there he remained three nights and three days until raging hunger forced him to quit his retreat.

Where, however, to go was the question—whom could he trust amongst so barbarous a people? One person alone came to his mind as likely to assist him in this extremity—in whose hands alone he conceived his life would be safe. Was it his brother or his sworn bosom friend? No; it was a man's never-failing, last, and best consolation, woman: one to whom he had been kind in his prosperity, whom he had been intimate with; and he felt assured that she would not be ungrateful, and never betray his confidence. Was he mistaken? No: she received him, fed him, washed his wounds, and for seven days concealed him when, at last, he was discovered and carried again before the chief.

After asking how he escaped, the governor said: 'I will keep you in my service, give you a horse, and see whether you will fight as well for me as you did for yourself'. Abdu Nibbe remained more than two months in this situation, drawing water, carrying wood, etc., when he heard that a caravan was about to leave Wadai consisting of a few merchants only, the remains of his own and former ones, who had bought their lives at a very high price. Taking advantage, therefore, of a dark night, he once more escaped and joined them. They lent him a gun and some ammunition to protect him from the wild beasts, which were very numerous, and advised his quitting the caravan before day for the woods: he moved nearly parallel with the caravan and at night again joined them. In this way he journeyed for five days, when the Wadai horsemen gave up the pursuit and returned without him.[16]

Earlier in the year, while El-Kanemi had been engaged against the Mangawa, a report had reached him that Wadai had an army in the

---

16. Ibid, pp. 457-9. Wadai's reputation for lawlessness and violence was not undeserved. The French official Moll and the British explorer Boyd Alexander were killed there as late as 1910.

field.[17] It proved to be false but the possibility was always there and in any case Baghirmi, on better evidence, was believed to be planning another offensive against Bornu.[18]

At this period, in fact, El-Kanemi had every reason to feel deeply anxious. In the Sudan he was surrounded by enemies, the Fulani Caliphate to the west and Wadai and Baghirmi to the east, so that if the Pasha were to decide to attack him from the north, as rumour still predicted, he could hardly hope to survive. What was equally serious for him was that his own people, despite his triumph in Manga and indeed to some extent because his success there had brought peace but no booty, were restless and discontented.

> The last expedition to Manga had been productive of no profit to the army, although the issue was of considerable benefit to their general interest. Looking, however, merely to the present moment, the Bornu people were certainly dissatisfied and they were encouraged in their expressions of discontent by the strangers whose only object was plunder. These were a numerous class and some of them high in favour.
>
> The Sheikh had, in the beginning of his conquests, seen the advantage of encouraging the discontented of other countries to settle in his new towns and, besides the Kanembu who accompanied him, he had Tuaregs, Arabs, and Baghirmis—and on those he appeared to rest his chief reliance. To check this warlike spirit was far from his wish or interest for, by indulging it, he not only enriched himself and his people, and strengthened his power, but might also hope to render it eventually a source of strength, prosperity, and permanency to his kingdom.[19]

Whatever private misgivings he may have had, El-Kanemi concealed them under such a bold front that the explorers never fully realised how precarious his position was. But, until he knew for certain what the Pasha's intentions were, he could not commit himself in any single direction. So he continued to make military preparations and, to hearten his followers, gave out that he was preparing a campaign against Baghirmi.[20]

Whether there was any basis in fact for the rumours about the Pasha's designs against Bornu it is now impossible to tell but the probability is that there was not. Certainly no supporting evidence had ever come to

17. Ibid, p. 381.
18. Ibid, p. 447.
19. Ibid, p. 442.
20. Ibid, p. 447.

light. Furthermore, it seems inherently improbable that the Pasha, having to some degree made himself responsible to the British Government for the safety of the explorers, should then make plans which, even if completely successful, would inevitably place them in danger. Finally there is the circumstance that in August 1823, when he was believed to be planning his military expedition, the Pasha was in fact writing a cordial letter, addressed to 'the learned and accomplished, the virtuous Imam, the jealous and zealous defender of the Moslem faith, our true friend the Sheikh Muhammad el-Kanemi', in which he begged him to continue to give to the English travellers his protection and assistance and went on to request him to arrange for them to visit Hausaland.[21] Admittedly, as already mentioned, this letter was almost certainly prompted by Warrington, the British Consul, in response to a message sent by Oudney after the Sheikh had first refused to allow the explorers to go to Hausaland, but even so, if the Pasha had been on the point of launching an expedition, he would hardly have troubled to send the letter, as he seems to have done, by special courier. But, real or imaginary, the rumours were taken seriously and for two months they threw a shadow over Kuka.

* * *

Apart from the military preparations however, life in the capital seems to have gone on as usual. On 17 August, for example, the Moslem festival of *Id el-Kebir*, commemorating Abraham's offering up of Isaac, was celebrated with the usual feasting and rejoicing and would have been dignified by the normal ceremonial procession if it had not been for the fact that the Sheikh was taken ill.

> Garments, according to the estimation in which the giver holds the receiver, are distributed by all great people to their followers. The Sheikh gave away upwards of a thousand gowns and as many bullocks and sheep. It is the custom on the morning of the festival for the sovereign with his suite to mount and, after praying at a certain distance from the town, to return to it with all his people skirmishing before him. The Sheikh had been suffering from an attack of the ague and therefore this ceremony did not take place. The people, however, drew bad omens from the circumstance and said that the Sheikh not having mounted and prayed with his people was not right.[22]

At about this time Denham watched, and indeed took some part in the celebration of a Kanuri wedding.

21. Ibid, II, pp. 420-2.
22. Ibid, I, pp. 404-5.

> This morning I rode out by daylight to see the ceremony of a Bornu wedding. The lady was from Ngornu and the bridegroom's friends, to the number of twenty or thirty, all mounted and in their best clothes, went to give her welcome. She was mounted on a bullock, whose back was covered with blue and white cloths, and followed by four female slaves laden with straw baskets, wooden bowls, and earthen pots, while two other bullocks carried the rest of the dowry which consisted of a certain number of cloths and gowns. She was attended by her mother and five or six young ladies who acted as bridesmaids.
>
> We galloped up to them repeatedly, which is the mode of salutation. The women cover their faces and scream their thanks. The men, however, wheel their horses quickly and return with their eyes cast to the ground, it being considered as extremely indelicate for them to look upon the bride. The lady, after this, proceeds to the bridegroom's house with her mother and there remains shut up until the evening when she is handed over to her justly impatient lord. For the whole day he is obliged to parade the streets with a crowd after him or sit on a raised seat *à la Sultan* in his house, dressed in all the finery he can either borrow or buy, while the people crowd in upon him, blowing horns, beating drums, and crying 'May you live forever! God prosper you! Grey hairs to you!', to all of which he makes no answer but looks more foolish than one could suppose it possible for any man in so enviable a situation as that of a bridegroom to do.[23]

After the festival, the courtiers took to amusing themselves by organising wrestling contests among their slaves.

> Since the feast day of *Id el-Kebir* there had been an evening assembly of persons before the Sheikh's gate when the most athletic and active of the slaves came out and wrestled in the presence of their masters and the Sheikh himself who usually took his post at a little window over the principal gate of the palace. Barka Gana, Ali Gana, Worma, Tirab, and all the chiefs were usually seated on mats in the inner ring and I generally took my place beside them.
>
> Quickness and main strength were the qualifications which ensured victory: they struggled with a bitterness which could scarcely have been exceeded in the armed contests of the Roman gladiators and which was greatly augmented by the voices of their masters, urging them to the most strenuous exertion of their powers. A rude trumpet of the buffalo's horn sounded to the attack and the

---

23. Ibid, pp. 397-8.

Ox-borne palanquins of the Shuwa Arabs remarkably similar to those described by Denham in 1823. Photos 1960. (See also Page 74)

combatants entered the arena naked with the exception of a leathern girdle about the loins. Those who had been victorious on former occasions were received with loud acclamations by the spectators.

Slaves of all nations were first matched against each other: of these the natives of Hausaland were the least powerful and seldom victors. The most arduous struggles were between the Musgau and Baghirmi negroes. Some of these slaves, and particularly the latter, were beautifully formed and of gigantic stature. But the feats of the day always closed by the matching of two Baghirmis against each other and dislocated limbs, or death, were often the consequence of these kindred encounters.

They commence by placing their hands on each other's shoulders. Of their feet they make no use but frequently stoop down and practise a hundred deceptions to throw the adversary off his guard, when the other will seize his antagonist by the hips and, after holding him in the air, dash him against the ground with a stunning violence where he lies covered with blood and unable to pursue the contest. A conqueror of this kind is greeted by loud shouts and several vests will be thrown to him by the spectators. On kneeling at his master's feet, which always concludes the triumph, he is often habited by the slaves near his lord in a gown of the value of thirty or forty dollars. Or, what is esteemed as a still higher mark of favour, one of the gowns worn by his chief is taken off and thrown on the back of the conqueror.

I have seen them foam and bleed at the mouth and nose from pure rage and exertion, their owners all the time vying with each other in using expressions most likely to excite their fury. One chief will draw a pistol and swear by the Koran that his slave shall not survive an instant his defeat and, with the same breath, offer him great rewards if he conquers. Both of these promises are sometimes too faithfully kept and one poor wretch, who had withstood the attacks of a ponderous negro, much more than his match, for more than fifty minutes, turned his eye reproachfully on his threatening master only for an instant when his antagonist slipped his hand down from the shoulders to the loins and, by a sudden twist, raised his knee to his chest and fell with his whole weight on the poor slave (who was from Hausaland), snapping his spine in the fall.

Former feats are considered as nothing after one failure and a slave that a hundred dollars would not purchase today is, after a defeat, sold at the market, maimed as he is, for a few dollars to any one who will purchase him.[24]

24. Ibid, pp. 417-9.

XIV

Hard Times

In the Sudan, the latter part of the rainy season, in August and September, is a tolerable but dangerous time. The almost insufferable heat of April and May are things of the past. Now the rivers are all in flood. Low-lying land is inundated. In the bush the elephant grass is high enough to conceal a woman with a calabash on her head while in the farms the millet and guinea corn easily out-top a man on a horse. Humidity is high and the air is full of flies by day and mosquitoes by night.

The explorers and the animals they had brought with them from North Africa suffered very severely from these conditions, both in hardship and illness.

> We had now been five days without rain. The thermometer was as high as 89° in the middle of the day in the shade and we began to think summer was again coming. It may appear incredible that with such a temperature we should wish for an increase of heat, but the dampness of the atmosphere and the millions of flies and mosquitoes, beyond all conception, that accompanied it, rendered it almost impossible to enjoy anything like repose, either by day or night. The annoyance of these insects I had experienced at Lisbon, Naples, and in other parts of Italy and Sicily, but neither in numbers nor in peace-disturbing powers were they to be compared with these.[1]

---

1. Among mosquitoes it is only the females that are the bloodsuckers. The intensity of infestation in any given place is nowadays measured by exposing one man in one room for one night and then, on the following morning, counting the

Towards the evening, a fire in the hut, made of damp straw and weeds, was sometimes the means of procuring a few hours' tranquility, but the remedy was in itself so disagreeable that it was only resorted to in dispair. A fire of this kind, however, seldom fails to expel the intruders from the thick and suffocating vapours which arise from it.

The horses also suffered dreadfully from the same annoyance and, to keep them from injuring themselves wherever they can reach with their teeth, the negroes are obliged to keep a fire the greater part of the day, particularly at the hours of feeding.... And, notwithstanding the natural dislike those animals have to flames and smoke, they will hang their heads over the fire so as to suffer themselves to be all but scorched in order to obtain a little rest from their persecutors.

Of scorpions we had seen but few, but the white and black ants were like the sands in numbers. The white ones made their way into every trunk, of whatever sort of wood they were made, as if it had been paper, and on the late expedition, during a halt of three days in a spot where they were more than usually numerous, a mat and a carpet on which I slept were completely destroyed by them. They tell a story of an Arab having lain down to sleep near old Birni just over a nest of these destructive insects, covered up in a barracan, and that in the morning he found himself quite naked, his covering having been eaten to the last thread. The wooden supports of a sort of shade, which I had erected in the front of my hut, in a little more than three months these destructive insects had perforated with so many millions of holes as to reduce it to a powder, and a new one was obliged to be placed in its room.

The black ant was no less persevering in attacks upon our persons; her bite was nearly as bad as a scorpion, and so sharp as to excite an involuntary exclamation from the sufferer. Indeed for weeks together my skin had, from these insects alone, more resembled that of a person afflicted with the measles than any thing else that I can compare it to. Oil, unfortunately, we had none, which is both a preventive and a cure. The only substitute I could obtain was

---

number of mosquitoes he has attracted. The results, expressed in blood-gorged females, surely one of science's more bizarre yardsticks, provide interesting statistics. The highest figure ever recorded in Nigeria is over 100. Tests have been made only in government stations, however, and it is probable that in lakeside villages, like those that Denham visited, the infestation rate is considerably higher. Be that as it may, anyone who has spent a night with even half-a-dozen mosquitoes inside his net will have no difficulty in imagining the torment that all the early African explorers must have suffered.

a little fat rubbed over the body and this seldom failed of giving me relief.²

The link between mosquitoes and malarial fever was not to be discovered for another seventy years. At this time it was not even suspected and malaria, as the name indicates, was believed to be caused by the miasmas or foul exhalations emanating from swamps. But, even if the explorers had recognized the danger, there was little that they could have done to protect themselves because mosquito nets had not then been invented. On the other hand, since the efficacy of quinine in the treatment of fever had long been known in Europe, it is strange that it had apparently not been included in Dr. Oudney's medicine chest. His remedy for fever, a drastic one, was to empty the stomach and open the bowels and his patients soon learnt to pay grudging respect to the volcanic power residing in one of his innocuous-looking prescriptions, tartar emetic.

> The season seemed now to prove very unhealthy both to the natives and ourselves, and from six to ten bodies were seen carried out daily from the city gates. My poor friend Mai Migami was attacked, among the rest, by this dreadfully prevalent complaint and he sent for me by daylight. I found him in an alarming state of fever with a fit of the ague on him at the time. After consulting with Dr. Oudney, who was unable to visit him, I gave him a strong dose of the emetic tartar and in two days had the pleasure of seeing him quite recovered.
>
> The effect of the emetic tartar was to him a matter of the greatest astonishment: at the first sight of the dose he was unwilling to take it and asked what a little white powder like that could do for him. He was very shortly, however, convinced that the quantity I had prescribed was quite sufficient. 'What wonderful medicine!' said he. 'Why, if I had swallowed so much', taking up a little sand in his hand, 'what would have become of me? Wonderful! wonderful! The English know everything: why are they not Moslems?'³

The malaria endemic to West Africa is one of the most malignant strains in the world. Its effect on Europeans is much more severe and more often fatal, than that of East Africa or Asia or indeed of any other part of the globe except perhaps parts of Central and South America. Eighteen years later for example, when the first British naval expedition was sent to the Niger, it was abandoned after only two months because

2. Denham, I, pp. 421-3.
3. Ibid, pp. 429-30.

there had been 48 deaths out of a complement of 148.[4] It is not surprising, therefore, that Denham's narrative of this period is full of accounts of illness and debilitation. Oudney was ailing; Hillman was intermittently ill and, even when well, was plagued by pricky-heat; Clapperton was prostrated most of the time by a fever that he was unable to throw off. As a result, Denham often found that he was the only one to appear at the mess bench for the evening meal. And even he, though his constitution was a tough one, suffered from recurrent head-aches and pains in the chest. To cure himself, he resorted to Oudney's heroic remedy.

> August 27—We still had excessive rains and, notwithstanding the great power of the sun for some hours in the middle of the day, so damp was the air that for several days together my blankets were never dry, the rain always coming through the roof of the hut at night.
>
> I was during the last twelve days attacked slightly by what would, I have no doubt, have terminated in that violent fever of the country, so prevalent during the rainy season, which we afterwards saw and felt the fatal effects of, both amongst the natives and ourselves, had it not been for poor Doctor Oudney's prompt and able advice and assistance. Two ounces of Epsom salts in a pint of water, with three grains of emetic tartar dissolved therein, I swallowed in about two hours, and from the effects of this, added to daily copious draughts of tamarind water, I attribute my complete recovery in less than six days.[5]

At Denham's behest the faithful Columbus also submitted himself to this treatment. Moreover, he too recovered.

As a doctor, Oudney was more successful in treating Denham and Columbus than he was in maintaining his own health. For a month he was unable to take any food save a little sour milk three times a day, or leave his hut except from necessity. Hillman, too, had one very severe bout of fever which culminated in delirium and afterwards left him in a state of excessive weakness. But it was Clapperton, in many ways the toughest man in the party, who now caused his comrades the greatest concern.

> Mr. Clapperton's illness had increased to an alarming height: he had upwards of twenty-four hours' fever and delirium without

---

4. In spite of the climate's notorious reputation, quinine seems not to have been used in West Africa until 1854 when the twelve Europeans in the Baikie expedition took it as a prophylactic. For the first time there were no deaths, a most important turning point.

5. Denham, I, p. 408.

> sensation. These attacks, just about the time the rainy season is at an end, are very prevalent and often fatal to the white people from the sea, as the Arabs are called. How much more violently must they affect the natives of more temperate lands! . . .[6]
>
> Mr. Clapperton's illness increased and one night, while all were asleep, he made his way to the hut where the only servant slept who was not sick, begging for water. His inside, he said, was burning. The delirium had just then left him; he was too weak to return to his hut without the assistance of Columbus, who supported him in his arms; he was still dangerously ill. Four persons of our establishment, besides Doctor Oudney, were confined to their beds at this time with this same disorder: the symptoms of all were similar.[7]

In early September the anxieties of the explorers were heightened by an outbreak of small-pox which raged amongst the slaves of two of their friends.

> The small-pox . . . amongst the slaves of two of our friends, added to the fever of the season. Out of twelve slaves who were seized, two had died and the only child of Muhammad el-Wurdi had now taken it from his slave. They are not ignorant of inoculation and it is performed nearly in the same manner as amongst ourselves by inserting the sharp point of the dagger, charged with the disease. They never give any medicine but merely roll the invalid in a barracan and lay him in a corner of the hut until the disorder takes a turn.
>
> The castor tree is found in this neighbourhood and is commonly used as a medicine. . . . Tamarind and trona (carbonate of soda) are, however, their chief medicines, and excellent ones they are.
>
> Writers of charms are more frequently applied to: they possess nostrums which not only heal wounds, bestow eloquence and the gift of persuasion, but which calm all agitation and distress of mind. A Mallam, or writer, with a ready wit and imposing manner is at no loss for employment. His medicine chest consists of a few herbs, a gourd or calabash for an ink bottle, and a reed for a pen: the nausea of pills and potions is not endured. Yet, notwithstanding, the people are generally handsome, well grown, and healthy. We have none of those miserable cases of chronic complaints and consumptions which meet us at every turn in our own country, not any of those dreadful hereditary disorders which repeatedly appear in Europe. Advice is cheap and the remedy is usually applied outside instead of finding its way into the stomach of the patient; no harm,

6. Ibid, pp. 420-1.
7. Ibid, p. 424.

therefore, can arise from the use of the prescription. The imagination is worked upon, which more than half performs the cure, and their extreme temperance and faith complete the restoration of the patient.

Writers of charms, however, do not stop here: they can produce children or cause barrenness; they can invigorate, or render impotent, by the magic of their pens; and, should anyone suspect the fidelity of his wife or mistress, they have a herb which, placed under the pillow of a sleeping woman at certain periods of the moon, causes her to reveal not only her infidelities but her tenderest predilections and desires.[8]

In the second half of September, however, with the rains virtually over, the condition of the Europeans at last began to mend.

> The weather continued to improve upon us, though the heat increased and some days the thermometer was at 97° and 98°, but we had fewer mosquitoes and a clearer atmosphere. Doctor Oudney had been violently attacked, first in his right and then in his left eye, with an inflammation which left him no rest by day or night; he, however, within the last two days, got out for an hour in the evening. Mr. Clapperton also, who had been in a state of extreme danger for many days, appeared to have passed the crisis of his attack—cool blood flowed once more in his veins and consciousness was restored to his mind. He was, however, emaciated and in a dreadful state of weakness, and his eyes could scarcely be said to have life or expression in them; he had been supported outside his hut for the last two days and we began to hope he would recover.[9]

Soon afterwards the following entry appeared in Denham's narrative: 'On Sunday we all met in the evening about sunset before the doors of our huts and enjoyed the cool breeze for more than half an hour. Even Dr. Oudney, whose eyes had ceased to be so painful, joined us—we had not enjoyed such a coterie for many months.'

But it was only with the arrival of the Harmattan, in early November, that the Europeans finally threw off their fevers.

> The cool winds which had prevailed for the last fifteen days had so purified the air that disease appeared to be taking its departure and a season of health about to succeed in its turn. These long-wished-for breezes generally came on about ten in the forenoon and

---

8. Ibid, pp. 425-6.
9. Ibid, p. 427. Oudney's eye disease was undoubtedly trachoma, still a scourge of the Bornu area.

continued until two hours after mid-day. They had a great effect on the natives and appeared considerably to invigorate ourselves. Both Mr. Clapperton and Hillman were now able to walk about with the assistance of a stick. They were both, however, sadly pulled down and enfeebled.[10]

The effect of the climate on the explorers' animals was even more deadly. At the height of the rains, three camels, a horse, and a mule all died within the space of ten days. Later Denham noted that the mortality, in nine months, had amounted to six horses, a mule, and thirty-three camels.[11]

* * *

Towards the end of September Oudney felt sufficiently recovered to make another formal request for permission to travel to Hausaland.

> During the confinement of Doctor Oudney, I had occasionally seen the Sheikh about every seven days. He was always anxious in his enquiries after him and seemed much surprised that, having such excellent medicines for other people, he should not be able to cure himself. As this day the doctor seemed to think himself a little better, we went together to the Sheikh. Dr. Oudney at once told him that he wished to go to Hausaland and, as he had not given me the slightest intimation of this being his intention, I was really as much surprised as the Sheikh himself.
>
> 'What is your object?' said he. 'Why, the courier had not yet brought the Pasha's directions.'
>
> Doctor Oudney replied: 'My wish is to see the country—I cannot live here—I shall die. While travelling, I am always better.'[12]

As El-Kanemi still had no definite information about the Pasha's intentions towards him, it is not surprising that he refused the request. He probably calculated that, so long as the Europeans were in Bornu, it was unlikely that an expedition would be sent against him; he may also have reflected that, if there were an unexpected attack, they would make useful hostages.

In October a caravan set out for Murzuk and Tripoli. Despite all their ill-health and the Sheikh's refusal to allow them to visit Hausaland, there was never any question of the Europeans joining it. They were still determined to pursue their explorations during the dry-season. But there

10. Ibid, p. 446-7.
11. Ibid, pp. 407 and 470.
12. Ibid, pp. 427-8.

was now nothing to keep the Arabs of the escort in Bornu and so they took their leave.

Such of the Arabs as remained of our escort, after their return from Manga, left Kuka with the first caravan for Tripoli. They were all my professed friends but, notwithstanding the miserable state in which they were, I had not the means of assisting them. The few dollars each man had received from the Pasha on quitting Tripoli, and all they possessed besides, being lost at Mandara, and they knew I was precisely in the same situation. One man in three or four sold his gun, an Arab's greatest treasure, to provide them with water, skins, and corn, for their journey. Added to this, they were all weakened by sickness and wounds. The fancied riches they were to be masters of, by Bu-Khalum's victories over the pagans, had vanished into air and they were about to return to their families, after a year's absence, even poorer than they left them.

That the desperation natural to an Arab should be excited by such circumstances was not to me a matter of surprise. I cautioned them, however, against returning to Tripoli with unclean hands. They promised fair enough and even shuddered when I reminded them of the Pasha's summary mode of punishing. All was, however, without effect for, on arriving at the Tubu country, they proceeded to the well Daggeshinga, a retreat which had been shown to Bu-Khalum in confidence on his last journey by Mina Tahr and the road to which they too well remembered, and surprising the flocks of the Tubus, and killing three of the people, marched off four hundred and upwards of their best camels. This exasperated the Tubus almost to madness and they filled up the wells, swearing they would be repaid or that no caravan should pass through their country. This news made us tremble for our supplies.[13]

The position of the Europeans in Kuka, already undermined by their lack of cash and by the loss of virtually all their animals, was weakened further by the departure of the Arabs and the danger that the closing of the caravan route by the Tubus would prevent their receiving help from the north. Their loss of status was reflected in the attitude of the people and, where previously their Christian faith had been passed over in silence, except by Mallam Chadili, it now became a cause of suspicion and friction to the more bigoted and superstitious Moslems.

The first indication of this change was comparatively trivial but is

13. Ibid, pp. 435-6.

worth recounting because of the light that it sheds on contemporary superstitions and the quacks and charlatans who exploited it.

> A very hale strong negro woman, the mother of Mr. Clapperton's servant, had taken the fever from her son, who had been more than a month laid on his back, and reduced her almost to death's door. She was a Kuri, from one of the islands to the east of Chad, and had sent for several Mallams who, after writing mysterious words, decided on her case as hopeless.
>
> At last an old *Haji,* more than seventy years of age, was requested to come to her. He was a miserable old wretch, carrying nothing but an ink-bottle made of a small gourd and a few reed pens, but he set about his business with great form and with the air of a master, and in the evening Zerega, my negro's wife, came to me quite in raptures at the following wonderful story. He said the woman was certainly enchanted, probably by the unbelievers, meaning the English, but 'By the head of the Prophet' he should drive the devil out of her. . . . He wrote a new wooden bowl all over sentences from the Koran; he washed it and she drank the water; he said 'Bismillah' forty times, and some other words when she screamed out, and he directly produced two little red and white birds, which, he said, had come from her. 'What did you do in that poor woman? She is not young' said the Mallam. 'Why perplex her? Why did you not come out of her before?'
>
> 'We did not wish to hurt her much' said the birds 'but she had been following strange gods, old as she is, and must be punished. There are others in her yet who will not come out so easily. But now, since you are come, she will not die but she had better take care for the future. We jumped into her when she went to the market and she knows what she did there.'
>
> The poor woman shed an abundance of tears and acknowledged that she had been a little thoughtless on the preceding market day. The Mallam was rewarded with her best Hausa shift and they were all made happy at the news of her recovery.[14]

Almost immediately afterwards however, another incident revealed to the explorers that the prejudice against Christians was widespread and that the Sheikh's favour, if they still enjoyed it, did not guarantee their immunity.

> A circumstance happened yesterday which, I acknowledge, a good deal irritated my feelings. A Tripoli merchant had entrusted to

---

14. Ibid, pp. 431-3.

one of the Mesurata [Arabs] a parcel of coral to take for him to Ngornu. It was, however, never forthcoming and he declared that he had lost it on the road. Koranic law would not, in that case, oblige the loser to make good the loss—a thing lost is God's will and nobody's fault. A servant of the owner, however, unluckily saw the coral afterwards in the Mesurata's house. The merchant therefore appealed to the *Kadi* as, if he succeeded in proving this, the value would be recoverable. This servant had been for some time out of employ and had assisted at our huts during the time that we had so many of the party sick. The *Kadi* took this man's oath and was about to decide when some one said: 'Why, he eats bread and salt with the Christians'.

'How!' said the *Kadi*. 'Is that true?'

'Yes' replied he, 'I have eaten their bread but it was because no one else would feed me. But I don't hate them the less for that.'

'Turn him out' said the *Kadi*. 'God forbid that anyone who has eaten with Christians should give justice by the laws of Muhammad!'

His evidence was accordingly refused and the merchant lost his cause. A Bornuese, a friend of mine, who was present asked the *Kadi,* with much simplicity, whether really these Christians were such bad people. 'They seem kind' said he 'and, if they are so very bad, why does God suffer them to be so rich and to know things so much better than we do?'

'Don't talk about them' said the *Kadi*. 'Don't talk about them—please God, those who are here will die Moslem. As to their riches, let them enjoy them. God allows them the good things of this world but to Moslems he has given paradise and eternity.'

'True! True!' was re-echoed from each and the *fatah* was immediately recited aloud.[15]

A little later a third incident occurred which confirmed these disquieting signs of public animosity.

We discovered too, or thought we discovered, that the people now treated us with less respect and were more lavish of the contemptuous appellations of Unbeliever, Dog, [and] Christian, both to me and to our servants, than formerly. . . . As the opinion of the common people in all these countries is usually governed by authority, I concluded we had also lost ground in the estimation of the chief. A Bornu boy whom I had taken some notice of, and who used to come to me almost every day to talk Kanuri, was hooted in

15. Ibid, pp. 433-5.

the streets and called *insara,* Christian. And, when we turned him from the huts for stealing nearly two dollars in strips of cloth, the money of the country, the people all exclaimed against such an act as, by consorting with Christians, they said that the misfortune of being supposed a thief had come upon him.[16]

There may well have been some truth in Denham's theory that at this period the explorers were out of favour with the Sheikh. Certainly for a time he ceased to furnish them with supplies.[17] Whatever his motive may have been, the action would certainly have become quickly known in every corner of the town and would have been taken as an indication that a coolness had sprung up. This by itself was enough to account for the liberties that the townspeople now began to take.

* * *

Denham does not state when the Sheikh received the letter which the Pasha had written in August asking him to arrange for the explorers to visit Hausaland. As there was no caravan, however, it must have been sent by the hand of one of the special desert couriers and probably arrived in November or early December. It certainly allayed the last of El-Kanemi's fears about the Pasha's intentions and brought about a sudden and radical change in his attitude to two unsettled questions. First, his military measures shed their defensive character and became preparations for offensive expeditions against his nearer neighbours. Second, after refusing for nine months to hear of Oudney's going to Hausaland, he suddenly swung round and not only granted permission but went out of his way to be helpful.

> Dr. Oudney, notwithstanding the extremely debilitated state to which he was reduced, determined on accompanying this [caravan] if the Sheikh would allow him. El-Kanemi not only gave his instant permission but did his utmost to forward his views and to secure his safety. He charged Muhammad el-Wurdi, the principal person of the caravan, to assist him in every way [and] gave him letters to the Emir of Katagum, the Emir of Kano and also to a Moor residing at Kano named Hat-Sallah with whom he had great influence and to whose care he confided them as friends of his own and the best of Christians.[18]

16. Ibid, pp. 436-7.
17. Ibid, p. 451.
18. Ibid, p. 460.

So sudden was El-Kanemi's *volte face* that we are entitled to speculate about his motives. In view of the hostility of his neighbours, his overriding concern was doubtless to ingratiate himself with the Pasha by giving prompt and willing effect to his wishes. He may also have realised however that Oudney was not exaggerating when he said that he would die if he were forced to stay in Kuka[19] and have appreciated that, if he did die after having several times being refused permission to go to Hausaland, he himself might be held responsible by the Pasha for his death. In short, after receiving the Pasha's letter, El-Kanemi had very strong reasons for packing Oudney off to Hausaland without delay and this, in fact, is exactly what he proceeded to do. The point is worth emphasizing because in the past some superficial historical judgements have been based upon this episode and the supposed liberality of El-Kanemi in allowing Oudney to travel from Bornu to Hausaland has been contrasted with Sultan Bello's subsequent refusal to allow Clapperton to travel from Hausaland to Bornu.

Oudney, accompanied by Clapperton, with whom incidentally he seems to have maintained closer relations than with Denham, left Kuka on December 14 in a caravan bound for Kano, the eighth that had taken the road for Hausaland since the explorers' arrival nine months earlier. They set out about noon and were escorted for the first few miles of their journey by Denham, the Arab merchants and many of the principal men of the town. Even Haj Ali Bu-Khalum, with whom they had had such serious quarrels in the past, turned out for the occasion.

None of Oudney's companions believed that he would survive the journey and when Denham said good-bye he cannot have expected to see him again. For over a month he remained without news of him and then on 23 January he received a brief, undated note in which Oudney admitted to being ill. "The acknowledgement of being weak and helpless" Denham wrote afterwards "assured me that he [Oudney] really was so, for during the whole of his long sufferings a complaint had scarcely ever escaped his lips."[20] In fact, Oudney was already dead, having succumbed on the road before even reaching Kano.[21]

Oudney remains a shadowy, diffident figure. His choice as leader of the expedition seems to have been made in a haphazard way. As a

19. Ibid, p. 471.
20. Ibid, pp. 470-1.
21. There is some evidence that Dr. Oudney died near the town of Madaci in Hadejia Emirate. See A.C.C. Hastings *The Voyage of the Dayspring*. (John Lane, Bodley Head Ltd, London 1926) Page 7.

scientist he was highly recommended by Professor Jameson to Mr. Barrow of the Africa Association, who in turn was instrumental in having him appointed.[22] But, as a man, his physical stamina was suspect from the start and, as a leader, his qualifications were apparently not examined at all. In some ways he seems to have been cast in the same sort of mould as another explorer-scientist, Wilson of the Antarctic and to have been a man of sterling character rather than strong personality. Being of humbler origins than Denham and Clapperton and having no advantage over them in years or experience, it was difficult for him to assert his leadership and it is clear that he was not equipped by temperament to do so. But, whatever his shortcomings as a leader, the fortitude with which he bore his sufferings and the resolution with which he held on until he dropped, helped to perpetuate the great tradition handed down by his fellow countryman, Mungo Park.

A week after the departure of Oudney and Clapperton for Hausaland, when Denham was feeling depressed at the loss of their company, he received unexpected news.

> December 21. To my inexpressible delight, Karouash came with intelligence that a small caravan had arrived at Wudi from Murzuk, that an Englishman accompanied them, and that this was followed by another, a more numerous one, which they had quitted at Zau.
>
> The following was a day of great anxiety and on the 23rd instant, very soon after daylight, I was overjoyed at seeing, instead of Mr. Tyrwhitt, whose bodily infirmities made me always consider his joining me doubtful, a robust, healthy-looking young man, with a double-barrelled gun slung at his back. When he presented himself at the door of my hut, his very countenance was an irresistible letter of introduction, and I opened the packages which were to account for his appearance with considerable eagerness. Mr. Tyrwhitt, I found, had been prevented by sickness from profiting by the consul's recommendation and, on application being made to the governor of Malta for a substitute, Mr. Toole, an ensign in the 80th regiment, had volunteered to join me and left Malta at twenty hours' notice. He had made the long, dangerous, and difficult journey from Tripoli to Bornu in the short space of three months and fourteen days, having left that place on the 6th of September, and overcoming all obstacles by perseverence and resolution, both at Murzuk and in the Tubu country, had arrived here with only the loss of five camels.

22. See John Barrow's 'Prefatory Notice' at pp. 203-6 in vol. II of Denham and Clapperton's *Narrative*.

> The arrival of this caravan with Mr. Toole, and the supplies which he brought, gave a most favourable turn to my situation at Kuka. I had now money, health, and a desirable companion. Even an attack might lead to our pursuing an enemy and, by that means, getting out of the Sheikh's dominions.... as, on the least favourable opportunity offering, I had determined to make a start in one direction or another. At one time, indeed, Pandora's sealed casket seemed to have burst over our heads—strife, war, famine, falsehood, and a thousand other evils, surrounded us. Still, however, hope remained in the box....[22]

From Denham's narrative one gets the impression that he had never wholly succeeded in penetrating the close circle between Oudney and Clapperton, fellow Scots and naval officers who had been friends before ever he had appeared upon the scene and that for this reason alone he was particularly glad to welcome a new companion who was not separated from him, as Hillman must have been, by barriers of class and education. Unfortunately however, though he was not disappointed in the quality of this companionship, he was not destined to enjoy it for very long.

23. Ibid, I. pp. 461-2.

Excursion To Logone
And The Death Of Toole

As soon as El-Kanemi became certain that the Pasha was not planning to attack him, he was able to utilise the defensive measures he had already taken as the basis for offensive plans against his eastern neighbours.

In Kanem some of the Shuwa Arabs, encouraged no doubt by the Sultan of Wadai and counting on his active support, were in rebellion against the Sheikh's authority. Their open challenge had in turn caused unrest and disaffection among the native Kanembu. For El-Kanemi, who had always regarded the Kanembu as the staunchest of his adherents, this was a serious development and he reacted vigorously. The offending chiefs were summoned to Kuka where, after they had been given opportunity of defending themselves, three of the ring-leaders were put to death by being taken into the courtyard of the Palace and strangled. 'On these occasions' Denham noted 'the Sheikh merely moves his finger which is the signal for immediate execution'.[1] Not content with making these examples, El-Kanemi pressed on with his plans for sending a military force to Kanem to subdue the rebellious Shuwas. This duly left Kuka early in December.

The Kanem expedition, however, was the smaller of the two enterprises that El-Kanemi was now planning. His main target was Baghirmi but his preparations seem to have been rather leisurely, probably because

---

1. Denham, I, p. 453 and 453n.

he was temporarily preoccupied with the trouble in Kanem, and in the event he allowed the Baghirmis to get their blow in first. Towards the end of November they crossed the River Shari in force and occupied the district of Logone. Moreover, by blandishments or threats, they induced the people to declare for them. For a time it was feared in Kuka that, as soon as the level of the other rivers fell, they would use the Logone bridgehead for launching an invasion of Bornu proper. In January, however, a counter-attack by the Kanuri did enough damage and created enough alarm to cause the Baghirmis to retire again behind the Shari. The people of Logone, thus left in the lurch, thought it advisable to buy their way back into the Sheikh's favour. This they did by hurriedly sending a deputation to wait on him with a congratulatory address and a present of 60 slaves and 300 bullocks.[2]

Denham, who had long wished to visit this part of the country, decided that his opportunity had now arrived. El-Kanemi, when approached, not only gave permission for the expedition but provided a mount for Toole whose own horses, like those of the other explorers, had both died within a few weeks of reaching Kuka. He also furnished a guide called Bellal but warned Denham frankly that he was going among people with whom he had but little influence.

Bellal proved to be a superior person and produced six slaves, two of them mounted, to serve as an escort. As for the explorers, they took with them only the faithful Columbus and as much baggage as two camels could carry.[3] On 23 January 1824, this little party set out from Kuka and headed south east.

They travelled first to Ngornu and from there, skirting the lake, they made their way to Ngala. This town could be described as the eastern gateway to Bornu; it had already seen one major battle and, before the end of the century was to witness two more.[4]

> The present Chief was the first friend and supporter of El-Kanemi and, twenty-five years ago when he was only a merchant, betrothed to him his daughter Miriam in marriage with a large dowery in slaves and cattle. The Chief, a most benevolent-looking

---

2. Ibid, pp. 452 and 467-8.
3. Ibid, pp. 467-70.
4. The first battle of Ngala was the one in which Sultan Dunama Lefiami was killed in 1817. The second, at this point of the narrative, was about to take place and will be described later. The third still lay far in the future and did not come until Rabeh invaded Bornu in 1893.

old black, received us with great kindness and hospitality and, as soon as we were lodged in the house of the chief minister, bowls of milk, rice, flour, and honey were brought to us. An abundance of eatables were also sent in the evening and the next morning a very fine fat sheep.

Miriam, now the divorced wife of the Sheikh El-Kanemi, was residing at Ngala and I requested permission to visit her. Her father had built for her a house in which she constantly resided and her establishment exceeded sixty persons. She was a very handsome, beautifully formed negress of about thirty-five and had imbibed much of that softness of manner which is so extremely prepossessing in the Sheikh. Seated on an earthen throne covered with a Turkey carpet, and surrounded by twenty of her favourite slaves—all dressed alike in fine white shirts which reached to their feet—their neck, ears, and noses thickly ornamented with coral—she held her audience with very considerable grace, while four eunuchs guarded the entrance and a negro dwarf, who measured three feet all but an inch, the keeper of her keys, sat before her with the insignia of office on his shoulder, richly dressed in Hausa gowns.

This little person afforded us a subject of conversation and much laughter. Miriam inquired whether we had such little fellows in my country and, when I answered in the affirmative, she said: 'What are they good for? Do they ever have children?'

I answered: 'Yes, that we had instances of their being fathers to tall and proper men'.

'Oh, wonderful!' she replied, 'I thought so. They must be better than this dog of mine, for I have given him eight of my handsomest and youngest slaves, but it is all to no purpose. I would give a hundred bullocks and twenty slaves to the woman who would bear this wretch a child'. The wretch, and an ugly wretch he was, shook his large head, grinned, and slobbered copiously from his extensive mouth, at this flattering proof of his mistress's partiality.[5]

After spending only one night in Ngala the explorers moved on again and two or three days later reached the Shari at a town called Chawi. At the time Denham estimated that the river was fully half a mile wide but on a subsequent visit he measured it and found the distance to be only 650 yards. The speed of the current he put at two or three knots. The Chief of the town received the explorers with great deference and, in accordance with instructions from the Sheikh, conveyed to him by Bellal, readily agreed to arrange canoes to take them downstream to the lake.

5. Ibid, II, pp. 1-3.

After a few days rest, they set off in a flotilla of eight canoes, accompanied by the Chief of Chawi, and eight hours paddling brought them to the large island lying at the mouth of the river. The country through which they passed was only sparsely populated, for the banks of the river were thickly clothed with stately trees standing in dense undergrowth and hung with creepers, and they noticed no villages. Game, on the other hand, was abundant and they saw hippopotamuses in the water, crocodiles up to fifteen feet in length on the sand banks, and on land bush-cow and antelope. They even shot an iguana, asleep in the branches of a tamarind, and later, on the island, counted no fewer than thirty porcupines. Water fowl were to be seen everywhere in immense numbers and of insects there were of course myriads, both by night and day.

They camped on the island, which was uninhabited, and for their supper had an excellent meal of fish, ducks and venison, all grilled or roasted round the fire. So great was the dread of the Buduma, the pirates of the lake, that two of the canoes kept guard all night but in the event they were not attacked or molested. Next morning, hoping to sail right round the island, they made an early start and took the north-west passage towards the lake.

> We passed several marshy, floating islands covered with rushes, high grass, and papyrus, apparently dividing the water into different streams, when we found ourselves in that sea of fresh water, the Chad, . . . into which the Shari empties itself. It was my intention to have proceeded quite round the island to the east and to have returned by the other branch but, after making about two miles in the open lake, a heavy swell from the northeast caused so much water to come into the canoes, and so much labour to the men, that we gave up that idea.
>
> The nearest Buduma island is said to be three days' voyage on the open lake from the mouth of the river, in a north-east direction, say ninety miles, during two of which these canoes lose sight of land. With an excellent telescope I could discern nothing but the waste of waters to the north or east. The Budumas are a wild and independent people, who carry on a piratical war with all their neighbours: they send out fleets of sixty or one hundred canoes and they are reported as terrible unbelievers.
>
> We now commenced our return and a laborious business it was, rowing or paddling against the stream. We had endured two days of burning heat and exposure to the sun and a night of watchfulness and torture from the insects. Added to this, we had lived entirely on

Indian corn, boiled in the canoes during the day. We were also constantly ankle deep in water, from the leaking of the canoes.[6]

Successful though this excursion had been, Denham was clearly not sorry to get back to Chawi. The next places that the explorers wished to visit were Kusseri and Logone. As they both lay up-stream from Chawi, it would have been possible to reach them by water if the Baghirmi town of Gulfei had not barred the way. As it was, to avoid Gulfei, they had to make a wide detour to the west. Setting out from Chawi on February 8, therefore, they made their way overland through Wulki and Afade and reached Kusseri on the fifth day. The track, which was little used, took them alternately through dense bush and extensive swamps. The going was arduous, now with deep fords to be crossed, now with the path so narrow and overhung with thorn bushes that the baggage became dislodged from the camels' backs. On the march the travellers were plagued by flies and sometimes bees, while at night they were tormented by mosquitoes. Denham, whose constitution must have been unusually strong, was able to withstand these rigours but Toole, who though fresher was less seasoned, now began to show disturbing signs of illness and was unable to stomach the coarse diet of fish and paste which was all that the travellers had lately been able to procure. Denham hoped, however, that a few days in Kusseri would restore his health and spirits.

*   *   *

Kusseri proved to be a large town situationed on the Logone near its confluence with the Shari. Its walls extended to the very banks of the river and had two water gates. Unfortunately its situation in a low-lying district which was always extensively flooded in the rainy season, gave it a very unhealthy climate.

> During several hours in the day the inhabitants themselves dare not move out on account of the flies and bees. The formation of the houses, which are literally one cell within another, five or six in number, excited my surprise, which was not a little increased when I found that they were built expressly as a retreat from the attacks of these insects. Still I was incredulous until one of our people, who had carelessly gone out, returned with his eyes and head in such a state that he was extremely ill for three days.

6. Ibid, pp. 7-8.

Kusseri is a strong walled town, ruled by an independent Chief named Zarmawa who has twice been in rebellion against the Sheikh. Bellal was obliged to take off his red cap and turban and enter the presence with his head and feet bare—a ceremony which had previously been dispensed with on our journey. The Chief merely peeped at us through a latice-work of bamboo but inquired particularly why I turned my face towards him as I sat. I, of course, replied that turning my back would be, in my country, a gross afront, at which he laughed heartily. We had a separate letter to this prince from the Sheikh: he seemed, however, to pay but little respect to it, or the bearer, Bellal, while to me he was most attentive. We had ten dishes of fish and paste, which regaled our attendants sumptuously, and one of his own household took up his residence at our huts.

Salt is here scarcely known and therefore not eaten with any of their meals. Out of the small stock I had brought the townspeople were always begging little lumps, which they put into their mouths and suck with as much satisfaction as if it had been barley-sugar.

I gave the Chief in the morning a parcel of beads, two pairs of scissors, a knife, two kerchiefs, and a turban, on which he said 'we were a great people, a race of sultans, and would bring good fortune to his dominions'.

I must not omit to mention a visit which I received from the Chief's sister. She had been some time divorced from her husband who had gone over to the Baghirmis. The officer in attendance on us announced her with great secrecy about ten o'clock at night. For the only light in our hut we were indebted to the pale moonbeams which shone through the doorway, as we had neither candles nor lamp and I had been some time fast asleep when she arrived. Her attendants, three in number, waited for her at the entrance, while she advanced and sat herself down beside my mat. She talked away at a great rate, in a sort of whisper, often pointing to my sick friend, who was at the further end of the hut, and did not appear at all to wish for any reply. After remaining nearly half an hour, and feeling and rubbing my hands, face and head, which she uncovered by taking off my cap and turban, she took her leave, apparently much gratified by her visit.[7]

In describing Kusseri's climate Denham noted that the woods were not cleared and concluded, in accordance with the beliefs of the day, that the wind consequently lacked the power to disperse the foul exhalations that arose from the unwholesome swamps. Though his premises were faulty, his general conclusion that the place was not one in which a man as sick

---

7. Ibid, pp. 12-15.

213 | EXCURSION TO LOGONE AND THE DEATH OF TOOLE

as Toole ought to remain was certainly correct. He was therefore faced with the most difficult decision of whether to go forward to Logone or back to Ngala. Logone was only fifteen to twenty miles away but there was no knowing whether the travellers would be welcome there or find it any more healthy than Kusseri. At Ngala they could be sure of being well received but the distance was much greater, over fifty miles. Nevertheless a return to Ngala was probably the safer course because an advance to Logone, if it turned out badly, would leave them further than ever from their base. Denham did not explain in his narrative how he weighed the pros and cons and what factors led him to his decision. He doubtless realised that, if he went back, even to Ngala, it was improbable that he would ever see Logone and this consideration may well have influenced him, perhaps subconsciously. Whatever his motive, it can be argued that, with his colleague seriously ill, he should have played safe and must bear some responsibility for the unhappy consequence of choosing the more hazardous course. In his defence, however, let it be added that, if there had been no men like him ready to take such risks, the exploration of Africa would hardly have been accomplished at all.

Having decided to advance, the travellers soon ran into difficulties.

> We moved on towards Logone the next morning. We could advance, however, but a few miles. Mr. Toole's sufferings were most acute: he twice fainted and we lifted him on and off his horse like an infant, so helpless had he become.
>
> What added also to our distress was that from this time, until the evening of the 16th the Shuwa Arabs who occupy the frontier of the Logone country refused to allow us to pass until the Chief had been consulted and a number of his questions answered as to the purpose of our visit. We were now close to the river and, notwithstanding the heat, the only means we had of defending either ourselves or our animals from the torture of the millions of insects that beset us was by lighting fires at the entrance of our tent and constantly supplying them with weeds and wet straw: the thick suffocating smoke arising from this description of fire afforded us temporary relief.[8]

After a most uncomfortable delay, the explorers were at last admitted to Logone.

> We entered the town by the western gate which leads to the principal street: it is as wide as Pall Mall and has large dwellings on each side built with great uniformity, each having a court-yard in

8. Ibid, pp. 15-16.

front, surrounded by walls, and a handsome entrance with a strong door hasped with iron. A number of inhabitants were seated at their doors for the purpose of seeing us enter, with their slaves ranged behind them. At first they took but little notice of us. Indeed our appearance could not have been very imposing: one of our party was laid on a camel and another supported on his horse by two persons, who walked on each side of him, while he raved most incoherently from the violence of the fever by which he was consumed.... We were at length conducted to our habitation, which consisted of four separate huts, well built, within an outer wall, with a large entrance hall for our servants. In the most retired and quiet spot I spread the mat and pillow of my patient who was in a sad state of exhaustion and irritation.

The next morning I was sent for to appear before the Chief. Ten immense negroes, of high birth, most of them grey-bearded, bare-headed and carrying large clubs, preceded me through the streets, and I was received with considerable ceremony. After passing through several dark rooms, I was conducted to a large square court where some hundred persons were assembled, and all seated on the ground. In the middle was a vacant space to which they led me, and I was desired to sit down also. Two slaves in striped cotton gowns who were fanning the air through the lattice-work of cane, pointed out the retirement of the Chief. On a signal this shade was removed and something alive was discovered on a carpet, wrapped up in silk gowns, with the head enveloped in shawls and nothing but the eyes visible. The whole court prostrated themselves and poured sand on their heads, while eight trumpets and as many horns blew a loud and very harsh-sounding salute.

My present, a red bornous, a striped cotton caftan, a turban, two knives, two pairs of scissors, and a pair of red trousers, was laid before him. He again whispered a welcome, for it is considered so extremely ill-bred in a Logone gentlemen to speak out, that it is with difficulty you can catch the sound of their voices.

He examined me very minutely and then the shade was again drawn. I begged for permission to embark on the Shari and was told he would consider of it. He particularly inquired if I wished to purchase handsome female slaves, which I assured him I did not, 'because' said he 'if you do, go no farther: I have some hundreds, and will sell them to you as cheap as any one'.[9]

Like Kusseri, Logone occupied an uncomfortable position between Baghirmi and Bornu, separated from the one by the Shari and Logone

9. Ibid, pp. 16-18.

215 | EXCURSION TO LOGONE AND THE DEATH OF TOOLE

Rivers and yet too remote from the other's centre of power to enjoy adequate protection. To avoid being crushed between the upper and the nether millstone, its mixed population pursued a policy not far removed from neutrality, acknowledging Bornu's suzerainty in peace but taking care not to provoke Baghirmi's displeasure in war.[10] Though he spent only a short time there, Denham painted a most interesting picture of the place and its sophisticated people.

> Logone has fifteen thousand inhabitants at least. They speak a language nearly Baghirmi. The Shuwas are all round them, and to them they are indebted for the plentiful supply of bullocks, milk, and fat with which the market abounds. These necessaries are paid for by gowns and blue cotton in stripes which the Logone people make and dye to a very beautiful colour. They have also a metal currency, ... the first I had seen in the Sudan. It consists of thin plates of iron, something in the shape of the tip with which they shoe race-horses: these are made into parcels of ten and twelve, according to the weight, and thirty of these parcels are equal in value to ten rottola or a dollar.
>
> The money market, however, has its fluctuations: the value of this 'circulating medium' is settled by proclamation at the commencement of the weekly market, every Wednesday, and speculations are made, by the bulls and bears, according to their belief of its rise or fall. Previous to the Chief's receiving tribute or duty on bullocks or indigo, the chief minister generally proclaims the currency to be below par; while, on the contrary, when he has purchases to make for his household preparatory to one of their feasts, the value of the metal is invariably increased. The proclamation of the value of the metal always excites an amazing disturbance, as if some were losers and some gainers by the variation.[11]
>
> The inhabitants of Logone of both sexes are industrious and labour at the loom more regularly than in any part of the Sheikh's dominions. Almost every house has its rude machinery for weaving, and the finer and closer linen is here produced; the width, however, is invariably the same as the Bornu strips, not exceeding six or seven inches. In one house I saw five looms at work: the free people usually perform this labour, while the female slaves prepare the cotton and give it the deep blue dye, so esteemed amongst them, by their incomparable indigo. The glazing is also another and very important part of their manufacture: the linen which, previous to

10. Ibid, pp. 23 and 32.
11. Ibid, pp. 18-20.

its being dyed, is generally either made up into gowns, or large shirts, or into lengths of fifteen or sixteen yards, . . . is after three steepings, and as many exposures to the sun, laid in a damp state on the trunks of large trees, cut to a flat surface for the purpose, and is then beaten with a wooden mallet, being at the same time occasionally sprinkled with cold water and powdered antimony. By this means the most glossy appearance is produced: the constant hammering attending this process during the whole day really sounds like the busy hum of industry and occupation.[12]

They are a much handsomer race than the Bornuese, and far more intelligent—the women particularly so—and they possess a superior carriage and manner to any negro nation I had seen. The ladies of the principal persons of the country visited me, accompanied by one or more female slaves. They examined everything, even to the pockets of my trousers, and more inquisitive ladies I never saw in any country. They begged for everything and nearly all attempted to steal something; when found out, they only laughed heartily, clapped their hands together, and exclaimed: 'Why, how sharp he is! Only think! Why, he caught us!' If they may be said to excel my Bornu friends in accomplishments, they fall far behind them in modesty. To give them their due they are the cleverest and the most immoral race I had met with in the Black country.

I was not a little surprised the next day at hearing that there were two Chiefs, father and son, both at the head of strong parties and both equally fearing and hating each other, that I had seen the son, but that it was absolutely necessary to give the elder at least as much as I had given the younger one. I remonstrated but Bellal assured me that his slaves were the most expert thieves in the kingdom—that no walls could stop them if the governor once gave the word 'Forage'.[13] There was no alternative so, putting ten dollars in a stocking and tying up in a French silk handkerchief two strings of coral and a few cloves with six gilt basket-buttons, I presented him with them and had the pleasure of hearing that his majesty was highly gratified by the present.

12. Ibid, pp. 31-32. In the central Sudan it was Hausaland, and particularly Kano, that was most renowned for these crafts of weaving and dyeing but it is clear from Denham's description that the people of Logone had also attained a high degree of skill. The glossy finish on the navy dye is still much prized and to this day is produced by the same laborious method described by Denham.

13. This form of oppression, under which unscrupulous chiefs extended their protection to gangs of thieves in return for a share of the booty, had been known in the Sudan for centuries. Mention of it will be found in some of the early Hausa folk-tales and late in the colonial era it was still cropping up in the reports of District Officers.

217 | EXCURSION TO LOGONE AND THE DEATH OF TOOLE

> Of the bad terms on which these rival Chiefs were, notwithstanding their consanguinity, I had pretty good proof by their both sending to me in secret for poison 'that would not lie', to use their own expression. The young Chief, as the son was called, sent me three female slaves, under fifteen years of age, as an inducement; whom I returned, explaining in pretty strong terms our abhorrence of such proceedings, for which I had the satisfaction of hearing myself, and all my countrymen, pronounced fools a hundred times over.[14]

On their third day in Logone, as Toole's condition had improved, Denham decided to make an excursion to the south.

> The river here is not more than 400 yards in breadth. The canoes are different from those of Chawi measuring nearly fifty feet in length and being capable of carrying twenty or twenty-five persons. . . .
>
> It was near noon, when we had ascended but a few miles, that a canoe was seen following our track with a speed denoting some extraordinary occurrence. And, on their reaching us and reporting the cause of this haste, such confusion took place amongst my party that, out of seven canoes which accompanied me, not one remained. All made for the shore and it was with some difficulty, that we could persuade our own to return with us to Logone. We now found that the Baghirmis were again on the Medba and coming towards Logone.
>
> The Chief, on our return, sent for us, and desired the Sheikh's people to quit his dominions *instanter*. I told him that I came expressly to remain some time; that Bellal might return; but that for myself I was his subject and must remain under his protection, added to which I had a sick friend and a sick servant and that I could not move. This, however, he would not hear of. Bellal was desired to quit Logone and to take all of us with him. 'More than half my people are Baghirmi' said the Chief. 'I have no protection to give—go, go, while you can'.
>
> Obliged to obey, I raised my suffering friend who was unable to assist himself in any way. We set him on a horse and, with no provisions but a sack of parched corn which the Chief gave us, at four o'clock the same day we quitted the walls, whereupon the three gates were shut upon us, one after the other, with great satisfaction, by an immense crowd of people.[15]

* * *

14. Ibid, pp. 20-22.
15. Ibid, pp. 22-23.

Denham now decided to make for Ngala, sixty-five miles away over the difficult terrain of swamp and bush that the party had already traversed. With the ever-present risk of being ambushed or captured by the Baghirmi, with Toole so weak that he could do nothing to help himself even when he was conscious and not sunk in the coma which possessed him for much of the time and with no proper food or shelter, the journey proved to be a terrible ordeal. On the first day, February 19, they marched far into the night and then stopped at some deserted cattle sheds. Denham made Toole as comfortable as possible and then sat up, keeping watch. During the next two days they pressed on, with little rest or food, but even so, after two and a half days of hard travelling, they were no further forward than Tilli and had covered only about half the distance to Ngala.

In these circumstances it was natural that Bellal should have chafed at the delay imposed by Toole's weakness and have been impatient to extricate himself of his charges from the exposed and dangerous situation in which they found themselves. If they were captured by the Baghirmis, the Europeans might have been spared but he and his slaves could have expected nothing but death or enslavement. With these thoughts in their minds, he and his people set a pace which Toole was quite unable to match. Denham, therefore, had to act as a link between the van and the rear of his party, restraining the one and urging on the other. In this way, travelling through the bush by night, they reached a river.

> Bellal proceeded to search for the ford preparatory to crossing the stream. To this I decidedly objected until our companions and baggage came up, knowing that our doing so must depend on the state of my patient. He made various objections but, as I dismounted and began gathering wood for a signal fire, he gave up the point. They answered immediately the glare of the flame and curling smoke by a shot and I proceeded in the direction of the sound for the purpose of conducting them to the spot we had rested on. A second and a third shot, however, were necessary before we could meet, so intricate were the paths. I found Mr. Toole perfectly senseless and we laid him on a bed of unripe indigo, near our fire, wrapped up in his blanket, while a little warm tea was prepared for him, and he soon after fell into a sound sleep.
>
> Bellal now recommenced searching for the ford, which I allowed him to do, fully determined, however, not to disturb my companion until morning unless the danger of our situation should increase. He

219 | EXCURSION TO LOGONE AND THE DEATH OF TOOLE

returned soon after midnight and pronounced the river not fordable, either above or below the town.[16]

Bellal, it seems, now convinced Denham that it was folly to remain in a place from which there was no escape towards the west. They therefore agreed to get on the move again at once and look for another ford further to the north. When Toole was woken from his sleep however, he protested that he was unable to go any further.

> Only once did he declare his incapability to proceed and refused to be lashed on the camel. But, when I sat down on the ground beside him and Bellal and the Sheikh's people prepared to leave us, he cried out: 'No! No! Heed me not: tie me on once more, but pray gently: you will not leave me alone and I shall [not] be the cause of others falling into unnecessary peril.'[17]

It is safe to say that Bellal, in pretending to be ready to abandon his two charges, was only bluffing in order to force their hand. He knew perfectly well, as indeed he told Denham, that if he allowed anything to happen to them he could never face the Sheikh again and would therefore lose his family, his home and all his possessions. Besides, he was a kindhearted man, as well as a brave one, and he felt enough concern for Toole to shed tears, on one occasion, at seeing him brought so low.[18]

After this incident, they pressed on at their best speed, still heading north-west.

> We passed the walls of Afade soon after daylight, from whence the people were flying in all directions, and rested for the night at Irun, after fording the river at Solon. Here the natives had determined on making a stand and three of the four gates were built up, while the fourth had only space sufficient left for a man to force himself through. The chief sent to invite us to remain and furnished us with milk and fresh fish, as well as with corn for our half-famished animals. We raised a tent over Mr. Toole where he lay on the ground and twice, during the night, gave him rice and tea, after which, to my inexpressible delight, he slept. On the following day, February 23, we reached Ngala, a place of comparative safety, and where we were sure of protection.... We took up our old quarters, at the house of the Chief minister, and Mr. Toole, on being told

16. Ibid, pp. 24-25.
17. Ibid, pp. 27-28.
18. Ibid, p. 25.

where he was, exclaimed: 'Thank God! Then I shall not die!' And so much better was he, for the two following days, that I had great hopes for his recovery.[19]

But later Toole himself seemed to know that he would not recover and to be reconciled to his fate.

> On the day previous to that of his death, when I mentioned to him his return to Kuka, he smiled, shook his head, and said: 'No! No!' Nearly his last words were expressive of hopes that, through Earl Bathurst's recommendation, his next brother might succeed to the ensigncy in the 80th regiment which would became vacant in the event of his death....[20]

Toole's premonition of his approaching end proved to be correct.

> About four o'clock, however, on the morning of the 26th of February, those hopes were at an end. A cold shivering had seized him and his extremeties were like ice. I gave him both tea and rice-water. There was but little alteration in him until just before noon when, without a struggle or a groan, he expired, completely worn out and exhausted.
>
> The same afternoon, just as the sun was sinking below the horizon, I followed his remains to their last resting-place, a deep grave, which six of the Chief of Ngala's slaves had prepared, under my direction, to the north-west of the town, overhung by a clump of mimosa in full blossom. The chief minister attended the procession with his staff of office and a silent prayer, breathed over all that remained of my departed friend, was the best funeral service circumstances allowed me to perform. After raising over the grave a pile of thorns and branches of the prickly mimosa, several feet high, as a protection against the flocks of hyenas, who nightly infest the burying-places in this country, I returned to the town.[21]

After the death of Toole, Denham decided to return at once to Kuka. With the Baghirmis scouring all the country round Ngala, no other course was really open to him. So next day he set out with his escort and on March 1 reached Ngornu where he found the Sheikh busy assembling an army with which to counter-attack the invaders. The people were in a state of great alarm, seeming to doubt the issue of the coming contest,

---

19. Ibid, pp. 25-29.
20. Ibid, pp. 28-29. Lord Bathurst duly arranged for the brother to succeed to the vacancy.
21. Ibid, pp. 26-27.

221 | EXCURSION TO LOGONE AND THE DEATH OF TOOLE

but El-Kanemi was composed enough to show his solicitude over Toole's death and send a message back to the capital saying that everything Denham desired was to be done for him.

On the following day Denham rode on to Kuka, to be met with the news of Oudney's death. At this, he too went down with fever.

XVI

Expedition To Kanem

Denham seems to have spent the whole of March recovering in Kuka from the physical exhaustion of his journey, the mental shock of Toole's death and the fever which now laid him low.

Meanwhile El-Kanemi and his army remained in the field near Ngala, guarding the eastern gateway into Bornu. The war between the Kanuri and the Baghirmis had now been going on intermittently for eight years. In the course of it the Baghirmis had been repeatedly defeated and had suffered some shattering reverses, notably when the Sultan of Murzuk had reinforced the Bornu army. In fact from first to last, according to the information given to Denham, they had lost 30,000 prisoners into slavery besides many towns destroyed and enormous quantities of booty carried away.[1] Nevertheless, all along, they had shown the most extraordinary resilience and now they were once more strong enough to take the offensive.

For El-Kanemi the war had a particularly bitter flavour because it had already cost the life of his eldest son. As for the courtiers and the people of the capital, the presence of the Baghirmi army on the eastern border made this a most anxious time: they knew that if the Sheikh were defeated, the enemy would be upon them and the town would fall. Understandably, therefore, the mood was one of great nervousness. One evening, for example, the unexpected reappearance of a man who was

1. Denham, II, p. 182.

EXPEDITION TO KANEM

thought to have been killed on an earlier expedition caused a commotion in his compound which almost led on to a general panic.

> The whole town was in commotion and the cries of 'the enemy! the enemy!' were re-echoed from a thousand voices. It happened just at twilight and my negro, Barka, dropping the mess of rice and fat which was intended for our supper, came running with his gun in his hand, and we were all for a few minutes in a sad state of agitation. When we had ascertained the cause of this alarm, and were a little tranquillized, the rice was thought of; monkeys, bloodhounds, and parrots had, however, feasted at their ease in the general confusion, and we went supperless to bed. We were able to muster about seven guns and three pair of pistols, and had plenty of powder and ball. As our huts were enclosed within a wall, we had determined on defending ourselves to the last. Our determination was no sooner known than I had messages from the wives of all the Sheikh's chiefs who were my friends saying that they should fly to me for protection, if the Baghirmis came, as I had guns and plenty of powder. So I might have had as numerous, and almost as formidable, an army as the Sheikh himself for, from what I had seen of both sexes in Bornu, I believe in my heart the women would have fought quite as well as their husbands.[2]

In the course of the month the Baghirmis came on several times and offered battle, but each time El-Kanemi refused, either because his muster was incomplete or because the tactical situation was unfavourable. At length however, when he judged that the right moment had come, he took up the challenge.

> It is said that, on the morning of the battle, the Sheikh appeared at the door of his tent, with the English double-barrelled gun in his hand and his English sword slung over his shoulders, clothed in the dress of a simple trooper, saying it was his intention to fight on foot, at the head of his Kanembu; that he expected all the Arabs to follow his example and encourage the slaves who were but young in the use of the firelock; that if it pleased God to grant their enemies victory, flight was out of the question: they had nothing left but to die before their wives and children were torn from them and escape so appalling a sight.[3]

The battle was fought on 28 March 1824 and, although Denham was not present at it, he has left us a good account of it.

2. Ibid, pp. 36-7.
3. Ibid, p. 39.

The Baghirmis became bold in consequence of the Sheikh's apparent unwillingness to fight and they at length ventured to attack him in the plain to the south-east of Ngala, on the edge of which he had halted. The caravan, which had departed for Hausaland, had deprived him of at least thirty of his Arabs. The few that remained, with some forty Musgau slaves who had been trained to the firelock, being his great dependence, he placed them on his flanks. No sooner had the Baghirmis cleared the wood than the Sheikh, hoisting his green flag in the centre and surrounded by his Kanembu spearmen, moved rapidly on, the two guns in front, which Hillman had mounted, with the Arabs and musketeers right and left of them.

The Baghirmis, also came on with great coolness, in a solid mass five thousand strong, with two hundred chiefs at their head. They made directly for the centre, where the Sheikh had raised the standard of the Prophet, but were repulsed by a discharge from his artillery. They now fell upon Barka Gana's flank which was attacked with such determined bravery that all except himself and a chosen band gave way. Here fell my friend and preserver Marami who, while in the act of drawing a spear from the body of one of their chiefs, received a thrust in his own which went quite through him.

The Bornuese horse who, on occasions of this kind when the road is opened for them, are most active, now took up the pursuit of the routed Baghirmis. The Arabs also mounted and joined them and, of the two hundred chiefs of Baghirmi, one only is said to have escaped alive. Seven sons of the Sultan were amongst the killed, and seventeen hundred of less note, whilst great numbers were put to death by the people of the towns to which they fled who now, as if by magic, all became the staunch friends of the Sheikh. The water of the little stream Gambaru, near which the battle was fought, also lent its aid in destroying these invaders and many were drowned in attempting its passage. The chiefs quitted their horses and their cumbersome armour on arriving at the river and, rushing into the water, pushed their retreat.

Here it was the Kanembu spearmen who were so destructive: they pursued closely their enemies, naked and most active. They were now more than a match for them: this stream is said to have been red with blood. 'The guns! The guns! Oh, wonderful! How they made the dogs skip! Oh, the guns!' were words in everybody's mouth. My friend the Sheikh, however, thought there was a little too much of this for, on the second day, he said: 'True, the guns are wonderful. Tis true—but I lifted my hands and said: *Sidi absolam, sidi abdel garda!* And from that moment the victory was yours. . . .'[4]

The plunder was said to have amounted to 480 horses and nearly 200 women, with two eunuchs and the baggage of the princes which was carried on bullocks and asses. Fifty of their women were *sirias* of great beauty (slaves worthy of being admitted into the seraglio) and these were all given up to the Sheikh.[5]

Among the prisoners captured was one of the leading Baghirmi champions. Denham's account of his execution reveals the superstitious awe in which such men were held once they had established their reputations in the very personal style of fighting that was still the rule.

> Dummutum, a very celebrated chief who put whole squadrons to flight with his single arm, was . . . taken prisoner by Kachalla Mustafa, a Kanemma leader. He had twice fought hand to hand with the Sheikh and once, on a retreat, had seized him from behind by the neck. The Sheikh on this occasion extricated himself by firing a pistol at him over his own shoulder. Mustafa would not kill him, but brought him bound to the Sheikh's feet.
>
> 'Ah! Ah!' said the Sheikh. 'You are humbled now, to what you were when last we met.'
>
> 'Do I look so?' replied the prisoner. 'Curse on my looks! Could you see my heart, it is as great as ever!'
>
> 'Where did I wound you last year?' said the Sheikh.
>
> 'Here!' said he, showing his right hand with the thumb and forefinger blown off.
>
> 'You have done me much injury' said the Sheikh. 'More than any of the chiefs of Baghirmi.' 'I swore to fight against you' said the negro. 'Would you have me break my oath? Give me death! It is my due, if you dare to strike!'
>
> 'Serve me' replied the Sheikh 'and you are free!'
>
> Dummutum laughed contemptuously and desired he might be killed, and by the Sheikh's own hand. This was of course denied him and, on the signal being given, he was dragged into an inner court, when he braved and defied his executioners. To this day they believe he was enchanted: neither spears nor daggers could penetrate his flesh and two pistols are said to have missed fire when presented at him. All this was reported to the Sheikh who, after consulting his book, said: He is charmed against iron, fire, or water; wood will kill him.' Several slaves were now ordered to despatch

4. Ibid, p. 37-9.
5. Ibid, p. 40.

him with their clubs. When he saw them approach he exclaimed: 'Now death is come upon me!'

In Kuka the victory was celebrated with uninhibited rejoicing and it was not long before the spoils began to appear in the market.

> April 4th—Nothing could exceed the joy of the people at having obtained the victory: the men walked about all day in their new gowns and the women danced, sang, and beat the drum all night. My hut was thronged with visitors, all recounting their own feats and bewailing their friends—sending the Baghirmis to the devil and asking for presents on their return, all in the same breath.
>
> I had a private interview with the Sheikh and offered him my hearty congratulations. He was as kind and as friendly as ever, talked a good deal about the signal manner in which the unbelievers had been delivered into his hands, and mentioned most feelingly the death of my poor companion, Mr. Toole, whom he was very partial to—asked if his mother and father were living and, turning to Tirab who was near him, said: 'How could they send him so far off?'[7]
>
> April 14—The rejoicing began to abate a little. The preceding market was crowded with slaves taken from the Baghirmis and they were cheap in proportion to their numbers. I saw several fine boys and girls sold for two or three bullocks—ten dollars. And a Shuwa was extremely anxious for the red cap off my head for which, with an old muslin turban, he offered me a very pretty girl, about fourteen years old.[8]

Here Denham added an illuminating note about the currency for such major transactions which was normally the bullock. A handsome slave would fetch thirty to forty bullocks, but significantly, the price of a good horse was very much higher at 100 to 150.

Soon after Dummutum's execution, news reached Kuka that another enemy chief, whose capture would have been very welcome, had been allowed to escape. This was Amanuk, the leader of the rebellious Lasala tribe of Shuwa Arabs. He was a mortal enemy of El-Kanemi who now again showed the harsh side of his character.

> In his [Amanuk's] escape after the last fight, his horse had fallen with him and some followers of the Chief of Mafate came upon him. They were about to finish him when he discovered himself

---

6. Ibid, pp. 185-6. Belief in the charm against metal, which in Hausa is known as *Maganin Karfe,* is as common in the Sudan as belief in the charm of invisibility.
7. Ibid, pp. 39-40.
8. Ibid, p. 49.

and, by a promise of one thousand bullocks, was allowed to escape, one of the men giving him a horse. This horse also knocked up previous to reaching the river and Amanuk saved himself by creeping into the warren of some wild hogs (foul disgrace to a believer) when, after remaining a night and a day, he ventured out and escaped by swimming across.

The story got to the Sheikh's ears and the Chief of Mafate was sent for. These worthies, having quarrelled in the division of the spoil, one of them betrayed the rest and all of them were hanged accordingly, even he who informed. And the Chief, having been kept in a state of great alarm for several days, was at length released on the payment to the Sheikh of twenty bullock loads of gowns, nearly one thousand dollars, for having such people in his kingdom.[9]

* * *

By this time Clapperton was in Sokoto, but Denham had no news of him and did not even know for certain that he was still alive. His thoughts therefore turned again to Wadai and the possibility of making his way there and then going on to Egypt.

I determined to see and talk to the Sheikh on the subject of an eastern journey. 'It is not in my power to send you to the eastward' said he 'or you should not want my assistance. You have seen enough yourself of the dispositions of the inhabitants of the countries towards me, and their power, to know that this is true. It has pleased God to grant me a victory now which may lead to quieter times. Even the pilgrims have not for years gone by Lake Fittri to the pilgrimage. I am as anxious as you are, and with more reason, to open a road with Egypt from hence. I cannot, nor can my people, now go to Mecca without passing through the Pasha of Tripoli's territories and there are reasons which make that disagreeable. Why not try it from Egypt, where you have many friends, and return from this way by Fezzan? That would be easier.' The Sheikh has a most singular manner of delivery and I scarcely ever met with any person who expressed himself so clearly and with so few words.

I replied 'that, if I could not proceed in the way I wished, I should return and either take his advice about Egypt or wait till better times; that the King of England, upon hearing from me of his kindness, his willingness to assist us, and his friendship, would send

9. Ibid, pp. 44-5.

some other Englishmen with proofs of his good will, who would claim his assistance in getting to Sennaar.'

'God keep you from evil!' said he. 'But tell your great king to send you again: here you are known and loved by the people, and know them and their language. We all will wish to see you again—what shall we do with a stranger?'[10]

But these enquiries by Denham served to recall the suspicions which were evidently never very far from El-Kanemi's mind. He summoned Columbus to the Palace, ostensibly to urge him to become a Moslem and then proceeded to question him about Denham and his motives.

'I have sent to speak to you and I think you will tell me the truth—what is this wish of Khalil's [Denham's] to go to Egypt? I think he is my friend, and I think the English are my friends, but a man's head is always his best friend. I fear they wish to overthrow the Moslem power altogether.'

The reply of Columbus was: 'As far as I know, they want to do no such thing. They wish to see and to describe the country with its inhabitants; and if the English are the first to do so, they will pride themselves greatly in consequence.'

'And is that all?' replied the Sheikh. 'Oh, Wonderful! No one would believe it—no one does here but myself—but I do because they say so, and they are not liars.'[11]

Soon afterwards another incident occurred which, though recorded with a light touch, reminded Denham of how suspicious the common people were of Christians and of how dependent he was on the Sheikh's favour.

I was sitting outside the door of my enclosure, as was sometimes my custom of an evening, when three women, wives of the Shuwa chiefs, passed by me on their return from some wedding or wake, for they otherwise seldom go out. After some consultation, it was determined that they should approach me. 'What do you here?' said the eldest. 'You do not buy or sell? Is it true that you have no female slaves? No one to shampoo you after a south wind?'

'Quite true' said I 'for I am a stranger and far from home and alone.'

'You are an unbeliever, Khalil' said she 'and it is you Christians, with the blue eyes like the hyena, that eat the blacks whenever you can get them far enough away from their own country'.

10. Ibid, pp. 41-3.
11. Ibid, pp. 42-4.

'God deliver me from this evil glance!' said a young girl who had just joined them. 'Is that true? Why they have been here now some time and don't seem very savage: would it not be better to give him a wife or two, teach him to pray like a Moslem, and never let him return amongst his own filthy race?'

'God forbid!' said the old woman. 'God forbid!' and some words passed between them which I could not thoroughly understand. Still, however, my friend the virgin was incredulous as to my perfect unworthiness. But at length the matron losing all patience with her companion, who defended me stoutly, exclaimed aloud: 'What infatuation is this? Why, I tell you again and again, he is an uncircumcised unbeliever! Neither washes nor prays! Eats pork! And will go to hell!'

'Oh, oh! The Lord preserve us from the infernal devil!' they all exclaimed and, screaming 'Y-hy-yo! Y-hy-ho!', they all ran off in the greatest alarm.[12]

In May the fast of Ramadan came round again. With thirteen hours of daylight, and the shade temperature well over 100°, it imposed the greatest hardship on the Moslems who had to observe it[13] and was the cause of a projected expedition being abandoned. Denham recorded that, an hour or two before sunset, a dozen or more labourers could be seen round any well, lying on the ground and having buckets of water sluiced over them to revive them and relieve their sufferings. All knew that the Sheikh admitted of no excuse for breaking the fast and that the most severe penalty awaited anyone who was detected in this sin.

Soon afterwards Denham happened to be at the Palace when a man and a woman who had been adjudged guilty of the double offence of adultery and fast-breaking received their retribution.

> While I was waiting in the palace ... a punishment took place [which is] probably only equalled in severity by that of the knout in Russia and which, as is often the case in that country, caused the death of the culprit before the morning. In this instance the unfortunate man had been found, by the spies of the *Kadi*, who are always on the alert, slumbering in his amours and was now to pay the penalty of his carelessness. In the middle of the day, during Ramadan, he had been seen asleep in his hut and the wife of

---

12. Ibid, pp. 45-6.
13. As Moslems follow the lunar calendar, the fast of Ramadan falls at different seasons of the year. In the Sudan, the hardship it entails is much the greatest when it comes in March, April or May when the humidity is at its lowest and the heat of the sun at its most intense.

another man, a merchant, who had been some time absent in Hausaland, stretched by his side. They were therefore without any hesitation presumed guilty of having broken the Ramadan. He was sentenced to receive four hundred stripes and his partner half that number.[14]

Her head was first shaved, her dress and ear-rings, armlets, leglets etc., were given to the informer; she was taken up by four men, with only a cloth round her middle, by means of which she was suspended in a manner not to be described, while a powerful negro inflicted the full number of lashes she was condemned to receive. This took place inside the court-yard of the palace; she afterwards was carried home senseless.

The man received his punishment in the square, suspended in the same manner, but with eight men, instead of four, to support him. An immense whip, of one thick thong cut off from the skin of the hippopotamus, was first shown to him, which he was obliged to kiss and acknowledge the justness of his sentence. The *fatah* was then said aloud, and two powerful slaves of the Sheikh inflicted the stripes, relieving each other every thirty or forty strokes. They strike on the back while the end of the whip, which has a knob or head, winds round and falls on the breast or upper stomach: this it is that renders these punishments fatal. After the first two hundred blood flowed from him upwards and downwards and, in a few hours after he had taken the whole four hundred, he was a corpse. The *Agas, Kachallas,* and *Kadis* attend on these occasions. I was assured the man did not breath even a sigh audibly.[15]

In the middle of the fast Denham received the news, as unexpected as it was welcome, that another European had crossed the Sahara and reached northern Bornu. On the following day he rode out to meet the newcomer and found that it was Tyrwhitt whom the British Government had sent out to reinforce the expedition. Tyrwhitt, it will be remembered, had been selected for this mission in the previous year but had fallen ill and been replaced, at very short notice, by Toole. Subsequently, although news of the deaths of Oudney and Toole had not then reached him, the perspicacious Warrington in Tripoli must have concluded that a further reinforcement would be useful to the expedition. Tyrwhitt had therefore been despatched with a fresh supply of dollars and presents.

14. In Ramadan, even normal conjugal relations are forbidden during the hours of daylight. If an adulterous union is consummated during the forbidden hours, each sin is aggravated by the other.

15. Denham, II, pp. 53-4.

EXPEDITION TO KANEM

To El-Kanemi, Tyrwhitt's arrival proved to be as pleasant a surprise as it had been to Denham. With him he brought the children who, through the intrigues of Sultan Mustafa, had for so long been detained in Fezzan. Their restoration relieved him of the last of his worries in the Northern sector. In addition he received the choicest of the presents that Tyrwhitt brought with him.

> On the 22nd (of May) we delivered the presents from His Majesty in full form, consisting of two swords of very beautiful workmanship, two pairs of pistols, a dagger, and two gold watches. The delight, nay ecstasy, with which these well-selected specimens of our manufactories were received by El-Kanemi was apparent in every feature of his intelligent countenance and in the quick glances of his sparkling and penetrating eye. The dagger and the watch with the seconds movement were the articles which struck him most forcibly. And when I mentioned that, agreeably to his request, a parcel of rockets had also been forwarded, he exclaimed: 'What, besides all these riches! There are no friends like these! They are all truth and I see by the Book that, if the Prophet had lived only a short time longer, they would have been all Moslem!'[16]

In June, with the fast over, preparations for mounting the previously postponed expedition were put in hand again. The real objective was the recapture of Mao, the capital of Kanem, which the pro-Wadai faction of Kanembu and Shuwa Arabs had recently wrested from the pro-Bornu faction. To conceal this from the enemy, however, it was given out that the purpose of the expedition was the subjugation of Amanuk, the dissident Shuwa who had fought with the Baghirmis.

The explorers had heard that Lake Chad was twenty days journey in circumference. Denham was now very keen to explore its further shore and Tyrwhitt was determined to accompany him. It was therefore agreed by El-Kanemi that they should accompany the expedition and that, if it proved feasible, they should be allowed to travel right round the Lake. Instructions were given accordingly to Barka Gana, who was again in command, and he was ordered to provide an escort of up to twenty horsemen to ensure the safety of the explorers who were again entrusted to the special care of Bellal.

The expedition set out from Kuka on June 17 and reached Ngala two days later. There Denham visited Toole's grave and found it undisturbed. Next day they reached Mafate. Denham had stayed there on his previous

16. Ibid, pp. 47-8.

journey and he was now glad to move into his old quarters again where he had been made very comfortable and welcome.

> The host, however, was from home, getting his millet into the ground. His eldest wife did the honours. She also gave me a little more of her company than before and told me, very good-naturedly, that she could not when the lord was at home. Nothing, indeed, could exceed the kindness with which my hostess, who was called Ittha, did all she could to show how welcome a visitor I was. 'Birma' she said 'must stay and get in the corn but she hoped I should not miss him.'
>
> During the first day she came repeatedly with her sister Funha, a negress with an expression of countenance more pleasing than I had ever seen before, of about eighteen who, Ittha said, was most anxious to see me from what she had told her formerly. Luckily, she added, Funha had divorced her husband only two days before or she could not have had that pleasure. Ittha, with all the familiarity of an old acquaintance, uncovered my hands, arms, and breast to show her sister my extraordinary whiteness. It seemed to surprise her greatly but nevertheless I was pleased to observe that it did not appear to excite either much alarm or disgust. But what certainly seemed to both the greatest wonder was the sight and touch of my head which had just been shaved: it was literally passed from the hands of one to the other with so many remarks that some minutes elapsed ere I could be allowed to replace my turban. When, at length, they left me, Ittha exclaimed, pressing my hand with both hers, that I was fit to be a sultan and that Funha should shampoo me and try to bring on sleep, as I must be tired and fatigued by the heat of the sun.
>
> This, however, was not all. Towards evening, more than a dozen of Ittha's friends, the principal ladies of the town, came in consequence of the liberty she enjoyed while the good man was away to have a look at the white man, each bringing me something—a few onions, a little rice, or a bowl of milk—as a present. Funha performed all the duties imposed on her to perfection. I had a supper of pounded rice, milk, and honey, with something like bread made into cakes, and verily I began to think, like Ittha herself, that I not only deserved to be a sultan, but that I had really commenced my reign.[17]

From Mafate the explorers accompanied the expedition to Chawi, where they crossed the Shari, and from there they skirted the southern

---

17. Ibid, pp. 55-7.

shore of the lake until they reached its southeastern corner at Tangalia. They were now in a district mainly populated by Shuwa Arabs and dominated by the rebel chieftain, Amanuk. He and his followers had gone to ground, however, and were nowhere to be found.

Only now did Denham learn that the defeat and capture of Amanuk was in any case not the expedition's real, or at any rate primary, objective.

> June 28—Although on our arriving at the camp of the Duggana a long parley was held, and a number of questions asked of Sheikh Hamed as to Amanuk's numbers and his hiding-place, yet the first object of the expedition did not appear until just before daylight this morning when the whole body mounted and in fifteen minutes were moving towards Kanem Mendu, one day from Mao, the capital, from whence the Wadais had driven the Sheikh's friends. Mendu had thrown off the Sheikh's government and Edirshe Gebere, nephew of the Fugbu that had been put to death by the order of Mustafa, the Sultan of Fezzan, now ruled as regent. The Sheikh's object had been to catch him by surprise and for this reason Amanuk and Lasala were always held out as the sole destination of the army.
>
> Mendu was nearly in my road and it was therefore necessary that it should be cleared first of these rebels. Barka Gana sent in the night for Bellal and desired him to acquaint me with his intention, saying that he should merely halt to pray and water the horses, from his starting until the sun should be three fathoms high on the following day, when he should surround Mendu; that the Sheikh wished me to remain where I was until his return, which would be in four days, when he trusted I should be able to proceed in safety. I should have preferred going on and, leaving Mendu to him, [passing] on round the Chad, but he would not hear of such an arrangement and, as I was kept in ignorance of this plan until the whole army was actually in motion, I had no alternative. Not a camel went with them, and all the baggage and concubines were left in the camp.
>
> Bellal now became the chief and, with the assistance of the Shuwas and Arabs, the camp was entrenched, trees cut down, and a sort of abbattis quickly formed for our protection. Our situation was, however, one of jeopardy and inconvenience, as nothing but their ignorance of our movements could save us from an attack from Amanuk's people to whom we should have been a fine booty and an easy prey. From our vicinity to the Chad, the swarms of flies in the day and mosquitoes at night were so great that we were

obliged to resort to our old remedy of lighting fires and living in the smoke in order to obtain a little peace.[18]

After passing an anxious and uncomfortable week at Tangalia, the explorers were relieved when Barka Gana at length returned. They learnt from him that, although he and his force had covered fifty miles in a day and a night in the hope of achieving surprise, the rebels had still been forewarned and had immediately evacuated Mao, taking with them all their women, children and cattle. Barka Gana had succeeded in locating them in the strongly fortified camp to which they had withdrawn but by that time his men had been so fatigued and so short of provisions that he had not ventured to attack. Instead, he had decided to abandon this part of the enterprise altogether.[19]

18. Ibid, pp. 61-2.
19. Ibid, pp. 68-9.

XVII

The Shuwa Arabs

The Shuwas, among whom the explorers now found themselves, were descendants of Arab pastoralists who had come to West Africa by way of the Nile Valley. Four or five centuries earlier, after the destruction of the Christian Kingdom of Nubia had opened the way, they had entered the corridor of the Sudan, between the Sahara and the equatorial forest belt, and made their way along it in search of water and grazing. In the Chad region they had found plenty of both. There, moreover, their westward flowing tide had encountered the eastward flowing tide of the Fulani who, being pastoralists like themselves, had already established a lien over the best water and grazing in Hausaland and Western Bornu.[1] So, as conditions in the Chad region suited them, the Shuwas had settled there.

Over the centuries the Shuwas had inter-married to a greater or lesser degree with the local people and become more sedentary in their habits. Nevertheless, as Denham's description of them shows, they had preserved their identity as a separate race, retained Arabic as their mother tongue and remained semi-nomadic pastoralists.

> The Shuwas have brought with them Arabic which they speak nearly pure. They are divided into tribes and bear still the names of some of the most formidable of the Bedouin hordes of Egypt. They are a deceitful, arrogant, and cunning race.... The strong resemblance they bear, both in features and habits, to some of our gipsy tribes is particularly striking. It is said that Bornu can muster

---

1. Johnston, pp. 74 and 81.

236 | DENHAM IN BORNU

> 15,000 Shuwas in the field, mounted. They are the greatest breeders of cattle in the country and annually supply Hausaland with from two to three thousand horses. . .

While they were waiting in the fortified camp at Tangalia for Barka Gana to return, Denham and Tyrwhitt succeeded in getting on friendly terms with the Shuwas of the Duggana tribe.

> June 29—The Duggana chief, Tahr, came to my tent today, attended by about twenty people. . . . He had a fine, serious, expressive countenance, large features, and a long bushy beard. These are the particular characteristics of these Shuwas—they differ from the Shuwas to the west who have mixed more with the natives. Tahr might have sat for the picture of one of the patriarchs. . .
>
> June 30—Tahr paid me another visit today. The Dugganas were formerly Wadais and were strong enough to have great influence with the Sultan but, by quarrelling among themselves, they lost their influence and became subject to the Wadai Sultans. They generally passed one part of the year in the Bahr el-Ghazal[3] and the other part by Lake Fittri: in these two spots had been their regular camps for several generations.
>
> Sheikh Hamed, father of the present chief, who had more than one hundred children, found that another tribe of Duggana had been intriguing with the Sultan of Wadai against him and that he was to be plundered and his brethren to share in the spoil. On learning this, he fled with his flocks and his wives, offered himself to the Sheikh, El-Kanemi, and had since lived in his dominions.[4]

Unfortunately, however, Tahr's geography was not as strong as his history. He stated, perfectly correctly, that Lake Chad was not drained by any river but he also affirmed, quite wrongly, that Lake Fittri was linked to the Nile system.[5]

* * *

After the complete failure of his mission against the Kanem rebels, Barka Gana was doubtless reluctant to return to the capital with nothing to show for his labours, no victory for the Sheikh nor any booty for his troops. He therefore decided, after all, to make an attempt to bring Amanuk to book. For this operation he was able to muster nearly 1000

2. Denham II, pp. 157 and 67.
3. A district east of Lake Chad, not to be confused with the better known province on the Upper Nile.
4. Denham, II, pp. 62-5.
5. Ibid, pp. 66.

of the Sheikh's men reinforced by about 400 Dugganas. In normal country, such a force would have been amply sufficient but, in the swamps of Chad, Amanuk proved to be just as difficult to tackle as Hereward the Wake in the East Anglian fens.

The Chad, which in this part forms itself into innumerable still waters or lakes of various extents and consequently leaves many detached spaces of land or islands, always afforded the Lasala Shuwas and the Budumas natural defences which their enemies had ever found it extremely difficult to conquer. In one of these situations these very Lasalas, with Amanuk at their head, kept the Sultan of Fezzan, with two thousand Arabs and all the Sheikh's army, several days in check and killed between thirty and forty of the Arabs before they surrendered.

On this occasion Amanuk had taken possession of one of these islands, to attack which, with horsemen alone in front of an opposing enemy, was the height of imprudence. A narrow pass led between two lakes to a third, behind which Amanuk had posted himself with all his cattle and his people, male and female. The lake in front of him was neither deep nor wide, but full of holes and had a muddy deceitful bottom on the side from whence the attack was made. The sight of the bleating flocks and lowing herds was too much for the ravenous troops of the Sheikh, irritated by their recent disappointment, and notwithstanding the declaration of Barka Gana that he wished to halt on the opposite side of the water and send for spearmen on foot with shields who would lead the attack, the junior chiefs all exclaimed: 'What! Be so near them as this and not eat them? No, no, let us on! This night these flocks and women will be ours.' This cry the Sheikh's Shuwas also joined in, ever loud in talk but rearmost in the fight, as the sequel proved.

The attack commenced; the Arabs, of whom there were about eighty, led the way with the Dugganas. On arriving in the middle of the lake the horses sank up to their saddle-bows, most of them were out of their depth and others floundered in the mud. The ammunition of the riders became wet, their guns useless, many even missed the first fire, and they were unhorsed in this situation. As they approached the shore, the Lasalas hurled at them, with unerring aim, a volley of their light spears, a very formidable missile, which they followed up by a charge of their strongest and best horses, trained and accustomed to the water, while at the same time another body, having crossed the lake higher up, came by the narrow pass and cut off the retreat of all those who had advanced into the lake.

The Shuwas, on the first appearance of resistance, had as usual gone to the right-about and left those, under whose cover they meant to plunder, to fight it out by themselves. The slaughter now became very desperate amongst the Sheikh's people. Barka Gana, although attacking against his own judgement, was of the foremost and received a severe spear wound in his back, which pierced through four gowns and an iron chain armour, while attacked by five chiefs who seemed determined on finishing him, one of whom he thrust completely through with his long spear. By crowding around him and by helping him quickly to a fresh horse, his own people and chiefs saved him and thirty of them remained either killed or in the hands of the Lasalas. But few of those who were wounded in the water, or whose horses failed them there, escaped. Yet still they defended themselves, still continued to strike their ironheaded weapons into the bodies of their enemies. Numbers, however, at length overpowered them and they fell tumbling on the bodies of each other, a heap of slain into a watery grave.

We found Barka Gana, with the other Chiefs, seated near the second water. He was in great pain from his wound and the whole army dreadfully disheartened: they had not more than forty followers in all. We waited vainly until sunset, in the hopes of the missing making their appearance but we were disappointed and returned to the camp. By this desertion of the Sheikh's Shuwas, the Dugganas suffered severely. Anxious to show their sincerity to the Sheikh, they had gone on boldly, and their loss exceeded one hundred. Eighteen of the Arabs were also missing. The night was passed in a state of great anxiety, from the fear of an attack on our camp; and the sense of our unjoyous situation was constantly awakened by the melancholy dirges which the Duggana women were singing over their dead husbands.

The Dugganas, from being the humblest of the allies, now became rather dictatorial and told the General very plainly that they could fight better without him than with him. They refused him both bullocks and sheep and said they must keep them to pay the ransom of their people.

Amanuk, who it seems had no idea of following up his victory by an attack on our camp, which he might have done successfully and carried off all the chiefs, concubines, and camels, sent word this evening that he would now treat with nobody but the Sheikh himself; that he had declared to the General before he had attacked him that he feared no one but God, the Prophet, and the Sheikh, and wished for peace. 'They would not listen to me' said he 'but attempted to take by force what was their master's before, for all

THE SHUWA ARABS

we had was the Sheikh's and is still. By God's help my people overcame them but that is nothing. I am to the Sheikh, in point of strength, as an egg is to a stone. If he wishes peace, and will no more molest me in my wilds, peace be with us—I will give up his people, his horses, and his arms, that have fallen into my hands. If not, I will keep them all and maybe add to their number. We are not easily beaten. By the head of the Prophet, I can and will, if I am forced, turn fish and fly to the centre of the water. And if the Sheikh comes himself against me, I will bring Wadai against him.'

If we were mentally in hot water during the day, we were bodily in cold all the night, for we had a most drenching storm which came on soon after dark. The fire under our rice and mutton was extinguished, not to be again kindled, and we were obliged to eat it, half raw, and soaked with rain water, about midnight.

July 8—The chiefs all refused to withdraw their forces on this offer of Amanuk: they sent word that he was not to be depended on, so often had he deceived them. Nothing but an unconditional return of all the spoil would satisfy them. In a long conversation which I had with Barka Gana, whose wound was now fast healing from the dressing of burnt fat and sulphur which I had applied, he assured me that they should not make another attempt on this bold chieftain. He, however, advised my returning to Kuka. 'The excursion' said he 'you wish to make was always dangerous: it is now impracticable. We must wait for the Sheikh's appearance before we can do anything and I think from the advanced state of the season, as the rains have now begun to fall, you will find that the Sheikh will not come and that we shall all return.'[6]

* * *

In spite of Barka Gana's advice, Denham and Tyrwhitt lingered with the expedition at Tangalia for a few more days. The women of the Shuwa Arabs are very handsome and Tyrwhitt in particular seems to have felt their attractions.

By being ten days encamped close to the camp of the Duggana Shuwas, we had a better opportunity of observing these curious people: they were a superior class to any I had met with, were rich in cattle and in camels, and seemed to live in plenty and patriarchal simplicity. The Sheikh had greatly encouraged their taking refuge with him on their disagreement with Wadai and had promised them protection, tribute free, provided they were faithful. Both the men

6. Ibid, pp. 70-6.

and women were comely, particularly the latter who, when they found that we paid for what we wanted in little bits of coarse amber, with which I had provided myself, brought us night and morning frothy bowls of milk which formed by far the best part of our repasts.

There is something so curious and singularly interesting and expressive in the Shuwa manners and language that I am at a loss how to describe it. A girl sits down by your tent with a bowl of milk, a dark blue cotton wrapper tied round her waist, and a mantilla of the same thrown over her head with which she hides her face, yet leaves all her bust naked. She says: 'A happy day to you! Your friend has brought you milk: you gave her something so handsome yesterday, she has not forgotten it. Oh! how her eyes ache to see all you have got in that wooden house!', pointing to a trunk. 'We have no fears now: we know you are good and our eyes, which before could not look at you, now search after you always. They bade us beware of you at first, for you were bad, very bad, but we know better now. How it pains us that you are so white!'

Another who was called Aisha, the daughter of a chief and descended from the Tahr, who brought her milk, begging coral and *kohl* in return, had made some impression on a friend of mine [presumably Tyrwhitt] .. She came to the tent two days after the fight, by daylight, and tears were rolling over her expressive features. 'A happy day to my friend!' she began. 'What can he think of Aisha's not having seen him for two days? But what could she do—eight of her father's house fell beneath the spears of Amanuk! She was obliged to stay and mourn over them but she mourned more in her heart that she was not with her friend. Still, they deserved her tears, for they were brave and beloved, but then the whole camp would have wept for them, and the stranger was alone and had nobody to bring him milk. No, no, she was wrong. Last night she would have come and had passed the barrier; she feared nothing but giving pain to him she thought of—but she knew not herself. The hyenas howled, they came near her; her heart was small, and she turned back.'

She was now pressed to enter the tent, probably with more warmth than usual. 'Wait' she replied. 'Sit down here on the sand. Aisha is now frightened at her friend: what does he ask her to do. Would he see her beaten with leather thongs till she bleeds? Would he have her brother's dagger red with her blood—the blood of her heart which now beats so strong and bids her go to him it beats for, while her head tells her to fear? Aisha's heart is weaker than her

> head; her eyes have seen her stranger friend and have seen none other like him.'
>
> This was serious I believe and alarmed as much as it interested the stranger. A present was offered her and she was advised to return to the camp. 'I go' said she 'for it is now day'. But smiling through the tears which were still hanging in her long black eyelashes, she added: 'What! Take pretty things from her friend now, when she knows his eyes have no pleasure in her? No, no! She now leaves him but, when night comes and all her house will be singing over the dead, then Aisha will have no fears—she will leave the tent, but her stranger must come with his gun and protect her from the hyenas.'[7]

Denham does not tell us how this flirtation, whether of Tyrwhitt's or himself concluded.

It was typical of El-Kanemi's methods that, in entrusting the command of the expedition to Barka Gana, who was a Hausa by origin, he should have appointed a Kanemma, Ali Gana and a Shuwa, Tirab, as his deputies. But this move had drawbacks as well as advantages because, although it insured the Sheikh against any intrigues being hatched against his person or authority, it also produced rivalries among the three leaders which had a disastrous effect on the central direction of the expedition. Convinced at length that he would achieve nothing, Denham and Tyrwhitt took their leave of Barka Gana and set out for Kuka. Two days later, considerably exhausted by the hardships of living in the open in those mosquito-infested swamps they were thankful to be welcomed back into their hospitable quarters at Mafate.

> July 12—Left Chawi and once more found ourselves at Mafate. The rest, and fish bazeen, with which were here regaled, with the deep shade of Birma's spacious mansion, greatly recovered us. The skin of my face all came off and I slept nearly the whole day after our arrival. The sun, rain, flies, and mosquitoes, altogether had fatigued me more than any former journey.
>
> Birma was at home and pestered me to death with his civilities, and twenty times over expressed his concern at my having been three days in his house during his absence. 'I must have been sadly provided for, as his wives—poor weak things!—were afraid to come near the room where I was . . . but they were shamefaced silly beings, and what could he do? Thank God, however, he was now

---

7. Ibid, pp. 77-80.

> here himself to do everything for me I might want.' I could not be otherwise than grateful, but he little knew how satisfied I would have been had I been left once more to their care and himself a hundred miles off.
>
> I was burnt with the sun, scarified by the bites of animals and insects, with my limbs aching from the frequent wettings that I had got, and I longed most earnestly for a shampooing. But the thing was impossible, for although Ittha came up to pay me a short visit of ceremony, by her husband's desire, yet I found the regulations of the family very different to what they were on my former visit. Funha, however, found means to make her appearance the next morning before my departure. She had returned to her husband, through Birma's intercession. After giving her a kerchief, which appeared to afford her but little satisfaction, and asking her what else she wished, her only reply was: 'I wish for nothing, except that it may please God to bring you here again once more.'[8]

After three days' rest at Mafate, they set out again and, on July 18, reached Kuka.

> On my arrival at Kuka I found that Captain Clapperton, with a small caravan, had returned from Hausaland. It was nearly eight months since we had separated and, although it was midday, I went immediately to the hut where he was lodged; but, so satisfied was I that the sunburnt sickly person that lay extended on the floor, rolled in a dark blue shirt, was not my companion, that I was about to leave the place, when he convinced me of my error by calling me by name. The alteration was certainly in him most striking. Our meeting was a melancholy one: he had buried his companion and I had also closed the eyes of my younger and more robust colleague, Mr. Toole.[9]

Clapperton had succeeded in reaching Sokoto and establishing very friendly relations with Sultan Bello, the ruler of the Fulani Empire. Despite his weakness, he now announced, to Denham's surprise, that it was his intention, after their return to England to go back there yet again.

8. Ibid, pp. 81-3.
9. Ibid, p. 84.

XVIII

The Journey Home

The explorers now began to prepare for the journey back to Europe. It was agreed that the newly arrived Tyrwhitt should remain in Bornu and act as British Consul but for Denham, Clapperton and Hillman, who had been in Africa for nearly three years, the time had clearly come to return to a temperate climate while they still had the health and strength to do so. They knew that towards the end of the rains, the caravan which was expected from Hausaland would be setting out for North Africa and they planned to attach themselves to it.

When these proposals were put to El-Kanemi, he accepted them readily enough.

> The Sheikh had consented to Mr. Tyrwhitt's remaining as Consul and, on my enquiring whether he would protect one or two English merchants if they came to this country, 'Certainly: why not?' said he 'and assist them to the extent of my power, but they must be small traders or the journey will never pay them'.
>
> He expressed his wish to write to the King and added: 'Whatever I can do in Hausaland, remember I am ready. I have influence there certainly which may increase and probably shortly extend to Nupe. As to yourself, I shall write to beg the King will send you here with any English whom he may wish to visit Bornu. You are known and might now go to anywhere in Bornu without fear. Even the Shuwas on the frontiers, and the Dugganas, all know Rais Khalil. But this has not been done hastily: you have been nearly eighteen months among us and you remember when you could not go to Ngornu

without inconvenience. I then thought you would never be as much at liberty as you are. Time and yourself may be thanked for this, not me, for I could not, by any orders I might have given, have done for you what your mixing freely with the people, and gaining their good will, has brought about and yet you are a Christian!'[1]

In the light of subsequent events, El-Kanemi's passing remarks about Hausaland and Nupe are very significant. They show that, despite the hostility of Wadai and Baghirmi in the east, he was already contemplating an attack on the Fulani Empire in the west with the object of recovering the lost suzerainty of Hausaland. This invasion was to be launched two and a half years later and was to ruin the prospects of Clapperton's second expedition to Sokoto.

On August 6, the festival of *Id el-Kebir* came round again. This time however, because of the reverses that the Bornu forces had suffered in Kanem and the severities with which the Sheikh had again been treating the women of Kuka, it was celebrated with little joy.

> This was the Id el-Kebir, the principal feast of the Moslems during the year, in commemoration of God's staying the hand of Abraham in the place Jehovah-jireh, when about to sacrifice his son Isaac. All who can muster a sheep or a goat, kill it on this day, after prayers.
>
> The Sheikh sent the day before to know if we kept the feast and, when we met, repeated his question. I replied that we believed the interposition of the Divine Power in saving Isaac to be a signal proof of God's mercy and love to all his creatures. 'For remember' said I 'he is the God of many, not of Moslems alone, and that our father Abraham's great and implicit faith in the existence of that mercy was what obtained for him all the blessings God promised him'. He sent us two very fine sheep, and we killed and feasted with the rest.
>
> Early in the morning the Sheikh, with his sons and all his Court, mounted, according to custom, to welcome the feast by praying outside the town and firing and skirmishing on their return. The assembly was not so large as on former occasions, in consequence of the absence of the chiefs in Kanem; indeed every thing went off extremely flat, owing to the defeat of the Sheikh's people. Contrary to custom, no presents were made by him and no dresses were distributed to the slaves. Instead of the glossy new gowns which on former occasions shone on the persons of the footmen who ran by the side of his horse, they were now clothed with torn, discoloured ones, and everything wore the appearance of gloom and disgrace.

1. Denham, II, pp. 85-6.

On these days, the custom is also for the women to assemble, dressed in all their finery, in the street before the doors of their huts and scream a salutation to the passing chiefs. It was one of the best parts of the ceremony but this year it was omitted. The Sheikh, whose unamiable trait was, as I have before observed, visiting the weaknesses of the female part of his subjects with too great severity, had during my absence given an order which would have disgraced the most absolute despot that ever sat on a throne: the gates of his town were kept shut at daylight one morning and his emissaries despatched who bound and brought before him sixty women who had a bad reputation. Five were sentenced to be hanged in the public market and four to be flogged, which latter punishment was inflicted with such severity that two expired under the lash. Those who were doomed to death, after being dragged, with their head shaved, round the market on a public day, with a rope round their necks, were then strangled and thrown by twos into a hole previously prepared, in the most barbarous manner. This diabolical act, for it deserves no better name, armed all tongues against him. The Bornuese, who are a humane and forgiving people, shuddered at so much cruelty. And so much influence had the ladies in general with their husbands that more than a hundred families quitted Kuka (to which place they were before daily flocking) to take up their abode in other towns where this rigour did not exist. In Kuka they declared there was no living, where only to be suspected was sufficient to be doomed to a cruel and ignominious death, and where malicious spies converted 'trifles light as air into confirmation strong'. Those who remained, though the women of his particular attendants, refused flatly to scream him a welcome, and the procession passed through the streets in silence.[2]

On the following day, moreover, when the explorers called on El-Kanemi, they found that an Arab had again sown doubts in his mind about the objects of their mission.

> In the afternoon we went to pay our respects to the Sheikh, in honour of the feast. He received us but cooly and I was scarcely seated on the sand when I saw near me a little Shereef from Morocco named Hussein who, though once or twice our friend, I was always in fear of, being aware both of his cunning and his influence. Almost the first question of the Sheikh's was as to the distance of our country from India and, when told it was four

---

2. Ibid, pp. 88-91.

months by sea, he said: 'What could induce you to go so far from home—to find it out and fight with the people?'

We replied 'that we had plenty of ships and were great lovers of discovery, that the French and the Dutch had been there before us, and that we were always jealous of our neighbours doing more than ourselves.'

'And now it is all yours' said he 'and governed by your laws!'

Our reply was 'that we only kept possession of the part near the sea—that their own laws were in full force—but that even Moslems often preferred the English laws to their own'.

'Wonderful!' said he. 'And you went at first with only a few ships, as friends?'

'We are friends now' said I 'and by trade have not only made ourselves rich but the natives also'.

'By God!' said the Moroccan 'they eat the whole country—they are no friends. These are the words of truth'. We had then a few remarks (not good-natured ones) as to the right of dictating to Algiers and the other Barbary powers. Algiers we described as unfaithful to their word and little better than pirates.[3]

The Sheikh had already given the explorers their parting presents. These had clearly been chosen with thought to the journey that lay ahead of them and consisted of a fine camel, a horse, two water-skins, two leopard skins, two dressed leather sacks, eight elephant tusks, and three rhinoceros horns. At the same time Denham, when consulted about the presents that they should take back to the King of England, had suggested that they should include a suit of the quilted armour in which both men and horses of the heavy cavalry were encased. This, together with the other presents, was formally delivered a few days after the festival.

>Soon after daylight Karouash, with Alhaji Mustafa, the chief of the Shuwas, and the Sheikh's two nephews, Hussein and Kanemi, came to our huts. Alhaji Mustafa had been one of the original four hundred who commenced the liberation of Bornu from the Fulani. They were attended by more than a dozen slaves, bearing presents for us, for King George and the Consul at Tripoli.
>
>I had applied for a *lebida,* after seeing those taken from the Baghirmis: the Sheikh now sent a man clothed in a yellow wadded jacket, with a scarlet cap, and mounted on the horse taken from the Baghirmis on which the Sultan's eldest son rode. He was one of the

3. Ibid, pp. 92-3.

finest horses I had seen and covered with a scarlet cloth, also wadded. 'Everything' Alhaji Mustafa said 'except the man, is to be taken to your great king.'

He also brought me twelve very beautiful gowns of every manufacture, from Nupe to Logone and Wadai, four parrots, and a box of musk. For the Consul he also sent six gowns and a small box of musk, worth thirty or forty dollars, with two parrots.[4]

While the explorers were waiting for the caravan from Hausaland, Denham picked up what is probably another echo of Hornemann—this time of his death.

> Muhammad Busgaye, an Arab who left this place with Doctor Oudney and Mr. Clapperton, came to my hut. He had gone on from Kano with four or five Arabs to Yauri and Nupe and had stayed some time at a place called Gusgei on the Niger, two days west-southwest nearly from Yauri. The Niger he described to be here as wide as to the market outside the walls and back, which must have been nearly two miles. They were all unbelievers, he said, but not bad people. The chief Mahmud had several hundred guns and powder, which were brought from the sea, and arrack (gin) in plenty, which was brought in large glass bottles. At eight days' distance only from Yauri, large boats came to a place called Yearban, but it is not on the sea. Katunga is the great port, which is at some distance from the sea. To both of these places people he called Americans came: they were white and Christians; they always demand gum arabic and male slaves for which they will pay as high as sixty and seventy dollars each. The Chief Mahmud produced to him two books, which he said were like mine, and told him that a man, whose beard was white, had lived nearly three years with no money, that he wished to go but had no means, and that he had died. Busgaye said the Emir had offered him the book, which he refused as he did not know what he could do with it, but that now he was going back and should bring it.

This little-known and hitherto largely neglected report is of major importance and merits the closest analysis in order to test its veracity to the limit.

According to Muhammed Busgaye, he had visited both Yauri and Nupe, stopping for "some time at a place called Gusgei on the Niger, two days west-southwest, nearly, from Yauri." It is hardly to be doubted that

---

4. Ibid, pp. 92-4.

the place referred to is the then flourishing river-port of N'gaski—now, alas, flooded by the lake formed by the Kanji Dam just south of Bussa.

By 1948, the ancient main town of N'gaski was actually some seven miles from the river, but the inhabitants insisted that this was not always the case. Similar shifts of the Niger to the west have been established beyond question, the most famous of course being in the area of Timbuktu, which is now some fifteen miles from the water. It should be noted also that the former capital of Yauri, Bin Yauri, founded by Queen Amina and with walls five miles and more in circumference, once had also been a flourishing river port. This fact played a part in the decision of the 35th Chief Abdulai Abershi (1888-1904) to establish his capital at Yelwa, a move which was made between 1889 and 1891.

Be this as it may, the fact remained that at N'gaski, a satellite town, also called N'gaski existed on the banks of the Niger and it is this place that was visited by Mungo Park in 1806. The town was some 35 miles from Bin Yauri by canoe and fits the description given by Muhammed Busgaye not only as to distance but also to direction; moreover, there are other points of coincidence.

In 1823, the Chief of Yauri was Mahammadu d'an Ayi, alias Besheru[5] who ruled from March 1799 to November 1829. This is the man whom Busgaye said was named Mahmud (a variant of Muhammadu) who also described him as the possessor of "several hundred guns and powder, which were brought from the sea, and [gin] in plenty—in large glass bottles".

To Mungo Park, this same Emir of Yauri had appeared as a powerful potentate. To Muhammed Busgaye he clearly equally was so. It was not, in fact until some forty years later that Yauri's wings were clipped by the appearance on the scene of the warrior chief Umaru Nagwamachi (1806-1876) who carved himself out the Emirate of Kontagora over which he and his successors ruled with a rod of iron mainly at the expense of Yauri and Nupe.

Busgaye's description, moreover, accurately fitted the Niger at this point, mid-way down the great island of Foge, itself over twenty miles long and ten miles wide—a feature yet again now submerged in Kanji lake.

When the British began the insertion of their power in the Niger valley north of Lokoja, Yelwa, the capital of Yauri as it then was, became a prime focus for their attention. In 1896 it was visited by Mr. (later Sir)

---

5. Kontagora Province Gazeteer; Waterlow, London 1920, p. 20.

William Wallace. N'gaski however was sufficiently powerful and sufficiently important to be regarded at this time as a separate Emirate.[6]

The accuracy with which Muhammed Busgaye describes the place, its environs, its position and the personalities thus demands that in the absence of proof to the contrary, the remainder of his report should be approached with respect and a readiness to acknowledge its accuracy if this be at all possible.

"Eight days from Yauri", he alleges, "large boats came to a place called Yearban, but it is not on the sea." Such a description can only apply to the river port of Jebba, a little less than 150 miles down-stream from Bin Yauri and thus a fair eight days journey from that point. To deny the association is to stretch reason beyond its bounds, in view of the informant's accuracy heretofore.[7] This, however is not the end of the matter.

Muhammed Busgaye then goes on to state that "Katunga is the great port which is at some distance from the sea". Katunga is the Hausa name for "old" Oyo, the seat of the powerful Yoruba potentate the Alafin of Oyo, held by some authorities to be the secular, as opposed to spiritual head of all the Yoruba people.

"To both these places" (i.e. to Jebba [Yearban] and to Katunga [Old Oyo]) Busgaye alleges, "people he called Americans came: they were white and Christians; they always demanded gum arabic and male slaves for which they will pay as high as sixty and seventy dollars each."

The fact that old Oyo is situated nearly two hundred miles from the sea is not material. What Busgaye intended by his understatement that it was "at some distance" from it can never be established. Moreover, all we have here is Denham's interpretation of Busgaye's information. The observation about the coming of the Americans, on the other hand, is fact, plain and unadulterated, and as reliable as any other fact which Busgaye has reported—a reliability, which as has been shown, is high.

Jebba is about 35 miles from old Oyo (Katunga) and is certainly the nearest river port of any note to it. It is also some 16 miles from Raba,

---

6. With regard to Ngaski, the author (DJMM) has personally seen an eighteenth century "footmans staff" which was given to an ancestor of the present Chief of Ngaski by Mungo Park, a fact which bears witness to the town's status.
As late as 1899-1900, Ngaski was still sufficiently important for it to be regarded as an independant Emirate. See Hall W.M., *The Great Drama of Kumasi*: Putnam, 1939.

7. It has been suggested that Yearban might also have been a misinterpretation of Yoruba (land).

later to become the seat of Mallam Dendo (died 1832), the power behind the Nupe throne; 20 miles from Mokwa an important Nupe administrative center and former capital and 32 miles from Bokani, the place where other reports indicate that Hornemann died. The suggestion, implicit in this report, that Hornemann died in Yauri is thus important. Whether or not Busgaye's report of the death of the white haired man is taken to mean that he actually did die there, the fact remains that his journals ("two books, which he said were like mine") probably were still surviving some twenty years after his death. A man—not a trader—white, living in this area for up to three years, at this period can only be Hornemann. No one else fits the bill.

The real item of importance in Busgaye's statement however, is the reference to "the Americans". If, from independent sources, its accuracy can be established, then our whole concept of the trade etc. patterns in the valley of the Middle Niger will require extensive re-appraisal.

* * *

On August 13 the caravan from Hausaland at length reached Kuka, having been fifty days on the road from Kano. It was the worst time of the year to traverse the low-lying, half-flooded plains of eastern Kano and western Bornu and the only reason that induced them to do so was that the slavetraders among the merchants wanted to lose no time in taking the road to Fezzan. The winter nights in the Sahara could be bitterly cold and they knew from experience that many of their slaves would die on the road if the season was too far advanced before they reached their destination. Needless to add, it was greed, not compassion, that drove them on.[8]

Denham, thwarted in his ambition to travel right round Lake Chad, was still hankering to fill the gap in his knowledge by visiting its north-eastern shores. To give him time to do this, he obtained permission from the Sheikh to set out ahead of the caravan and join forces with it after making his excursion.

> On Monday, the . . . 16th of August, we took our final leave of Kuka, and not without many feelings of regret, so accustomed had we become, particularly myself, to the people. In the morning I had taken leave of the Sheikh in his garden, when he had given me a letter to the King and a list of requests. He was all kindness and said he had only one wish, which was that I might find all my friends well and once more return to them. He gave me his hand at parting,

8. Ibid, p. 94.

which excited an involuntary exclamation of astonishment from the six eunuchs and Karouash who were the only persons present.

I preceded the caravan for the following reason: I had, ever since my return from Tangalia, determined to attempt the east side of Chad, by Lari, previous to returning home. Many had been the objections, many the reports of danger from the Wadai people and Amanuk, who had now boldly forsaken the Lake and was encamped at no great distance from Barka Gana to whom he twice paid a night visit and had been beaten back. I, however, told the Sheikh I could take no present, or promise to the execution of any commission, unless this duty was accomplished, or at least until I had done my utmost, and that I would take care not to go into danger.

Bellal, my old companion, was once more appointed to attend me, and we moved with two camels, lightly laden, for the more train, always the more trouble and the more expense. All my friends then in Kuka mounted to escort me from the town; the women assembled outside the gate and screamed an adieu; and I am persuaded our regrets were mutual.

On Wednesday we slept at Kaliluwa, and on the 23rd came once more on the Yobe, now a considerable stream, full of water and running towards Chad at the rate of three miles an hour. My feelings on seeing this river for a second time were very different to what they had been when I first looked on its waters. We then had an escort of two hundred men and yet could not feel ourselves in perfect safety one hundred yards from our tents. Now I had only one attendant—the people about me were all natives—and I wandered about the banks of the river with perfect freedom and slept with my tent door open in as great security as I could have done in any part of England had I been obliged so to travel. Other feelings also obtruded themselves: I was about to return home to see once more dear friends, and a dear country, after an absence of nearly three years on a duty full of perils and difficulties. Two out of four of my companions had fallen victims to climate and disease, while those who remained were suffering, in no small degree, sickness and debility from the same causes. I was in health and, notwithstanding the many very trying situations in which we had all been placed, some of them of great vexation and distress, yet had we been eminently successful...[9]

On August 25 Denham reached Wudi, on the north-western corner of the Lake and there he found Barka Gana who had arrived from the

---

9. Ibid, pp. 96-9.

opposite direction with a much depleted force. Barka Gana's account of his campaign showed how Wadai, which already dominated eastern Kanem, had now almost succeeded in wresting away western Kanem as well.

> At Wudi I met Barka Gana, Ali Gana, and Tirab, with their forces on their return from Kanem. They had been out, some of them five months, had made the complete tour of the Lake, and were in a sad plight with scarcely thirty horses left, having literally fought their way. Amanuk had twice attacked them ... and they were so reduced as not to be able to do anything to prevent him. They were so badly off for everything that they were obliged to come down on Kanem for supplies. The people refused them any assistance and, after being half starved, they were obliged to make a running fight of it and get home as well as they could. The Kanem people were all in a state of mutiny and the Duggana had gone off towards Wadai.
>
> This was sorry news; Bellal wanted to turn back. I saw Barka Gana who said: 'It is dangerous but I think you may go on if you wish it. I would give you eighteen men but you are better without them: they expect the Sheikh and, going with Bellal, wanting but little, and paying for that, for the crops have failed them, you will have little to fear. But you cannot go beyond the Bornu Kanembu with less than one hundred men.'[10]

A lesser man might have felt that honour had already been satisfied but Denham's conscientiousness forced him to undertake new tasks of supererogation. He therefore set off again towards the east but, after covering about fifty miles in four days, even he was obliged to turn back. This last excursion achieved little but the account of it is nevertheless interesting because it gives us another glimpse of those strange people, the Budumas and shows the state of abject misery to which the tug-of-war between Bornu and Wadai had reduced the unhappy people of Kanem. It also reveals Denham's resolution and fortitude in the face of the most acute physical discomfort.

> August 30th. After a night of intolerable misery to us all, from flies and mosquitoes, so bad as to knock up two of our blacks, we mounted and advanced; and leaving our tents, for Bellal would not carry them on, we proceeded to Garuwa and Mabah which are full of people and, though annually pillaged by Tubus and Tuaregs, yet still they will not quit their native soil.
>
> The character of the country here, which is different to the south or west sides of the lake, extends to Gala, where the land is again

10. Ibid, p. 101.

varied and a little higher. For many miles on this side we had one continued marsh and swamp. I was at the northern most part of the lake and, pursuing a course first to the west and then to the eastward of south for five or six miles, nearly up to the body of the horse in water, and with reeds and high grass overtopping our heads, I at last got a sight of the open Lake. We disturbed hippopotami, buffaloes, enormous fish, and innumerable hosts of insects. At the commencement of the water it had a taste of natron which, as we advanced, became gradually sweeter.

Completely fatigued, we returned to the village of Chirgao near which our tents were pitched; this was a most distressing day and we had been on our horses nearly thirteen hours. Garuwa is twelve miles from Zogani and Mabah twenty. We were some way in advance of the latter but to Kuskuwa I could not induce my guide to venture. . . . So many proofs had I seen, not only of his bravery but his desire to satisfy my curiosity, that I could not doubt his fears were just. Notwithstanding our fatigue, no rest could we obtain, and another night was passed in a state of suffering and distress that defies description: the buzz from the insects was like the singing of birds; the men and horses groaned with anguish; we absolutely could not eat our paste and fat from the agony we experienced in uncovering our heads. We at last hit upon an expedient that gave us a little relief; as they came at intervals, in swarms, we thought they might also be driven off in the same quantities, and we found, by occasionally lighting a line of fires with wet grass to windward of our tents, that the smoke carried off millions and left us a little at ease. I do not think our animals could have borne such another night: their legs and necks were covered with blood and they could scarcely stand from the state of irritation in which they had been kept for so many hours.

On Friday we returned to Lari by the lower road where there are frequent large detached pieces of water, strongly impregnated with natron. On the road today we fell in with a tribe of Budduma who had, during the last three months, taken up their abode on the Sheikh's land and asked for what was instantly granted them, permission to remain. Internal wars cause these fallings off of one tribe from another, which the Sheikh encourages. Only one of their chiefs could ever be induced to proceed so far as Kuka. The Sheikh takes no notice and suffers them to do as they please. He sent them gowns and a Mallam and desired they would learn to pray. And they are now beginning, as my guide said, to have the fear of God.

They were the most savage beings I had seen in the shape of men, except the Musgawa, and we had sat some time under a tree before they would come near us. The men, until they are married, wear their hair and collect as many beads and ornaments as they can which they wear round their necks. Their hair is long and plaited or twisted in knots; they have ear-rings also and this collection of beads and metal is always given to the wife on their marriage. The upper part of the face is very flat and the eye sunk; they have large mouths and long necks; a sulky, reserved look about them, anything but agreeable. They have no style of salutation like other negroes, who greet strangers over and over again, sitting down by them. These stand up, leaning on a spear, and look steadfastly at you without speaking. I gave a little boy some white beads which were directly tied round his neck, I suppose as the commencement of his marriage portion. They, however, at length, produced some sour milk; and some of them came round my horse when I mounted and nodded their heads at me when I rode off, which I returned, much to their amusement.

When we arrived at Lari, which was comparatively free from flies, the horses lay down, and, stretching themselves out, fell asleep in a way, and with an expression of enjoyment, I never saw animals do before, and did not look for their nosebags until after midnight. We here found that one of Barka Gana's people had the night before lost his horse, which had been stolen by the Buddumas we saw. . .

Kanem, the most persecuted and unfortunate of negro countries, was daily becoming more miserable. They were pillaged alternately by the Tuaregs, the Fezzaneers, and the Wadai people. Between the latter and the Sheikh they hung for protection, and from neither could they obtain what they sought. The country was becoming abandoned and the villages deserted, part taking refuge in Wadai and part the Sheikh's dominions. The land communication between Bornu and Kanem was too difficult and distant, either by the south or north, for the Sheikh to render them any effectual support. An army almost every year went to Kanem for this purpose, but they usually returned with the loss of horses, camels and men, and were seldom able much to annoy their enemies, the Wadais.

This year his expedition had been upon a large scale and his losses were greater than on any former occasion. In consequence of the waters, which fill the rivers at this season, the ford across the Shari had become impassable, and they were therefore obliged to return home through Kanem. Not the least assistance would any of the towns give them, except Gala, and a more wretched state I never saw men in: some of the chiefs on foot, without horses, and those who were mounted bestriding sorry animals with torn appointments. They all said fighting without the Sheikh was useless as he alone could lead them to victory.

Sept. 3—I had now been six days at Wudi, waiting the arrival of my companions with our camels and the caravan of merchants whom we were to accompany to Fezzan. Wudi is no very pleasant place of sojourn, as the Budduma have a sort of agreement with the chief of the town to be allowed to plunder all strangers and travellers provided the property of the inhabitants is respected. We were, however, told to be on our guard, and not without reason. Our tents were pitched near each other and a look-out kept the whole night, notwithstanding which they paid us a visit, during a storm of thunder and rain and, from the entrance of Bellal's tent, only eight paces from my own, stole both his horses. Although six or seven negroes were sleeping quite close to them, they got completely off and had an hour's start before even the loss was discovered. Bellal pursued them with about a dozen people quite to the lake, tracing their footsteps in the sand, which was not difficult after the rains. But, finding here that they had embarked, the pursuit was given up.[11]

This was to be Denham's last experience of Bornu because soon afterwards, the caravan caught him up. Turning their backs on the Sudan, he and his companions now had to face the Sahara again.

* * *

The caravan completed the passage of the Sahara between Chad and Murzuk in the good time of sixty-nine days. As soon as they left the Lake, with its dense vegetation and myriads of insects, the character of the country changed abruptly and before long they found themselves in the desert once more.

At Bir Kashiferi, nine days out, they entered the territory of the Bunda Tubus and had another encounter with their old ally, Mina Tahr.

> We made the well soon after midday and, fortunately for us, we brought some water with us, for the power of our friend Mina Tahr here began to appear. This well was guarded and we were told that, until the Sheikh Mina appeared, not a drop was to be drawn. It required some exertion of patience and forbearance in a sultry oppressive day, with the thermometer at 110° in the tent, to be obliged to drink muddy water from goat skins when a well of the

11. Ibid, pp. 103-109.

best water between Kuka and Bilma was under our feet. But we were inured to hardships and contradictions and submitted, I hope, like good Christians.

Towards evening Tahr appeared on the hills to the north-west, attended by his troop. He seemed vastly glad to see us; said 'the well was ours, that our water-skins should be filled and camels watered before anybody, and for nothing, and then' said he 'Sultan George the Great must be obliged to Mina Tahr, the wandering Chief of Gunda, and that will give more pleasure to Tahr's heart than payment, and who knows' said he 'but when Sultan George hears this he may send me a sword?' . . .

In the evening Tahr came for his present. I gave him a Hausa gown, a red cap, and a kerchief. The gown and cap he looked at and said: 'Ah! This is very well for me—I am one but my wives are three—what shall I do with one kerchief?' Tahr now began a speech: he was greatly distressed that he had nothing to send Sultan George. 'By the head of Mustafa!' said he 'I consider him as much my master as the Pasha—aye and more—for you say he sent you to see me, which is more than the Pasha ever did. I can send him a tiger-skin and I will write him a letter—for Tahr's enemies are never quiet—and he has no time to kill ostriches now. The well Bir Kashiferi, whose waters are here like gold, and better than gold, and all that Kachalla Tahr and the Gunda Tubus have to give shall always be, as long as he or his children govern, at the service of Sultan George Inglesi.'

He now asked for water and began washing the ink from a paper which had previously been ornamented with a charm, drinking the dirty water, and rubbing it over his head and neck. When this was finished, he laid the paper in the sun, and I was a little amused when I found that it was on this dirty scrap that he intended writing to King George.[12]

Slighting though the reference to the Pasha was, it showed that these Tubus in the southernmost Sahara still acknowledged the suzerainty of Tripoli.

After Bir Kashiferi the caravan had to traverse one of the worst stretches of the whole route, four waterless days' journey through fine sand. The camels were loaded with as much water as they could lift and Denham's animal, in addition to its normal load, had to carry no less than seventeen water skins. A little further north there was an even worse stretch, a belt of over fifty miles of shifting dunes, which severely taxed

12. Ibid, pp. 109-111.

the stamina of both men and animals. Both were successfully negotiated, however, though not without alarms and narrowly averted perils, and on October 11 the caravan reached the oasis of Bilma.

In Bilma a danger of a different kind suddenly flared up.

> Two Mesuratas (Arabs of a town near Tripoli) who had killed a Tubu chief and his followers two years before, were of our party and, although the Tubus had revenged themselves by murdering twenty-five for eight, five of which they had assassinated in the night since our passing the road, yet they contended there was blood between them and we all feared a disturbance.
>
> This morning it broke out and was very near being serious, the Arabs' guns were twice presented, and had any blood been spilt on either side we should probably have been all prisoners to the Tubu or, if victorious, have sacked their whole town. A relation of the deceased chief went to the tent of one of the Mesuratas and, talking of the death of his kinsmen, shook his spear at the Arab, who quickly seized his gun, shouted out *baroud* (powder), beat the drum, and everybody ran to arms. The Tubu was thrust out of the camp, on which he was joined by one hundred of his fellows; others flocked to them from the town and for a short time things looked very warlike indeed. The Tubus were, however, evidently afraid of the Arabs who began skirmishing about, throwing their guns over their heads, sometimes pointing them, and playing a thousand very useless and aggravating antics.
>
> I quickly saw the disposition of the Tubus and, sending away my double-barrelled gun, I followed the example of a Fezzan merchant who seemed to me to have more coolness and courage than any of those drawn up in battle array. We went together, unarmed, amongst the Tubus and, pointing out the man who had offended, whom they had endeavoured to conceal, desired them to take him away and punish him. This had the effect of calming and eventually dispersing them. The Arabs cried out violently when they saw me go towards the Tubus with their drawn knives, saying that they would murder all the whites. Their fears, however, were groundless: the chiefs, and particularly the brother of the Emir, Lawal, stepped forward to meet me, paid the greatest attention to what I said, and not the slightest insult was attempted.
>
> The Arabs themselves teach these people to be rogues: they go through their country, drink at their wells, which as they say, and say truly, are better than gold mines, pay them scarcely any tribute, and generally insult them into the bargain.
>
> October 17—We had another day of rest and were pretty tran-

quil. The women came in throngs to our tents and were willing to sell us corn and dates, for either dollars or Hausa gowns, at one hundred and fifty per cent profit. Two lean goats they asked me four dollars for; and for a sheep, six.

A great deal of bustle was made about the settlement of the dispute with the Mesurata Arabs and the Tubus. The Koran was to be referred to but Haj Muhammad Abdu, the brother of the *Kadi* at Murzuk, would not open the leaves until the relations of the deceased swore to rest satisfied with his decision. This preliminary being arranged on Monday morning, the parties all assembled. The *Kadi,* Haj Ben Hamet and Ben Taleb, the chief merchants of our caravan, were present. They found, by the Koran, that if any man lifts his hand higher than his shoulder, in a menacing attitude, though he should not be armed, the adversary is not to wait the falling of the blow but may strike even to death. The law was of course in favour of the Arab, as he proved the Tubu's having his hand, armed with a spear, raised above his head when he shot him dead. On this being declared, the Arabs ran about, throwing their guns over their heads, shouting, and what we should call crowing, to such a degree that I fully expected the Tubus would be aggravated to renew hostilities.[13]

Denham noted that the return journey was far more exhausting than the outward passage.

The fatigue and difficulty of a journey to Bornu are not to be compared with a return to Fezzan: the nine days from Izhya to Tegerhy, without either forage or wood, is distressing beyond description, to both camels and men, at the end of such a journey as this. The camels, already worn out by the heavy sand-hills, have the stony desert to pass. The sharp points bruise their feet and they totter and fall under their heavy loads. The people, too, suffer severely from the scanty portion of provisions, mostly dates, that can be brought on by these tired animals, and altogether it is nine days of great distress and difficulty. There is something about El-Wahr surpassing dreariness itself. The rocks are dark sandstone of the most gloomy and barren appearance; the wind whistles through the narrow fissures which disdain to afford nourishment even to a single blade of wild grass; and, as the traveller creeps under the lowering crags to take shelter for the night, stumbling at each step over the skeleton of some starved human being and searching for level spots on the hard rock on which to lay his wearied body, he

13. Ibid, pp. 121-124.

may fancy himself wandering in the wilds of desolation and despair.

On the evening of our making El-Wahr, and the two following days, camels in numbers dropped and died, or were quickly killed, and the meat brought on by the hungry slaves. Caravans are obliged to rely on the chance of Tubus and Arabs from Murzuk hearing of their having passed the desert and bringing them supplies; should these fail, many poor creatures must fall a sacrifice for the salvation of the rest.[14]

Nevertheless, on November 14, the travellers safely reached Gatrone.

To do them justice, the Fezzan people seemed as glad we were come back as we were ourselves. 'To go and come back from the black country! Oh, wonderful! You English have large hearts! God bless you! The poor doctor to die too, so far from home! Health to your head! It was written he was to die and you to come back—God is great! And the young Rais Ali (Mr. Toole) Ah, that was written also—but he was a nice man—so sweet spoken! Now you are going home: well, good fortune attend you! How all your friends will come out to meet you with fine clothes—and how much gunpowder they will fire away!'[15]

A week later the caravan arrived in Murzuk to find that a new Sultan, Sidi Hussein, had succeeded Bu-Khalum's old enemy Mustafa. As the Court was in mourning for one of the Pasha's wives, there were no official celebrations, but from their Arab friends the Europeans received a heart-warming welcome.

The two Idzaris, Muhammad and Yusuf, Captain Lyon's friends, were amongst the foremost to pay us attention, as well as old Haj Mahmud, who exclaimed continually: 'Thank God you are come back! Who would have thought it! How great and good God is, to protect such unbelievers as you are! Well, well! Notwithstanding all this, I love you all, though I believe it is haram (sin). Oh, that some miracle would cause a change in you and that you might be Moslem, and then you would not go to the fire, as all the rest of you must, miserables!' All this he would finish by coming up close and whispering: 'Say, when you are alone sometimes, "*La illa il Allah, Muhammad rasul Allah!*", that will be better than nothing.'[16]

The explorers spent over three weeks in Murzuk and did not move on

14. Ibid, pp. 128-9.
15. Ibid, p. 131.
16. Ibid, pp. 132-3. "There is no god but Allah and Muhammed is the prophet of Allah"

again until mid-December, celebrating their fourth Christmas in Africa on the road and reaching Sokna just before the new year of 1825. There Denham again had reason to note that domestic slavery in Africa often had its compensations.

> Arrived at Sokna, I was lodged in the house of Haj Muhammad Bufas, a place with four white-washed walls and date beams; but, by the help of a brass pan and a hole in the ground, I managed to keep a pretty good fire without much smoke. I had neither host nor hostess. The house was in charge of one Baghirmi slave who had been twenty-four years in bondage: he was pleased greatly when he found that I had been near his home, and the names of some of the towns made him clap his hands with pleasure. But, when I asked him whether he should like to return, he had sense enough to answer: 'No, no! I am better where I am. I have no home now but this and what will my master's children do without me. He is dead: and who will take care of the garden for his wives and daughters if Musa goes? No! He is a slave still and so much the better for him. His country is far off and full of enemies. Here he has a house and plenty to eat, thank God! And two months ago they gave him a wife and kept his wedding for eight days'. The concubine of a Sokna merchant who had gone to Hausaland, leaving her pregnant, had by becoming a mother gained her freedom and, taking Musa for a husband, they were put in charge of his mistress's unoccupied house for a residence.[17]

In Sokna, as in Murzuk, Denham found that the death of Bu-Khalum was deeply and widely mourned.

After resting for ten days in Sokna, the explorers set off again. By this time, of course, news of their safe return had preceded them to Tripoli and in the last week of January they themselves were approaching the city.

> On the day after, we reached a well within ten miles of Tripoli and, previous to arriving there, were met by two *chaoushes* of the Pasha with one of the Consul's servants. We found the Consul's tent, but he had been obliged to return on business to the city, and the satisfaction with which we devoured some anchovy toasts and washed them down with huge draughts of Marsala wine in glass tumblers—luxuries we had so long indeed been strangers to—was quite indescribable.
>
> We slept soundly after our feast and on the 26th of January, a few miles from our resting-place, were met by the Consul and his

17. Ibid, pp. 140-1.

eldest son whose satisfaction at our safe return seemed equal to our own. We entered Tripoli the same day where a house had been provided for us. The Consul sent out sheep, bread, and fruit to treat all our fellow-travellers, and cooking and eating and singing and feasting were kept up by both slaves and Arabs until morning.

We had now no other duties to perform except the providing for our embarkation—with all our live animals, birds, and other specimens of natural history—and settling with our faithful native attendants, some of whom had left Tripoli with us and returned in our service. They had strong claims on our liberality and had served us with astonishing fidelity in many situations of great peril...

Our long absence from civilized society appeared to have an effect on our manner of speaking of which, though we were unconscious ourselves, occasioned the remarks of our friends. Even in common conversation, our tone was so loud as almost to alarm those we addressed, and it was some weeks before we could moderate our voices so as to bring them in harmony with the confined space in which we were now exercising them.

Having made arrangements with the captain of an Imperial brig which we found in the harbour of Tripoli to convey us to Leghorn, I applied through the Consul-General to the Pasha for his seal to the freedom of a Mandara boy whose liberation from slavery I had paid for some months before, the only legal way in which a Christian can give freedom to a slave in a Moslem country. The Pasha immediately complied with my request and, on Colonel Warrington's suggesting that the boy was anxious to accompany me to England, he replied, with great good humour: 'Let him go, then; the English can do no wrong'. Indeed on every occasion this prince endeavoured to convince us how rejoiced he was at our success and safe return.[18]

After consigning the animals and baggage to England by the direct sea route, in the care of Hillman, Denham and Clapperton embarked for Leghorn. In the face of storms, the voyage took four weeks and on arrival they were detained for a further twenty-five days in quarantine. Their travelling companions complained bitterly of the little *taverna* where they were all lodged, but to them the cooking seemed perfect and the beds so comfortable that for two days they could hardly bring themselves to stir out of them.

From Leghorn they crossed the Alps and travelled overland to Calais and thence to England. At last, on 1 June 1825, they were able to present themselves to the Secretary of State, Lord Bathurst and report the accomplishment of their mission.

18. Ibid, pp. 150-3.

Epilogue

The exploration of Bornu by Denham and of Hausaland by Clapperton was a turning point in the opening up of Sub-Saharan Africa. After Mungo Park's first journey, nearly thirty years earlier, there had followed a depressing series of failures coupled with a heavy toll in the lives of brave men. Hornemann, it was thought, had simply disappeared. Park on his second venture had perished with all his party. Nicholls had died in Calabar. The expeditions led by Captain Tuckey, Major Peddie and Dr. Ritchie had all come to grief. Laing, after reaching Timbuktu, had been murdered on his way home and all his papers had been lost. But now at last success had been achieved and, after so many setbacks, the lives of Oudney and Toole did not seem an exorbitant price to pay for the information which their comrades brought back. In London the explorers found themselves famous.

Africa however, though it had been forced to yield up some of its secrets, was still far from being vanquished. Tyrwhitt, who had been left in Bornu as British Consul, soon succumbed. Next Clapperton, when he returned to Hausaland to establish a Consulate at the Court of the Fulani Sultan, lost four out of his five companions on the journey from the coast and later died himself in Sokoto. Then Richard Lander, the sole survivor of that expedition, and his brother John, were to perish on the Niger River, in respect of which both of them had accomplished so much by completing Park's unfinished task. Finally, in 1842 a British philanthropic and naval expedition to Lokoja had to be abandoned when the climate killed over a third of the Europeans in three months. Not until the early 'fifties, when for the first time quinine was taken as a prophylactic, was the threat of deadly disease mastered and the way opened up for extended intercourse, not only in West Africa but in other parts of the continent as well.

The long list of failures which both preceded and followed the Denham-Clapperton discoveries makes theirs stand out all the more brightly. What they accomplished ranks with Mungo Park's journeys as the two outstanding events in the first half-century of African exploration and it was the more remarkable because, in point of time, they were made so much earlier than the great explorations of East and Central Africa which followed at least a generation later.

Yet, paradoxically, if, as this study shows, Muhammed Busgaye's story was true, Africa was not entirely the unknown entity that Denham and Clapperton supposed.

The "Americans" were clearly not casual or exploratory visitors. They came for a purpose and they knew therefore what they were seeking—gum and slaves.

It is hard for us these days to contemplate the major role which gum arabic played in the eighteenth and nineteenth century. It helped fill the space between solids such as bone or metal and malleables such as wax and rubber. It was, in fact, used in conjunction with woven silk or cotton and latex for all the purposes for which plastics are nowadays employed. Especially was this the case in the then burgeoning medical and pharmaceutical professions, in the last of which it had other uses as well, e.g. as an emulsion stabilizer.

Why was it therefore that the "market surveys" which these Americans had made had not become better known? Why is it that what must have been profitable connections were not more widely exploited? Where are the reports and the accounts which such visits as were described must have generated? Or, were there any, and if not why not?

Such questions are beyond the scope of this work either to analyse or to attempt. If, however by posing them it suggests new lines of research for future scholars, then its preparation will have been more than justified.

For intending explorers, Denham laid down the following code of conduct: "A determination to be pleased, if possible, is the wisest preparatory resolution that a traveller can make on quitting his native shores and the closer he adheres to it the better. Few are the situations from which some consolation cannot be derived with this determination and savage indeed must be that race of human beings from whom amusement, if not interesting information, cannot be collected".[1] Denham certainly practiced as he preached: he made the best of every situation in which he found himself, and, each time his circumstances threatened to become intolerable, he called up his lively sense of humor to sustain wilting zest or waning resolution. Though no scientist, he had an enquiring mind and a broad range of interests. Moreover, having already travelled widely, he was able to compare what he found in Africa with what he had seen in other parts of the world, to the great benefit of his narrative. In general he was a practical man rather than an intellectual but he had an excellent grasp of the principles of the Christian religion so that, in the theological disputations into which he was sometimes drawn, he was able to defend his ground without giving offence to his Moslem interlocutors. He was also most diligent and industrious in the pursuit of knowledge: not only did he work hard to improve his Arabic and to acquire some Kanuri but he was also tireless in collecting, sifting, and recording all the information that came his way. As for his English, the prose in which his narrative was written may sometimes have lacked polish, but he had a good eye for a scene or a trait of character and so his writing made up in vividness what it lacked in style.

As a man, Denham was well endowed with those two priceless qualities, tolerance and sympathy. His tolerance he managed to preserve, without in any way debasing his values or judging by double standards, while his sympathy enabled him to ignore superficial blemishes and to penetrate to the basic qualities of his African hosts. "If . . . it may be thought that I have spoken too favourably of the natives we were thrown amongst" he wrote at the end of his narrative "I can only answer that I have described them as I found them, hospitable, kindhearted, honest, and liberal. To the latest hour I shall remember them with affectionate regard, and many are the untutored children of nature in central Africa who possess feelings and principles that would do honour to the most civilized Christian".[2]

It clearly emerges from between the lines of Denham's narrative that he was greatly assisted in his work by being blessed with an uncomplicated personality. Forthright and free from inhibitions himself, he had no difficulty in establishing easy relations with all manner of men. On the Sahara journey, he got much closer to the Arabs than any of the other explorers and, on reaching Bornu, it was he, rather than the admittedly

1. Denham, II, p. 151.
2. Ibid.

ailing Oudney, who made his mark with the Sheikh. More striking still, after some early and serious clashes with Mallam Chadili, he succeeded in winning the grudging admiration even of that formidable old bigot.

Humour was never absent for long from Denham's narrative. His genuine admiration for El-Kanemi did not prevent him from poking gentle fun at the Sheikh's occasional lapses into pretentiousness. Similarly he mocked, though not unkindly, the bombast and boastfulness of the Arabs. Best of all, he was always able to summon up a wry or quizzical smile at his misadventures and set-backs.

Apart from Livingstone, whose main driving force was religious fervour, we know little of the personal motives that impelled the great African explorers to face such fearsome risks and daunting hardships. Denham was typical of his kind. There is no self-analysis in his writings. All we gather is that he had a sincere conviction that the opening up of the continent was pioneering work of historic importance which would transform the lot of Africans and would also have the incidental advantage of bringing commercial rewards to Great Britain. This was the conventional nineteenth century formula of "philanthropy and five per cent" and Denham propounded it faithfully when he described the expedition's arrival in Bornu.

> We were at last within a few short miles of our destination; were about to become acquainted with a people who had never seen, or scarcely heard of, a European; and to tread on ground the knowledge and true situation of which had hitherto been wholly unknown. These ideas of course excited strong hopes of our labours being beneficial to the race amongst whom we were shortly to mix; of our laying the first stone of a work which might lead to their civilisation, if not their emancipation from all their prejudices and ignorance, and probably at the same time open a field of commerce to our own country which might increase its wealth and prosperity.[3]

To this theme of civilisation through commerce Denham returned in the summing-up contained in the supplementary chapter of his book.

> I consider the establishment of a friendly intercourse with this potentate beyond the great desert, by whose means the unknown part of Africa may at no distant period be visited, of the greatest importance in every point of view. By encouraging a commercial intercourse, all the objects of African discovery must be advanced.

3. Ibid, I, p. 207.

> Not alone will the cause of science and research be benefited but the real philanthropist must see that an opening is now made by means of which, with judicious arrangements, thousands of his fellow beings may be saved from slavery. The results to which the maintenance of this intercourse may lead are incalculable. . . . [4]

Time, of course, has brought many disappointments and Africa, though it has freed itself from one set of shackles, is no nearer to being emancipated from prejudice and ignorance than other continents. Nevertheless, if its present state is compared with the past, it can be seen that in many respects, Denham's vision gradually is being realized and that his belief that he and his companions were blazing a trail across an historic watershed was fully justified.

Unhappily he did not survive for long to enjoy the satisfaction of his achievements. Soon after Clapperton had embarked on his second journey, Denham was promoted to the rank of Lieutenant Colonel and selected by Lord Bathurst, the Secretary of State, to fill the new post of superintendent of liberated slaves in West Africa. He reached Freetown, his headquarters, in 1827. Next year, while at the island of Fernando Po, he learnt from Richard Lander of Clapperton's death in Sokoto. But in 1828, soon after being appointed Lieutenant-Governor of Sierra Leone, he too succumbed to the climate. Like all his companions therefore, with the sole exception of Hillman the shipwright, he finally left his bones in Africa.

4. Ibid, II, p. 196.